KENFIG FOLK. Part III

KENFIG BOROUGH
THE LAST YEARS
1700 – 1886

Barrie Griffiths

THE KENFIG SOCIETY

Published in the UK by the Kenfig Society
3 Cwm Cadno, Margam, Wales SA13 2TP, UK

Registered Charity no. 702279

Website: www.kenfigsociety.org

ISBN: 978-0-9567701-3-4

A CIP catalogue record for this book is available from the British Library

The cover picture shows Morfa Beach seen from Sker Point

Printed by ImprintDigital.net, Exeter EX5 5HY, UK

BARRIE GRIFFITHS 1942–2009

Barrie was that best of amateur historians — enthusiastic, knowledgeable yet sceptical about what he read and saw. As a retired police-sergeant it came naturally to him to question the evidence, especially the earlier writings of those prone to mystic fantasy. Nor would Barrie accept the confident assertions of 'experts'; only by weighing the evidence would he come to a conclusion.

In this series of books Barrie lays out the depth of his knowledge and understanding of Kenfig over a period of 700 years, from the coming of the Anglo-Normans to the mid-Victorian era. Barrie, a colourful character in life, wanted to explain Kenfig and its story, but also what was going on in the wider world and how it affected the town. He does this in his own inimitable style, and has produced a highly readable account, which should please both the general reader and the historical specialist alike.

Never one to shrink from controversy, after 20 years or more of close examination and reflection on the evidence, Barrie was able to form many new insights and interpretations, which will be found in these pages. But this is not done in a rancorous way — reasonableness and good humour shine out from Barrie's account of the life of Kenfig Folk.

Note from the editing committee:

We have retained Barrie's text, but made significant changes to the 'packaging'. Barrie was rightly proud of the immense detail he discovered about the families who lived at Kenfig, and included this in his narrative. We made a decision that all this detail was a distraction from telling the tale of what happened in and around the Borough of Kenfig.

These facts about the families and places, mostly farmhouses of Kenfig have not been lost, however! Collected together, they will appear as the 4th (and final) part of this series of Kenfig Folk, and will no doubt be of great interest to family historians.

Of course such major changes would normally be checked and approved by the author. Instead we formed an editing committee consisting of Terry Robbins, Ken Williams, Brian James, Keith & Janis Edger and Dennis Jones. But as the person in overall charge mine is the final responsibility for any errors or omissions.

Conall Boyle,
Publications Secretary,
Kenfig Society

June 2013

CONTENTS:

Chapter 1

A Miserable Half-century 1700-1750

Back in the 1980s when I was engaged in my project on the manors of Stormy and Horgrove I gradually became aware that the first half of the 18th century had not been an easy time for the people of that district. It was also not an easy period of the area's history for this particular local historian to research either! The probate inventories that had provided some wonderful insights into the lives of people in the late 17th century began going out of fashion, dwindled in number, and then ceasing altogether. Contemporary archives from the Margam estate collection dry to a trickle for the 1730s and 40s. For more reasons than one therefore I came to think of this fifty year period in local history as something of a Dark Age.

A similar situation with regard to documentation prevailed in my study of Kenfig Borough, and it seems that here too people were suffering from the same set of circumstances that affected Stormy and Horgrove leading to decay and large scale emigration. There was no single factor that caused this – it was simply a case of several sets of circumstances coming together to make the half century between 1700 and 1750 a truly miserable one for the burgesses and their fellow inhabitants. This chapter takes a general view of these traumas that afflicted Kenfig during this period with a more detailed picture of what this actually meant to the people who lived here in the ones that follow.

Kenfig in the 17th century was a rural community that relied upon agriculture for its existence with farmers and simple crofters alike engaging in cross-channel trade with Bristol and the West Country via the little port at Newton. Upon their prosperity depended not only the livelihoods of the regular and part-time agricultural labourers within the community but also that of the local craftsmen such as weavers, blacksmiths, carpenters and suchlike. If money was scarce people put off repairing property, buying new equipment, or purchasing new clothes and furniture. It followed therefore that if the prosperity of the farming community suffered then so too did that of everyone else. This, in a nutshell, is exactly what happened during these early decades of the new century.

Nationally, the agricultural industry was already sliding into recession even before 1700. The price of wheat fell by 46.5% between 1695 and 1702, and wool prices went down by roughly the same amount (Cambridge, 1985). Some products rallied for a time in the decade after 1708, but having gone down, the price for wool stayed down, and in only one of the years leading up to 1750 did it ever command a price comparable with its 1695 value. The decline in the value of butter was not so dramatic over the same period, but nevertheless in the early decades of the century it remained roughly 10% down on what it had been in the mid 1690s until rallying in the 1740s. Beef values also declined and were generally 15–20% down throughout the period. Wool, butter and beef were the three staple products of our district, so the fall in the value of these goods would, in itself, mean that local producers inevitably felt the pinch. What made it far, far worse was that suddenly and inexplicably the trade with the West Country also totally collapsed.

Why this should have occurred, and whether or not it was just a local phenomena is a question I lack the competence to answer. All that I can say is that it happened. In the sequence of Port Books relating to the Port of Newton there is a long gap in the entries after the year 1683. At that time trade was still mostly butter, wool, and stockings being shipped out in quantities similar to those I noted then. There is no indication whatsoever of the approaching collapse.

The Port Book sequence resumes over twenty years later with some documents I traced at the Public Records Office which cover the years 1705 to 1711 (PRO E190 1290/12 to 1293/6). Just a cursory glance was sufficient to show how dramatically trade had altered during the intervening period. Far fewer vessels were using the port. Those that did were shipping out cargoes that consisted mainly or exclusively of coal. When agricultural produce was loaded it was taken on almost as an afterthought or make-weight. In 1705 the *Five Brothers of Newton* made a voyage to Bristol with a cargo that included animal skins and 30 casks and pots of butter. *The Orchard Galley of Watchet* took four casks of butter when she loaded coal here the following year, and **these were the only agricultural products to leave the port during those two**

years! The cross-channel trade that had enabled local farmers and crofters to prosper was dead.

Agriculture was not just the most important industry at Kenfig and the surrounding area – it was the only one. When it collapsed it brought down the economy of the entire district with it. Land that had been carefully nurtured for generations became valueless; rents that may formerly have been considered 'a little steep' suddenly became impossible. Some farmers and smallholders sold up and left to seek a better living elsewhere. Others hung on in hope of better times around the corner but sank steadily deeper and deeper into debt. Freeholders mortgaged their property to raise money to live, and when that ran out and the good days had not returned were forced to sell their land for a pittance just to clear their debts.

Then, when this crisis was at its height the people were hit by an event that has been called Britain's last great demographic crisis. What this means in plain language is that during the period 1728-30 the number of deaths exceeded the number of births so that the population of the country actually reduced in number by a significant amount. Not the least fascinating thing about this national disaster is that it is something that has been brought to light not from accounts in contemporary newspapers and documents, but through painstaking research by modern historians. (Appleby, 1978).

Their work has identified the principal culprit for this mortality as famine, but local food shortages were apparently so commonplace in the past that nobody thought it worth recording the fact even when it happened on a national scale! Yet, all across the county parish registers tell the same story – a massive increase in burials during these two years. They also show a marked decrease in the number of baptisms, which is why famine has been identified as the culprit. During outbreaks of plague or disease the birth rate (as indicated by the registers) tends to remain stable but, as modern aid workers are aware, famine causes a decline in the birth rate. It is something to do with chemical changes that occur naturally in a woman's body at such times. These inhibit conception and are nature's way of preventing children being born into a situation where they have little hope of survival.

Locally, a study (Jones, B 1981) of the registers of parishes in West Glamorgan indicates that between the years 1727 and 1731 the population reduced by about 800. Not, it might be thought, a particularly large number to get excited about until it is realised that at this period of history we are looking at a figure that probably represents some 8 - 10% of the total population.

The crisis started here twelve months earlier than elsewhere in Britain because of an outbreak of disease – influenza being the most likely suspect. Abnormally high numbers of burials are noted at Margam 1727 and in Pyle & Kenfig parish over the same period a total of 21 are recorded – nearly double the average of 11.8 per year over the preceding five years.

Losses on this occasion were offset by a high number of births indicating that the mortality was probably due to disease, but over the three years 1727, 1728 and 1729 a total of 66 burials in the parish are offset by only 31 baptisms. The figures are not as dramatic as some that might be quoted, but the reduction of the population by 35 has to be taken in a context where it is highly unlikely the entire population of the parish was much above 500. In fact, a return of 1763 states that at that time Pyle & Kenfig was home to just 67 families, which suggests a total population of around 350 or less. (Guy, 1991: 47)

This was not to prove famine's only visit to our area during this period though the one that occurred in 1740/41 was not as severe and was more local in character. It originated in the winter of 1739/40 which was a particularly harsh one for Wales. "Wine froze in cellars, birds dropped dead from the skies, and snow was still falling in May". One night the temperature fell as low as 2ºF (-17ºC) and the ground remained frozen into April (Stratton, 1969: 74-). The mortality amongst the livestock that were the mainstay of Welsh agriculture was devastating, and corn crops were ruined. To compound this the winter that followed was extremely wet and by the Spring of 1741 food riots were reported across the Principality including one at Bridgend.

Taking a purely detached view we can say that the physical effects of these famines made little or no lasting impression upon the history of the people of Kenfig Borough. At the same time coming as they did on top of the stagnation in the agricultural industry the events of 1728-9 must have brought untold misery. The parish registers tell us the names of those who died, but those who survived had done so only after enduring the agonies of starvation and watching with hopeless despair the deaths and sufferings of family and friends.

Kenfig and their Landlords, the Mansels

As if all this were not enough many Kenfig people also encountered further problems because they were tenants of the Margam estate during what was to prove a none too glorious period of its history. At the same time it would only be fair to say that the Mansel family were themselves enduring a crisis that was not entirely of their own making.

Things started in a small way in the early decades of the century during the time of Thomas Mansel who proposed introducing a new method of maintaining the estate's property. Hitherto, as the story of Catherine Gamage's running battle with the manorial court* illustrates, responsibility for maintaining estate properties rested with the tenants whilst Margam provided any raw materials required for the work. Mansel now altered this so that initially the tenants met the entire cost of any repair work out of their own pockets and then claimed this back from the estate.

THOMAS MANSELL, 1ST BARON MANSELL OF MARGAM
BY MICHAEL DAHL (THEPEERAGE.COM)

Thomas Mansel's agent saw only too clearly the problems inherent in such a system particularly in view of the agricultural recession. He favoured a method whereby such maintenance work would be carried out by a workforce of tenants employed by the estate

---

* this story can be found in Part 2 of *Kenfig Folk* 178-9

and wrote to Mansel advancing this idea in 1712. Many tenants, he pointed out, were in no position to raise the money necessary for repairs in the manner he envisaged. "Your lordship" he wrote, "has several tenants so far in arrears they will hardly ever be able to pay". His words were ignored but proved deeply prophetic. At a time when local farmers were struggling just to find the rent, how indeed could they afford money to thatch roofs, whitewash walls, or renew fences and gates in their fields? By 1750 many properties owned by the estate were in a state of considerable decay.

It was Thomas Mansel's death in 1723 however that really marks the start of Margam's woes. He had three sons — Robert, Christopher and Bussy*. Robert was the eldest and therefore his heir, but unfortunately had already died earlier the same year. The estate therefore descended to Robert's son Thomas who, having only been born in 1719 was just a toddler.

As was normal practice Trustees were appointed to administer the estate on the child's behalf until he reached the age of twenty-one, and the two principal ones were his uncles Christopher and Bussy. Such minorities were rarely good news for tenants. Far too often those appointed looked upon the task as a golden opportunity to line their own pockets and notwithstanding the fact that young Thomas was their nephew Christopher and Bussy proved no exception to this general rule. During the years of Thomas's minority from 1723 to 1740 his Trustees demonstrated they were interested only in securing the maximum return for the minimum outlay.

Young Thomas lived with his mother and her second husband John Blackwood at Charlton near Greenwich, and even when he came of age seems to have taken little or no interest in his estate. So far as is known he never even visited South Wales. Bussy, it seems, 'kept an eye on things' from his home at Briton Ferry and when Thomas died without a heir in 1744 matters went from bad to worse.

Under the terms of his grandfather's will Margam passed to his uncle Christopher who was a bachelor living at Newick in Sussex. He therefore had little interest in Margam other than as a source of revenue and in any case died only months after his nephew. Christopher in turn was replaced by his brother Bussy who retained control of the estate

---

* this unusual name 'Bussy' can be found in previous generations of Mansels; its origins are French.[ed]

until his own death in 1750 when it passed to the Revd Thomas Talbot of Lacock Abbey who was the eldest son of his sister Mary.

Bussy was a politician who served as the Tory MP for the Glamorgan Boroughs from 1727 to 1734 and then as the member for the County from 1737 until elevated to the peerage on inheriting the title of Lord Mansel in 1744. He was well aware that his possession of Margam was only temporary. In 1706 he had inherited the Briton Ferry estate and although there were no sons to succeed him, there was a daughter, Louisa, who married Lord Vernon in 1757. Therefore while Margam was in his grasp he did not hesitate to utilise his influence to feather his own nest on her behalf.

For the twenty-seven years following the death of Thomas Mansel senior in 1723 were, as a consequence, marked by decay and neglect by those who were Margam's owners and custodians. They were interested only in what it could be made to yield, and gave no thought for its long-term future. Once Christopher and Bussy got their hands on the property, first as Trustees and afterwards as owners in their own right, tenants' rents were hiked up to previously unheard of levels.

At Stormy and Horgrove manors, my history (Griffiths, 1990) shows that rent receipts actually fell slightly during the early part of the century prior to 1728 but thereafter climbed a staggering 70% over the next twenty-two years! Similarly the receipts for the manor of Kenfig Borough dipped from just over £34 a year to under £31 between 1690 and 1734 but then almost tripled to £88. 8s. 9d. by 1746 – an increase of well over 150% in just twelve years! Unfortunately alterations in the composition of the manor of Higher Kenfig mean I cannot offer comparable figures for the rents there over the same period.

Christopher and Bussy were able to force rents up quickly because they phased out the hitherto common practice of renting out estate property on leases that ran for the duration of the lives of those named in them. Existing agreements were not renewed and new ones not granted which meant an increasing number of properties were held 'at will' where tenancies were, in theory, renewed annually allowing alterations to the level of rent and duties demanded.

Under leasehold tenancies such payments were fixed from the time the agreement was made and remained the same until it expired. Normally a tenant was granted a lease for the lives of himself, his wife and one of their children. This security of tenure encouraged him to invest in his farm secure in the knowledge that it would in due course pass to them with every chance that they in turn would be able to renew the agreement in due course. Consequently leasehold farmers tended to keep their land in good heart and the farmhouse and outbuildings in good repair. Tenancies at will, on the other hand, encouraged a 'smash and grab' mentality. What was the point in investing time and money in a holding that might not be yours in twelve month's time? Furthermore, any who did improve their farms to increase production and profitability pretty soon found their rents being raised accordingly, robbing them of the fruits of their labours.

This policy of exploiting the tenants for every penny was backed up by court warrants obtained against those in arrears with their rents, ordering seizure of their goods, crops and livestock in lieu. Hitherto references to such actions are generally rare in the estate records, but become quite common in the early 18th century. Allied to Thomas Mansel's system placing initial responsibility for keeping land and property in repair on the shoulders of the tenants it is little wonder that many local farms and cottages became ruinous and often lay vacant for years on end.

Christopher and Bussy also began plundering the estate of some of its most profitable holdings. My research is not sufficiently extensive to indicate its true extent, but certainly it happened in Kenfig Borough.

The Talbots, when they eventually acquired Margam were at a loss to understand how two of the largest farms in Kenfig Borough – Llanmihangel and Marlas – had been removed from the estate and become the property of Bussy Mansel's heirs at Briton Ferry. Writing about the year 1820 one of their employees (presumably the estate agent) freely admitted that it was a complete mystery to him. His best suggestion was that "on the death of Lord Christopher Mansel his brother & heir, Bussy Lord Mansel, claimed & possessed the same … as tenant in tail, consequent as is supposed of an error in suffering a recovery by Thomas Lord Mansel in 1741"(PM 6662). He got the year right, but that was all! Lurking in the Margam archives was a document (PM 1532) that showed beyond a shadow of doubt that the transfer had not come about through accident or neglect, for it is nothing less than a deed of sale for Llanmihangel and Marlas dated 10th April 1741!

Let me confess straight away that I pretend little knowledge about the legal side of property transfers but that said, this to me is a very fishy document indeed! Young Thomas Mansel, as we have seen, showed little interest in Margam even though he had reached the age of twenty-one a year earlier. What more natural therefore than Uncle Bussy, living 'just round the corner' at Briton Ferry should keep an eye on things for him? The names of these two farms meant nothing to young Thomas, and if advised that they should be sold for £200 to help keep the estate solvent, he is unlikely to have raised any objection. The money was paid him by Elizabeth the wife of the Earl of Bristol "out of her separate estate", but what he may well not have realised was that the actual purchasers were his uncles Christopher and Bussy!

Furthermore, it seems to me that the two properties were acquired at what can only be described as a bargain price. According to this deed of sale the land at Llanmihangel comprised two hundred acres, and that at Marlas a hundred acres without the houses and farm buildings. The general rule of thumb by which the estate calculated the value of land is indicated in a document relating to property at Kenfig offered for sale to Thomas Mansel by Charles Aylward in 1712 (PM 5976). He reckoned it to be worth 10 shillings per acre which the Mansel steward thought was a bit on the high side, as to his mind the land in question was "very much worn". Nevertheless he arranged for a proper valuation and the sale went through at the price Aylward wanted.

Calculated on this basis the price Christopher and Bussy paid for the lands of Llanmihangel and Marlas was just over six shillings per acre even without taking the value of the buildings into consideration! The previous year (1740) the estate had purchased the 108 acres of New Park Farm near Sker at a price which works out at £9. 4s. 3d. an acre (PM 3611). In 1742 over eighteen shillings an acre was paid in another deal involving seven acres of land in Kenfig (PM 1539). The price the Countess of Bristol paid on behalf of the two uncles was, in anyone's language, a rock-bottom minimum!

The excuse the two seem to have used to effect the sale was that the estate was heavily in debt and maybe it was, but this had not apparently prevented them snapping up other vacant properties in the district on behalf of young Thomas during the same period! Besides New Park farm young Mansel also bought the manor of North Cornelly and had presumably made both purchases on Bussy's recommendation.

Again, amongst the Margam archives is a survey (PM 3646) made in March 1744 of various parts of Margam estate headed "Proposed as the fittest and most convenient part of the Estate to be sold for payment of debts". The annual income from these properties was in excess of £1,000 per annum at a time when the total yearly receipts from the estate amounted to about £4,800! Were Christopher and Bussy up to their tricks again, stripping the estate of yet more of its assets? This was the year in which both young Thomas Mansel and his uncle Christopher died leaving Bussy in sole (if temporary) possession, and it is probably significant that nothing more is subsequently heard about this proposed sale! Bussy now knew that he was only 'keeping the seat warm' for the Revd Thomas Talbot who was increasingly taking an interest in affairs as the decade of the 1740s drew towards its close. In a letter dated 10th February 1744 (for 1745) the Margam Agent, Edward Savours wrote to Sir Charles Kemeys-Tynte, "Lord Mansel is laid up in the gout, both hands and feet and can't move either. Mr Talbot is now here and ... his father with him. An Act of Parliament is now solicited in order to invest them with power to grant leases of the Margam Estate"(Grant, 1978: 118) It would have been one thing to bamboozle the distant and (disinterested) Thomas Mansel, quite another to fool somebody who was keeping a watchful eye on his future inheritance.

Bussy was careful to keep Talbot in touch with matters relating to the estate and hearing that the latter was planning to marry in 1746 warned him not to make a too generous settlement upon his bride-to-be because of the massive debts the estate had accumulated. Just how massive these were became apparent at his death in 1750. Despite the crippling rents being extorted from the tenants it stood at £39,340! From an annual income of about £4,800 some £1,700 was being paid out just to service the loans that were keeping the estate afloat! (Martin, 1995: 17-8) As the year 1750 dawned the Margam estate, like the local economy, was also in a state of near collapse.

Chapter 2

Taming the Sands

The relationship of the burgesses of the Borough of Kenfig with the Mansels of Margam, who were their Lords of the Manor, was always a difficult one. They didn't want their Lord to take too much interest in what they were up to, yet at the same time, it was invariably to him they turned when help was needed. In short, there were benefits and there were drawbacks. The years between 1700 and 1750 were to prove difficult ones both for the people of Kenfig and the Margam Estate. Since the latter is not seen at its best during this period of our history, perhaps it is as well that I start my account with an event in which the estate's influence is portrayed in a positive light.

We have already seen [in *Kenfig Folk* Part 2] how as the 17th century drew to a close the encroaching sands were continuing their steady and inexorable advance further inland. Every year, or so it seemed, it drove onwards a little more. Fields of pasture and arable; common land; Castle Cottage; the hamlet at Millhill – all had gone. The growing threat to Mawdlam that had prompted the burgesses to seek a new location for their town was now obvious to all, and its eventual abandonment seemed only a matter of time. Then, with the inevitable climax apparently imminent – nothing! For the local historian it is rather like turning a page in the last chapter of a crime thriller and finding only blank pages! The sand had halted! Finally containing the sand was one of the few positive notes in an otherwise dismal half-century, and the burgesses' success owed a great deal (albeit indirectly) to Margam and the Mansels.

The weapon that brought about this remarkable transformation was a humble plant that the burgesses called 'sedge' but is actually a species of rush with the Latin name *arundo arenaria*, and it is virtually certain that they learnt about it through operations by Margam Estate in Higher Kenfig. Here the ecological situation was identical in every respect to that in the lower Borough save one - the sands of Margam Burrows had not moved and were still confined to a relatively narrow strip of land adjoining the coast. Yet, like Kenfig Burrows, that coast had been subject to the abnormally high tide levels of the 14th and 15th centuries, and also the prevailing westerly winds that could have

*Arundo
arenaria 587.*

driven the dunes further inland. That they had not was because, unlike the dunes south of the river, there was no adjoining urban settlement, no livestock grazing and no rabbit warren. It was therefore a picture of what Kenfig might have looked like had the town never been built there in the 12th century.

Urban settlement and intensive farming only arrived in Higher Kenfig with the refugee burgesses in the 15th century and even when these new-arrivals created a permanent settlement it seems the monks did not allow them to establish a common upon which to pasture livestock. This in itself would have done much to preserve the fragile ecology of the dunes, but even more importantly the monks never created a rabbit warren here either.

That this is so was due to a remarkable stroke of good fortune because in 1344 the Abbot of the day had indeed obtained permission from the Lord of Glamorgan to create such a warren in Margam Burrows. For whatever reason the option never seems to have been taken up and the river Kenfig, small as it was, formed an effective barrier against these pests spreading here from Kenfig Burrows on the opposite bank.

Had things remained that way it is likely that little more would have been needed to keep the dunes confined to the coast, but then the Mansels of Margam embarked upon an ambitious land improvement scheme for their coastal property between the rivers Kenfig and Afan. This involved draining the marshes between the dunes and the Water Street ridge thereby turning them into lush pasture-land. Although this was a major piece of engineering work very little seems to be known about it. From random bits of information I have collected all I can say is that it was in place by 1633. The Dutch were past-masters at this sort of development, so possibly it had been carried out during the reign of Elizabeth I when relations between Britain and the Low Countries were particularly cordial.

The engineers constructed a series of connecting ditches to drain the marshland and built roads and bridges to give access to the fields thus created. It was a massive undertaking most of which now lies beneath the Port Talbot steelworks and Eglwys Nunnydd Lake. At the same time those employed for this work seem to have recognised that what they were doing would inevitably upset the fragile ecology of the area. The marshes had played an important part retarding sand movement further inland and so, in stark contrast to their counterparts south of the river, Margam Burrows had only inched forward at a snail's pace.

The drainage scheme effectively removed the watery barrier that had helped contain the dunes but it seems that from the first, measures were put in place designed to retard subsequent sand movement. Planting sedges to reinforce the existing dune vegetation was perhaps the most important of these, but it was backed up by the erection of a substantial sea wall and rather more fragile 'frith' fences. These were lightly built fences incorporating hurdles and gorse, erected at strategic points in the dunes to catch and trap windblown sand heading inland towards the reclaimed land.

Eventually the fences themselves became buried in dunes of their own making and fresh ones had to be erected to take their place. Renewing these, planting the sedge and maintaining the drainage ditches in the moors would have been a labour-intensive and expensive operation had not the estate come up with rather an ingenious solution. Maintenance was made part of the 'duties' due to Margam from its tenants in Higher Kenfig and other farms that adjoined the new development.

These 'duties' were a relic of the feudal system that survived well into the 18th century and were services and payments due to the Lord of the Manor from his tenants over and above their rent. They are also sometimes known as 'boon works' implying a gift or favour, and the term gives us an insight into how they originated. In the dim and distant past tenants had carried out such work voluntarily to help their master but, human nature being what it is, landlords began demanding such gifts as of right. The term 'boon work' therefore had a bitter and cynical ring to it in later centuries. These 'Duties' involved such things as working for a certain number of days on the Lord's land; 'gifts' of poultry (or the cash) at certain times of the year; or carrying timber and other materials to his house or elsewhere on the estate as required – all unpaid, of course!

When the marshes were drained the Mansels scrapped many of the duties owed by their tenants in Higher Kenfig and replaced them with a new set. 'Ditch Duty' meant that the tenant was made responsible for scouring a particular length of ditch in the moors – keeping it clear of weeds, maintaining the banks etc. How and when this was done was a matter for each individual, but failure to keep their portion of ditch in good repair could (in theory) cost them their farm! 'Burrow Duty' (often rather confusingly written as 'Borough Duty') involved remedial work in the dunes – renewing the frith fences and planting sedge. 'Carriage Duties' had been in existence since time immemorial, but were now applied to the haulage of material for such maintenance work in the burrows. There was a whole raft of them. Mary Cuffe, who took out a short-lived lease on Marlas Farm in 1680, was required to spend up to two days a year hauling "ffurze (gorse), thornes, rushes, stakes and other neccessaries to the Burrows of Margam" whenever this service was demanded of her (PM 734).

By such means the Margam estate ensured that its improvement of the coastal moors and marshes did not result in the kind of ecological disaster that was happening in Kenfig Lower. Eventually the burgesses took note of what was going on and as a result began implementing certain measures of their own.

It was beyond the Borough's power to adopt the Margam scheme in full, as financially the burgesses would have found it difficult to acquire the materials necessary for the erection of sufficient frith fencing to significantly reduce the amount of wind-blown sand being carried inland. Sedge planting, however, they believed to be well within their capabilities. It therefore became one of the duties of being a burgess to turn out annually, rain or shine, to "plant sedges where they shall be appointed according to ye ancient custom"(B/K 11). Failure to do so (and the female burgesses were not exempt) meant a fine of a shilling.

Perhaps surprisingly there are only two instances of the practice recorded in the Borough Minute books between 1729 and 1852. Both are in the 1730s, right at the commencement of the first surviving ledger. This may indicate that, despite the reference to it being an 'ancient custom' the practice had only recently been adopted. Thereafter the annual planting sessions became so much part of the burgesses' way of life that it was pointless recording them. A photograph in Frederick Evans' book *Tir Iarll* (published 1912) shows row upon row of newly planted sedge in the dunes, confirming other testimony that the practice continued well into the Borough's twilight years – and it was a success! There was still some movement within the dunes system itself, but wherever the sand began heading for housing or enclosed land the burgesses moved quickly to block its progress with sedge.

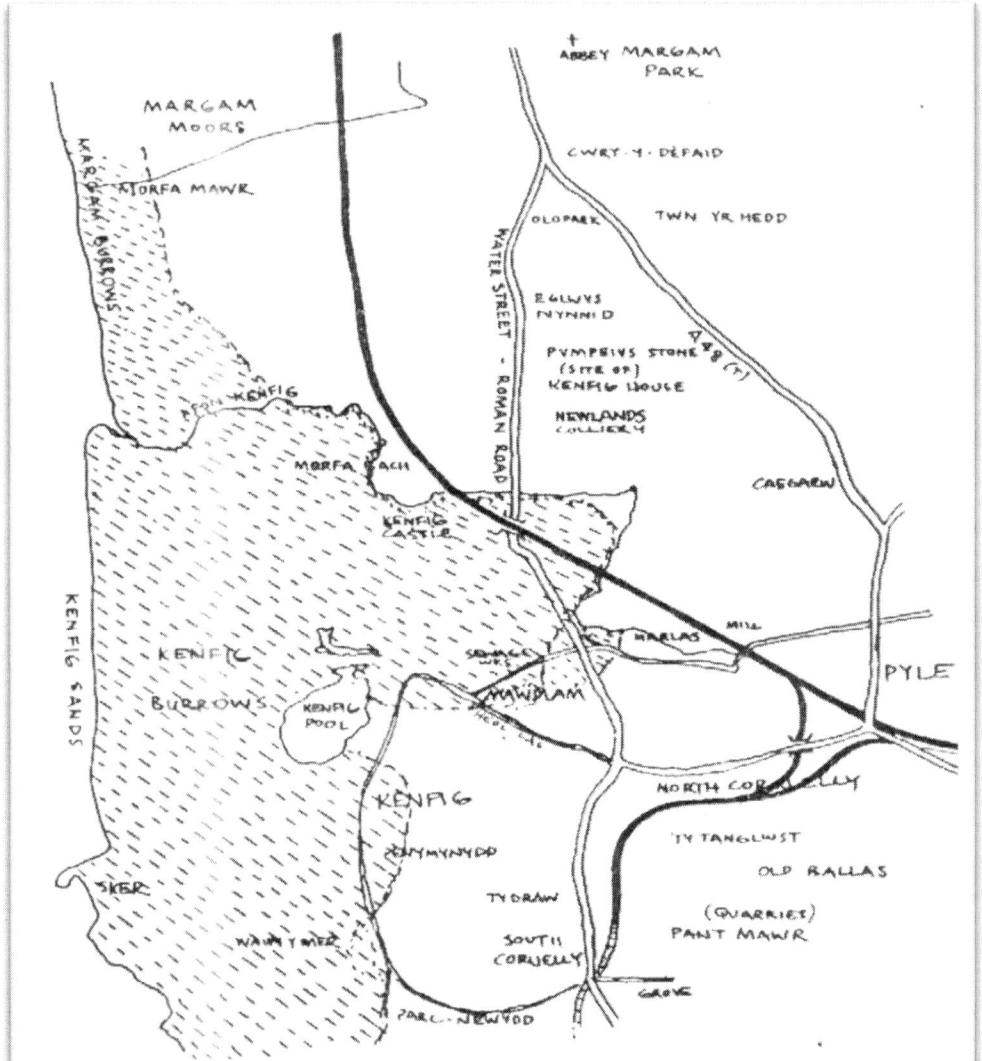

A SKETCH MAP SHOWING THE DUNE AREAS APPARENT AT KENFIG DURING THE SECOND HALF OF THE 20TH CENTURY.

IT WAS DRAWN BY THE LATE ALBERT EVANS ("ALBIE") OF NORTH CORNELLY WHO FOR MUCH OF THIS PERIOD WAS THE HAYWARD OF THE COMMON EMPLOYED BY THE KENFIG TRUSTEES. HIS KNOWLEDGE OF THE AREA AND ITS WILDLIFE WAS IMMENSE, AND I FOUND THE MAP IN A FOLDER OF HIS NOTES RELATING TO KENFIG'S HISTORY. IT SHOWS QUITE CLEARLY HOW THE ADVANCE INLAND OF THE SAND NORTH OF THE RIVER KENFIG WAS FAR LESS THAN IN THAT PART OF THE BOROUGH TO THE SOUTH, AND THE WAY IN WHICH KENFIG POOL ACTED AS A SHIELD TO THE LAND ON ITS EASTERN SIDE. THE MAP IS VALUABLE TODAY AS, BECAUSE OF THE PRESENT STABILITY OF THE DUNES, IT IS DIFFICULT TO ASCERTAIN THEIR TRUE EXTENT.

With constant vigilance and the aid of the humble *arundo arenaria* (or sometimes a sea sedge or marram grass called *ammophila arundinacea*) the burgesses successfully contained their deadly enemy and reshaped the landscape of the dunes so that by the 1940s only about 40% of their area was open shifting sand. Developments since then have reduced this percentage still further to a point that it is now causing serious concern. The land on which the burgesses formerly grazed their cattle is today a nature reserve created as a haven for plants and insects that actually thrive in the arid dunes and are now all but extinct elsewhere in the country. Myxomatosis has all but wiped out the rabbit population and together with the absence of common grazing, has allowed other vegetation to flourish and significantly reduce the sandy area. As a consequence the future survival of these increasingly rare dune species is now somewhat in the balance.

The date when the burgesses adopted this practice of planting sedge is not known, but as suggested above, the fact that the only two references in the minute books date occur in 1731 and 1733 indicate it may then have been a fairly recent introduction made during the previous half century or so. Our list of Portreeves prior to 1729 is rather fragmentary, but several I have identified during the period 1675-1725 came from Higher Kenfig. In their capacity as estate tenants of Margam they would have had first-hand knowledge of the manner in which Margam was controlling the dunes there. Any one of them may therefore have introduced the practice to the lower Borough, but it is interesting that the two references to sedge planting in the minute books occur during the Portreeveship of Thomas Griffith* who held office from 1729 to 1734. He was tenant of a farm in Higher Kenfig and so liable for duties connected with Margam Burrows, but also had another good reason to appreciate the importance of the sedge. Indeed, were it not for that reference to it being an 'ancient practice' I would have few reservations about suggesting that it was he who actually introduced the planting of it in Kenfig Lower. When the practice of blocking up rabbit holes on the common was introduced later in the century, a few entries were made in the minute books when the custom was new. Thereafter these cease and the only evidence for its continuation are one or two stray allusions to it later in the record. It

---

* More details about Thomas Griffith and many other Kenfig residents can be found in the companion volume *Kenfig Folk 4: People & Places*

may also be significant that the minute calls sedge planting "ye ancient custom" (as opposed to 'our ancient custom') which may therefore simply be a reference to the fact that the practice was already well established in the district, at Newton as well as Higher Kenfig.

Following some particularly violent storms during the winter of 1722/3 however, Thomas gained an even more comprehensive insight into the complexity of Margam's coastal defences when he himself was placed in charge of effecting the necessary repairs. The most obvious problem was that the sea had destroyed a section of the sea wall and a feature graphically described as "the anal key"(PM 2421). This was a kind of wooden trough by which excess water from the drainage system in the moors passed through the dunes and sea wall. To haul timber to the site Thomas invoked the 'Carriage Duties' due from certain tenancies, but in rather a nice touch lashed out ten shillings of the estate's money to supply the people involved with free ale.

Repairing this damage was, however, only part of the work involved. Where the sea breached the wall it had also broken into the dunes beyond. Remember the effect of the incoming tide on the sandcastles of our childhood? Well the result on the dunes would have been rather similar, dissolving the heaps of sand and spreading them around, burying existing vegetation. In dry weather this would provide large areas of sand for the wind to sweep inland. So, having repaired the wall and replaced the anal key, the next task was to plant the affected area with sedge. As this work was additional to the normal annual planting sessions by the tenants Thomas used hired help, but there is no mention of any frith fencing being erected. This was perhaps because these were normally put up on the inland side of the dunes rather than along the edge of the foreshore.

Similar repairs were necessary in the vicinity of the anal key after further storms during the winter of 1730/1, though there is no indication whether or not Thomas Griffith was put in charge on this occasion. Nevertheless from his earlier experience he would have gained an invaluable insight into how and why the dunes moved inland and the best means of combating it. If it was not he who introduced the practice of using sedge to the burgesses of the lower Borough, then he would certainly have helped by showing the burgesses how and where to plant them to secure the maximum advantage from the process.

Whilst many burgesses will have undoubtedly looked on the annual planting sessions as a chore they would rather avoid, others, particularly when the weather was fine and dry, probably welcomed the event as a break from the usual daily grind. Willingly or unwillingly however they did a marvellous job. The four hundred year long advance of the Kenfig dunes was finally halted, and from this time onwards ceases to be an element in the story of the Borough.

It had indeed been a close run thing for the village at Mawdlam. A large house at the rear of The Angel Inn, and just beyond the boundary wall of the churchyard, stands on the site of a farm known as Ty'n y Towyn – 'The House in the Sands'. Just beyond that, to the east, many of us remember a huge overgrown dune sufficiently large to have a bungalow on top, both of which were removed in the 1990s. When, at the eleventh hour the advance of the dunes was stopped both church and village must have been on the point of being engulfed by this monster.

Chapter 3

Bussy, the Last of the Mansels 1744-1750

Edward Harris of Llanmihangel Catherine Lyddon's second marriage to Edward Harris gives us a rather neat introduction to a rather interesting character I would like to bring before you in this chapter. He was the Edward Harris who may have been the son of Catherine's second husband as both were carpenters who hailed from Margam. Edward junior first appears at Kenfig in a Land Tax return for 1737 though there are records of one or the other of them being employed as a carpenter at Margam from 1724 through to 1731. This period may be (and probably was) a lot longer – it just so happens that a batch of estate records relating to this brief period still survives. A Land Tax return of 1737 (PM 4937) lists the younger Edward for sums of 4d and 8d in the lower borough suggesting that his holding was quite modest – probably just a cottage with a few acres of land. His comparatively lowly station in life at this time is further confirmed by the fact that he served as a Borough Aletaster which was a post that persons of any standing normally avoided. Edward Harris junior, however, was a man on the way up.

In 1736 Harris was commissioned by the Margam estate to make a survey of the land attached to Marlas Farm. This was one of the properties that five years later Bussy Mansel quietly removed from the estate and attached to his own, so it is quite likely that it was he who ordered the survey to be carried out. Morgan Waters was still the tenant here at the time though not for much longer for he had moved back to Stormy by 1739 having sunk deeply in arrears with his rent. He nevertheless still retained a curious connection with Kenfig as will be related in a later chapter.

Harris's survey of Marlas (PM 3806) is an interesting document in itself but made all the more entertaining by his weird and erratic spelling. He calculated the area of the various fields in "ackers" (acres), and it took me a little while to work out that "the orget" was in fact 'the orchard'. Others field names like 'Caskebore' (Cae Scibwr – The Barn Field) and 'Catower' (?Cae Towad – The Sandy Field) took even longer!

THE BRIDGE OVER THE RIVER KENFIG AT LLANMIHANGEL MILL
(E.H.Q.SMITH, 1973. REPRODUCED BY KIND PERMISSION OF HIS NEPHEW CHARLES SMITH)

Because so few estate documents survive from the 1730s and 40s it is difficult to be sure of Harris's standing with Bussy Mansel, but one suspects that the two were quite close and that Bussy had a hand in his subsequent advancement. When the Talbots took charge of the estate after 1750 Harris was in receipt of an annual salary "for looking after the timber and repairs" (D/DP 35). In all likelihood this was a post he had held for some time previously. One suspects therefore that it was his standing with Bussy Mansel that led him to being admitted as tenant of Llanmihangel corn mill in 1739 to which was added a corn drier (that stood somewhere on Mont Mawr) and land at Coed y Collwyn.

This mill was now the only one in the district, and with 'suit of mill' still in force was an attractive proposition even in view of the general recession. It is about this time that the lovely little mansion that adjoins the mill today came into being, so Harris was able to live in some style and as the Margam estate began to disintegrate snapped up vacant tenancies in the manner of the late John Thomas of Marlas. It is difficult not to infer from all this – the tenancy of the mill; the new house; the additional tenancies; and the employment with the Margam estate – that Harris was very much Bussy's man. By 1741 he had been sufficiently elevated in status to be appointed Portreeve of Kenfig Borough.

Bussy had been an MP prior to his elevation to the peerage in 1744 (after the death of his brother), and continued to dabble in politics thereafter. He would therefore look to Harris in his capacity as Portreeve to deliver the vote of the Kenfig burgesses for whichever candidate he favoured. The lack of estate documents from this period does not allow me to quote any examples, but in 1754 (in the days of the Talbots) there is record of a payment reimbursing Harris "for what he paid for the expenses of the burgesses to and from Mr Mackworth's election at Cardiff". (PM 9691)

Edward Harris was to hold the Portreeveship for fourteen consecutive years – by far the longest continuous period of office on record. This too can be seen as Margam influence. The estate controlled the Higher Kenfig burgesses, which ensured that their preferred candidate was at least nominated for the post annually, and since the Constable of the Castle was also their steward his subsequent selection, if they so desired, was a foregone conclusion.

During his term of office Harris certainly seems to have been held in some awe by the other burgesses. Not until after he was safely in his grave did they dare to conduct an enquiry into how it was that their Aletasters now had two sets of weights and scales available for use. Evidence was called which showed that the second set (completely superfluous to requirements!) had been 'donated' by Harris to make up a short-fall in his accounts! This he had done completely on his own initiative and, such was the shadow that he cast even in death that, having noted the facts the enquiry seems to have been content to let the matter lie. There was certainly no mention of returning the scales to his widow and demanding the missing cash!

Yet I think I would be doing an acute injustice to Edward Harris if I depicted him merely as Bussy Mansel's 'Trojan Horse' in the

Borough organisation, or that he ruled the burgesses with a rod of iron. As I showed more fully in Chapter 1 on the difficulties experienced by the Margam estate itself during the last years of the Mansels, he probably did much to offset the devastation caused by its near-collapse for tenants in the Borough. It also seems that whilst he well knew on which side his bread was buttered, he was no mere Bussy Mansel sycophant. Amongst his accounts for work done to the Town Hall is a payment of ten shillings to a tiler called John David: "For 10 days painting the ruff of the sd Hall & white limeing ye same against Mr Talbot Coming of aig" (B/K 11)

This certainly seems to reflect anticipation by Harris and his burgesses that the arrival of the Talbots would usher in better times for all. Bussy may have been instrumental in securing him his position as the Borough's Portreeve in the first place, but Harris was evidently well aware, and very proud of Kenfig's history and traditions. Concerned about the state of some of the Borough's archives, for example, he arranged for copies to be made of the Borough's charter, ordinances, the survey of 1661 and "a table for the wait of bred" (his spelling had not improved with time!). It is also typical of him that he should take the trouble to meticulously record that he purchased the six skins of parchment from a Swansea stationer named Francis Price, and that the actual copyist was a man named James Gideon.

In the early 1750s there are several entries in the estate accounts of an annual payment of £1. 10s. 0d to him "for keeping a boar at Lanmihangel Mill for the use of ... Mr Talbot's tenants" (D/DP 63). Most residents of the borough kept a pig or two and would have been glad of the chance to use the services of the boar to breed from. No charge seems to have been made for this, and one cannot help wondering again if Harris perhaps had a hand in initiating this useful service.

Edward Harris therefore seems to have had a charisma that was entirely his own. The property he acquired; the house in which he lived; and the authority he wielded was equivalent to that enjoyed by any local gentleman and more than most. Yet he never awarded himself such a title, nor did he even aspire to the more lowly status of 'yeoman'. Right to the end of his life he was content – proud even – to style himself simply as 'a carpenter'.

Little things like these culled from dry lists of payments bring Edward Harris very close to us across the centuries and shed a light on his character that is not otherwise apparent in his activities for Margam and the Borough. He may indeed have originally been installed as Bussy Mansel's man in the Kenfig Corporation but I suspect that when he died in 1756 many if not all the burgesses will genuinely have regretted his passing.

Thomas Turberville Although not a Kenfig person, an important departure from the district in 1742 was that of Thomas Turberville of the Hall in North Cornelly. Like all his family he had been staunchly Roman Catholic and had been brought down financially by the crippling fines that this imposed upon him. Leslie Evans (2008) found reference to a fugitive Jesuit priest in the area as late as the 1730s but Thomas's departure apparently marks the end of organised recusancy in the area. The dissenting community had also lost its place of worship at Kenfig Farm when Charles Aylward moved out, so the Anglican church now faced no organised opposition within the parish. This is not to say, however, that Pyle & Kenfig was now a thoroughly orthodox community. There were clearly many individuals here who held Nonconformist views that were to resurface later in the century.

Bussy's Cunning Plan? Document No 3646 in the Penrice & Margam Collection is a curious one. As the heading proclaims it is a survey of various Margam properties in Glamorgan "humbly proposed as the fittest and most convenient part of the estate to be sold for payment of debts". The income from the holdings listed in the survey totals over £1,000 per year and they included extensive landholdings at Llangewydd, St Brides Major, Newcastle, Horgrove and Llangynwyd. The author is unnamed, but was evidently a senior member of the estate's administration and probably the steward or agent.

Was Margam in such a parlous state that it had become necessary to consider selling off property from which it derived over 20% of its annual income? Just two years previously it had bought the Manor of North Cornelly and other property from Thomas Turberville when he sold up and quit the area (PM 1542 & 9780-3). Was Bussy Mansel seeking to line his own pockets again? We shall never know for the sale never went ahead. The document is dated 4th March, 1744 which is the year in which both Thomas Mansel and his legal heir and uncle Christopher died within weeks of each other leaving Bussy holding the entire estate but with the new heir-apparent – the Revd Thomas Talbot - monitoring his every move. Talbot, as subsequent events were to show, had no intention of selling up any portions of his inheritance – far from it!

When he succeeded Bussy in 1750 Thomas Talbot introduced a radical programme of reform aimed at putting the ailing estate on a more economic footing. In *Sturmi's Land* (Griffiths, 1990) I showed how this entailed rescuing many of the major farms from the derelict state into which they had fallen. In one instance Talbot himself endorsed a lease (PM 8396) to Evan Lewis in his own hand promising to "rebuild the farm and cowhouse at Stormy and put the dwelling house in tenantable repair as soon as the same may conveniently be done". The farmhouse at Pencastell that formed part of the holding could, he added, be allowed to "go down". That such personal intervention was necessary is in itself an indication of how trust between tenant and landlord had sunk during the Bussy Mansel years.

In the case of Stormy and Horgrove the leases and the estate accounts for the 1750s present a picture of considerable decay, dereliction and neglect, but strangely I have so far found little corresponding evidence from the two manors contained within the Borough of Kenfig. In 1751 the mill at Llanmihangel was repaired and the building re-thatched. The following year Talbot paid a proportion of repair work totalling under £3 deemed necessary to some houses lately in the tenure of Thomas John (alias Jones), and thatch was salvaged from a cottage in Higher Kenfig that was apparently being allowed to fall into ruin (D/DP 24). In 1753 Thomas Jenkin's house in Higher Kenfig was re-thatched (D/DP 37), and in 1754 the pine end of Eleanor David's former cottage was rebuilt (D/DP 50), but these are virtually 'running repairs' typically found in the estate accounts for any given year.

Nevertheless the same accounts indicate that some major repairs were necessary to Kenfig holdings in the period 1751-5. The tithe barn on Heol Las was re-thatched; the boundary wall about the rick yard rebuilt; and new hinges made and fitted to the barn doors. Marlas and Llanmihangel were now, of course, part of the Briton Ferry estate and in 1755 the Talbots managed to secure repayment from Bussy Mansel's executors for work done to them prior to his death amounting to nearly £25 (D/DP 44). Because of the confusion over the status of these farms the Margam agent had apparently continued authorising remedial work necessary at both properties after Bussy's death, and later still a further £20 was also successfully reclaimed under this heading (D/DP 44).

The other property that appears to have been in need of considerable repair was Caeau Gollen (Glasfryn). From 1727 it had been held by Evan John who was the sole survivor of Eleanor Mitchell's family that had been all but wiped out in the famine year of 1728. By 1739 he had added a smithy formerly in the tenancy of Hopkin John (which Evan then apparently sub-let) and is mentioned as a freeholder in the lower borough. The indications are in fact that he actually lived at this freehold property on Heol Las so the dereliction at Glasfryn was therefore largely due to his own neglect. Evan, in truth, does not seem to have been one of the most active inhabitants of Kenfig when it came to maintaining his property! The complaints made by the juries of the various courts held at the Town Hall about the state of his hedges adjoining roads in the borough and the fencing of his plot of hay at Waun Cimla are as frequent as they are monotonous.

After Evan's death (about 1748) his widow Mary Miles continued as the tenant for a time but in 1751 tenancy of Caeau Gollen was taken up by a bachelor named John Abraham, who was thereupon immediately admitted as a burgesses and appointed one of the Aletasters. Payments by the Margam estate in the years 1752 (D/DP 24) and 1755 (D/DP 50) reflect the amount of work done putting the farm in order. A carpenter named Charles Rich was paid £1. 5s. 6d. for work on the house and on the land (probably replacing gates) whilst John himself was compensated to the tune of £1. 9s. 2d. "for work done in halling of stones from Cwmmalwg Quarry, and for making an oven therewith for the use of the house". The work concluded in 1755 with payments totalling £2. 10s. 5d for re-roofing the barn and cow-house with thatch.

All in all therefore Kenfig Borough seems to have escaped the worst effects of estate neglect so prominent at Stormy, Horgrove and elsewhere in our locality. For this the person the tenants probably had to thank in no small measure was Edward Harris of Llanmihangel Mill. In the early 1750s it will be remembered he was paid a salary of £20 per annum "for looking after the timber and repairs on Margam Estate".

Although replaced by Talbot after 1753 he had probably held the post for some years previously and in this capacity would have been in a position to ensure that his fellow burgesses got the best of whatever dwindling resources the ailing estate was able to provide.

Margam's Kenfig tenants had nevertheless also suffered from the spiralling rent demands made upon them by the estate and there was another effect of the Margam's malaise that was to have repercussions within the community. This was a process whereby under the Talbots, small farms were amalgamated to make larger and more economic units. In a previous chapter we have also seen how, towards the end of Bussy's life, Thomas Talbot was instrumental in issuing leases upon holdings in Higher Kenfig to create larger and more economical farms. Throughout the period we have been studying, certain individuals had from time to time added vacant tenancies to their own as and when they became available. Such arrangements were usually of a temporary nature and often dissolved on the holder's death.

In an effort to make their property more attractive to prospective tenants the Talbots now actively encouraged this process, bringing together groups of small farms to create larger ones and (as with Pencastell quoted earlier), allowing the farmhouses on the lesser holdings to 'go down'. Within the Borough, however, these smaller farms rated as 'burgages', so the number of burgesses dwindled. As the next half-century progressed the Corporation was obliged to find alternative methods of keeping the number of burgesses up to the maximum number.

The Last Year of Bussy As the year 1750 dawned Bussy Mansel's life was ebbing fast, and at Llanmihangel Mill the sands of time were also running out fast for Edward Harris who was now in his ninth consecutive term as the Kenfig Portreeve.

The death of Bussy Mansel was recorded thus:

> We present the death of the Right Honourable Bussy Lord Mansel, Baron of Margam and late Lord of this said Borrough, who dyed sins last Court; and we present the Reverend Mr Thomas Talbot to be Lord of this said Borrough in his stead.,

This was undoubtedly the major event of 1750, and the above entry was duly made in the Borough minutes at a Court Baron held on 21st December. Not only is this a reflection of the importance of the event, but perhaps too a reflection of the feeling within the ranks of the burgesses that it perhaps heralded the dawn of a new age for the estate and those associated with it.

Was it perhaps the installation of Talbot as the new owner of Margam that prompted the Portreeve, Edward Harris, to lash out the sum of £10 to have the roof of the Corporation House decorated with lime-wash as recorded in his accounts? The entry in his accounts for this period actually states that the roof was decorated to celebrate Mr Talbots "coming of aig" an event that had actually taken place in 1740. His son, Thomas, was only born in 1747, so as it stands the entry makes no sense. It may simply have been a slip of the pen by Edward Harris or perhaps reflects the remoteness that had developed between the last Mansels and the local population so that the latter were not quite sure what exactly was going on.

Whatever the reason this expenditure of four year's income from the general rate to honour The Reverend Thomas Talbot is a clear indication of the considerable goodwill towards the new Lord of the Manor amongst the burgesses' ranks.

Chapter 4

The Borough in the 1700s

The State of the Borough in the Early 1700s

In this chapter we have looked at how even with the advent of the Talbots the events of the half century between 1700 and 1750 were pressing upon the Borough organisation in a way that was to force the burgesses to make changes in the decades that followed. Most significant was the dwindling number of 'burgage' properties. They could have simply accepted this situation, and allowed their number to reduce still further, but were apparently reluctant to do this. In addition they seem to have been greatly concerned that this reduction in burgage properties had been greatest in Higher Kenfig, significantly reducing the proportion of burgesses representing that area.

Another aspect that seems to have also bothered them is the manner in which the Portreeveship had been held for so long by Edward Harris who, whatever his good points had been a 'Margam man' through and through.

Although they were still cautious of committing their deliberations to entries in the minute books we can nevertheless deduce from them the manner in which they attempted to combat these perceived threats to their status and independence as will be outlined in a later chapter of this history. With hindsight we can see that these measures were ultimately to lead to the degeneration of the borough in its final years. That they had become necessary was due almost entirely to the events of the dreadful half century from 1700 to 1750.

This point in my narrative seems a suitable one therefore to discuss the workings of the Borough of Kenfig as it existed in 1750, bringing together the stray elements we have noted in earlier records with those from the early 18th century. Of the latter, it is the borough's minute books that are the most important but, because of the burgesses obsession with secrecy, it is largely a case of interpreting the contents rather than quoting from actual resolutions adopted by the Portreeve and his council!

What was a 'Burgess'? When I set out on this voyage of discovery into the old Borough of Kenfig I was as guilty as anyone of referring airily to 'the burgesses' with little or no idea of who or what they were. In truth it would seem I was in very good company, for I found few clues in published material relating to the borough as to how one became a burgess of Kenfig, and what the role entailed.

We have already seen (in Part 2 of *Kenfig Folk*) that they fell into two categories – 'out-dwellers' and 'in-dwellers' – depending on whether they lived inside or outside the borough boundary. The first group we can safely ignore as they are only peripheral to the story of Kenfig. It is the latter, numbering no more than 57 or 58, who were the 'real' burgesses and whose status concerns us here. We saw too how, following the abandonment of the medieval town, farms throughout the borough and certain cottages in Kenfig Lower were recognised as having the status of burgages entitling the occupant (who was not necessarily the owner) to be admitted to the burgesses' ranks. This practice still continued during the early 18th century.

Upon occupying such a property the new resident's name was put forward as a suitable person to be admitted as a burgess, and once approved they were required to pay the necessary admission fees and take the burgesses' oath agreeing to be ruled by the Portreeve and the town's charters. Admission was not always a foregone conclusion, but those during the first half of the 18th century seem to have been fairly straightforward.

Burgesses enjoyed many perquisites denied other inhabitants, even those living within the borough boundaries, but they also took on certain responsibilities. It is possible that the Borough rate was paid by all householders living within the boundaries, but personally I doubt that this was actually the case. A burgess who failed or refused to pay could be disciplined by being disenfranchised, thereby loosing his status and the various privileges that went with it. Against this, not only is there no record of collection or rates from mere inhabitants but none concerning any action being taken against them for defaults either.

How much these payments amounted to is nowhere recorded. What we do know is that once the money had been collected then the sum of £2. 10s. 0d. was paid by the Portreeve into the treasury and he retained what was left. Towards the end of the 18th century this practice was reversed. The Portreeve took £3, and the remainder of the collection went into the coffers. Given therefore that the burgesses (including the 'female burgesses' who also paid rates) never numbered more than 58, the average rate per head must have been in excess of two shillings, but probably no more than half a crown (2s. 6d.). It is probable too that this was not a flat rate payment but determined by the size of the property a burgess occupied so that the wealthy farmers perhaps paid more than simple cottagers.

In addition to this rate, the burgesses could be called upon to perform duties determined by the Portreeve and council. Once a year, for example, they were required to turn out and plant sedges in the sand dunes to retard their movement. Later, because of the nuisance and danger caused by rabbits on the dunes, they were also required to present themselves armed with spades to spend a day filling in their burrows on the common. This latter chore was later commuted to a charge known as 'the rabbit hole rate'.

'Female burgesses' were also liable for this work on the borough common, but their sex debarred them from sitting on the council or having to serve as one of the Corporation officers. As we have seen the council of Eight Elected Burgesses was appointed by the Portreeve from a panel of twelve nominated by the burgesses to transact the business at any given meeting.

The officers of the corporation were appointed at the Autumn Leet. The posts 'up for grabs' were those of Portreeve, Sergeant at Mace, Hayward, two Aletasters, and that of Petty Constable. Whilst virtually everybody wanted to be the Portreeve, and many of the smaller farmers and cottagers would have had their eyes on securing that of Hayward, I think it true to say that nobody would have been exactly falling over themselves to fill the other three vacancies!

There had been some changes in the method of appointment since medieval times. Now the burgesses made nominations for all these offices, with the Constable of the Castle making the final selection from the names put before him. Usually three names were advanced for each office – a total of four in the case of the two Aletasters. In theory this was done by the burgesses as a whole, but the earliest records of elections after 1729 mention the presence of two 'electors'. Their function is not clear, but it could be that prior to the actual court sitting these had taken soundings of the views of the burgesses and put forward the nominations on the basis of what they had been told.

The Portreeve was effectively the mayor of the town whose word was law within the borough boundaries, though he was expected to take into consideration the advice of his eight councillors. He was responsible for the collection of all rates and taxes from the borough inhabitants, and accounted to the Margam estate for the rents of the freeholders in Kenfig Lower. In addition he paid the estate a nominal ten shillings 'burgage rent' and ten shillings ground rent due in respect of Kenfig Down, the two usually lumped together as a single payment.

Most Portreeves at this time held office for a period of several years, being re-appointed annually. Generally they were local farmers of some standing, though Evan Lyddon who held the office on several occasions in the early decades of the 18th century was a carpenter. The simple criteria seems to have been the respect and esteem in which these persons were held both by their fellow burgesses and the Constable.

By virtue of his office the Portreeve was also a magistrate for the Hundred of Newcastle, and Coroner of the lower borough. This last only comes to light in the records towards the end of the 18th century, so I have been unable so far to discover how long they had been carrying out these duties previously.

As stated earlier, this was a salaried office with the Portreeve retaining any money above the sum of £2. 10s. 0d. collected under the general rate. He and the Sergeant also received two shillings each per annum for ensuring the safe custody of the suit roll for the manor of Kenfig Borough, though this may have been discontinued when the estate itself took responsibility for rent collections (other than those of freeholders) after 1692.

The Portreeves were required to submit an account of their income and expenditure to the Corporation though they often had to be badgered for years before they complied! In perusing these I have been struck by the fact that normally the only money they had at their disposal was that raised by the Borough rate and (later in the 18th century) payments due from burgesses allocated vacant plots at Waun Cimla. In the case of the Rabbit Hole Rate we know that the person awarded the contract was himself responsible for its collection, but there would have been other income that is never referred to in the Portreeves' accounts. These included payments by non-burgess to use the common, fees payable on the admission of new burgesses, and fines due from those who failed or neglected to turn out at the annual sedge planting. I can only presume therefore that such payments were made directly to the Recorder in his capacity as the Borough Treasurer.

The Sergeant at Mace. Whilst in theory the Portreeve was responsible for collecting the rates and taxes, it was the Sergeant who actually made the collection with the aid of the two Aletasters. As his title suggests he was responsible for the borough mace, and traditionally was the only person allowed to handle it – bearing it before the Portreeve on civic occasions. He received no payment for his duties other than the two shillings for custody of the suit roll.

The Hayward. He was, so to speak, the 'policeman' for Kenfig's Commons, and such was the importance of his role that he was paid a small fee for his services. Besides ensuring that the rules, regulations and customs relating to the common land were observed he was also responsible for seizing any stray animals and placing them in the common pound adjoining The Prince of Wales. To gain their release owners had to pay a fine – sixpence in the case of a sheep, more for cattle and horses. This was then paid by the Portreeve to the Lord of the Manor. In theory any unclaimed stock were also sent to Margam and on neighbouring manors that is what normally happened. At Kenfig, however, the Portreeve had the option of taking possession of any unclaimed animal found in the lower borough on payment of the appropriate fine.

Since there was no common land in the manor of Higher Kenfig, the Hayward was invariably a burgess living south of the river, and the fact that the office earned a small income meant that it was a post which was sought after by smallholders and cottagers alike. A Hayward who did his job well and to the satisfaction of his fellow burgesses was often continued in office for several years consecutively. In this it was unlike those of Sergeant, Aletaster or Constable where rarely is there an instance when anyone either wanted, or was expected, to take the job two years running!

Although there was no common land in Higher Kenfig by the early 19th century the manorial court there was appointing no less than two Haywards annually. Their sole function seems to have been the seizure of strays which they presumably took to the pound at Margam. There is no mention of these officers in the earlier records of this court which end in 1703, and unlike their counterpart in Kenfig Lower they were generally local farmers who were not paid for their services.

Aletasters There were two of them, and besides assisting the Sergeant collect the rates and taxes and tasting the ale at local hostelries, they acted as the Borough's 'Weights and Measures' officers. The measures they used to ensure that retailers were complying to the local standards are now housed at St Fagans Folk Museum.

The Petty Constable. This was one office that could be (and occasionally was) held by a non-burgess. As his title implies he was, for his year in the post, the Borough's policeman though he only had jurisdiction over that portion of the Borough south of the river. The burgesses of Higher Kenfig appointing one of their own at their manor court. In truth he was not an officer of the borough at all, for he was answerable to the Magistrates' Court for Newcastle Hundred. That the constable was appointed at the manorial Court Leet is a peculiarity of our district as normally they were selected at the parish vestry. In Pyle & Kenfig parish there were, for example, four constables each responsible for the manors of Pyle, Kenfig Borough, North Cornelly and South Cornelly.

Like the Aletasters the constable carried out his duty unpaid, and there was a small cell beneath the external stairs of the Town Hall where he could confine prisoners until they were brought before a magistrate. He would also, incidentally, have been responsible for supervising the punishment of certain local offenders by placing them in the stocks in accordance with the sentence of the court. These were situated in the churchyard at Mawdlam, and there is a mention of them being replaced sometime between 1742 and 1745.

The Recorder was an important officer who was not appointed annually – in fact only rarely are any changes in this office noted in the minute books that he was responsible for maintaining. He was the 'town clerk' and 'treasurer' rolled into one, and because of the need to have somebody both educated and utterly trustworthy in this post it was another that carried a small salary. In addition there were certain other perks such as a payment from every new burgess for entering their name on the roll. Only occasionally is it possible to identify Recorders in the records, but I have to admit that I have never had much difficulty in reading their hand-written minutes. The same cannot always be said of their spelling however!

One series of entries particularly tickled my sense of humour. The Recorders invariably made an entry in the minute books of any stray animals placed in the pound by the Hayward, and noted their subsequent disposal. Usually these were sheep, and the Recorder in question duly noted whether they were 'ewes', 'rams', or '*lams*'. He continued his misspelling of the latter for some time until eventually somebody pointed out to him the error of his ways. Thereafter he wrote of 'ewes', '*rambs*' and 'lambs'! It wasn't long before somebody picked up on this and patiently informed him that whilst 'ram' and 'lamb' might sound the same there was no 'b' on the end of the first. Thoroughly mystified by the vagaries of the English language the Recorder decided his first idea was as good as any, and reverted to 'rams' and 'lams' for the remainder of his years in office!

Burgesses' Rights So much then for the duties of the burgesses, but what of the perquisites? Foremost amongst these was the right to pasture livestock on the common. As we have seen when looking at the farmers and smallholders of the 17th Century this was no small concession. It enabled men (and women) with just an acre or two of land to pasture cattle, sheep, pigs and even horses. Occasionally non-burgesses were allowed to avail themselves of this facility on payment of a fee, as noted inside the cover of one of the Borough minute books (B/K 12) when Evan Jones paid to be allowed to pasture his pigs and geese in 1791.

Then there were the parcels of hay at Waun Cimla and parcels of fern on Kenfig Down. The first consisted of 29 x 3 acre plots. No rent was paid for these, and they remained with the family of the burgess to whom they were allocated so long as the holder or one of his descendants continued to live in the borough. Any plots that fell vacant were re-allocated to the most senior burgess without one, and during the 18th century it seems that such new owners made a one-off payment of £2 paid in equal instalments of 6s 8d over six years. Burgesses could hold no more than a single plot, and could only rent or sell them to a fellow burgess. The minute books show that such sales often occurred when plot-holders were planning to move elsewhere.

The enclosure at Waun Cimla was entered by a gate in the vicinity of the former level crossing on Prince Road in Kenfig Hill. It was secured by a padlock and there are frequent references in the minutes to the repair or replacement of both this and the gate. Frequent too are the threats against lazy or neglectful plot-holders for not maintaining the fences about their property!

The parcels of fern on Kenfig Down were more numerous, 53 are listed when the system was reorganised in 1839. Because this was common land these were un-enclosed, their locations indicated by marker stones erected by the holders one of which is preserved in the garden of a bungalow on Heol Ton Kenfig. There were more than enough plots to go round for those burgesses who wanted one, several of those on the 1839 list being vacant. Probably for this reason no charge was made to a new holder upon admission. Nevertheless this source of winter fodder seems to have been highly prized, and was held subject to the same restriction as those upon the parcels of hay.

These were the main benefits an individual would derive from being a burgess, but there were other lesser perquisites too. From the middle of the 18th century there was, for example, a washing pound provided by the Corporation at Kenfig Pool for burgesses to dip their sheep prior to shearing, and there were also probably other such minor benefits that do not find their way into the borough records.

The right to vote: Whether the right to vote for an MP to represent the Glamorgan Boroughs was a blessing or a curse I'm not quite sure! Elections became more frequent as the century progressed, but they were held at Cardiff which was a long and arduous journey, particularly if you were merely attending as 'cannon fodder' for the Margam estate's preferred candidate. I suppose one's view would have largely depended upon whether this was regarded as a chore or the chance of a day out!

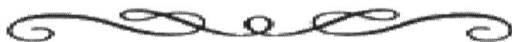

Chapter 5
Shipwrecks on Kenfig Sands

Despite the fact that Kenfig lies on the coast of Swansea Bay the sea (other than its secondary role in spawning and advancing the sand dunes) does not seem to have figured to any great extent in the everyday lives of the inhabitants. Although it is generally held that there was a commercial port associated with the medieval town of Kenfig, having reviewed such evidence [in Appendix II of *Part I* of *Kenfig Folk*] that there is, I personally am highly sceptical about its existence. Occasionally vessels may have landed or collected a cargo at the Kenfig river-mouth (which was outside the boundaries of the old borough anyway) but I can find little evidence to support the existence of sea-borne commerce on a regular basis.

[In this Chapter I have gathered together all of the stories of wrecks which Barrie re-told in his original, with one exception. In 1781 the *Caterina* with its valuable cargo was beached in a storm. What happened next had a major impact on the people and reputation of Kenfig; it will be explained in full in Chapter 10, and was probably the most exciting event in the whole of the period covered by this book! Otherwise, wrecks along this coast were a sad but frequent event, which had little impact on the lives of the locals. If you just want to follow the story of Kenfig Borough you can skip on to the next Chapter. Ed.]

Legends and stories current in the district mention that both cockles and mussels were harvested from the beach in the past though the first-mentioned shellfish have long vanished. According to a local legend collected by Frederick Evans (Evans, 1912:103) this happened when there was a 'falling out' between two local housewives whilst gathering shellfish. As the argument grew more and more heated their voices grew ever louder and shriller until the molluscs decided that there must be quieter places in which to live and promptly decamped!. Oysters too were formerly found here and the Margam accounts for the year 1707 (PM 5853) contain an entry of sixpence paid for "oysters from Kenfigg". In 1713 Thomas Cory's accounts (PM 2207) for the estate show that a man named John Owen, who is probably a Kenfig wheelwright and burgess of that name, was paid a total of £1. 2s 0d. for keeping the house supplied with oyster "to this day". Neither local traditions nor documentary sources suggest, however, that Kenfig folk ever fished the sea from boats.

That this was so is understandable, and indeed one of the reasons I tend to disbelieve in the existence of a medieval 'port of Kenfig'. The eastern side of Swansea Bay has been a graveyard for shipping since time immemorial. Prevailing winds here are Westerlies creating a lee shore that was deadly to any sailing ship trapped upon it. Whether by dragging their anchors whilst sheltering across the bay at Mumbles Roads or by sheer bad navigation, many a fine vessel's last voyage ended in disaster on Sker rocks or Kenfig sands. No sailing ship ever built could sail 'against the wind' and the crew's attempts to avoid being driven onto the beach were hampered both by Sker Point and the shoals further out in the bay such as Scarweather Sands and the Hugo Bank. Few that got close enough to land to see and hear surf breaking on Kenfig Sands ever escaped to boast of the experience.

But 'One man's meat is another man's poison' as the saying goes, and the wrecks that occurred from time to time were all part of the sea's bounty to the people of Kenfig, delivered by strong winds and fortune's caprice practically to their own doorsteps. What the vessel might be carrying by way of a cargo was merely a bonus. A wreck meant that at the very least there would be good seasoned timber, rope, cables, canvas and copper nails for anyone quick enough to take advantage. For a humble community like Kenfig these in themselves were riches indeed, and the fact that 'the authorities' regarded such salvage work as looting and theft worried them not in the least. 'What,' they would probably have argued, 'was the difference to taking possession of an abandoned vessel on the high seas to appropriating bits of one abandoned on the sands?' Legally, of course, there is indeed a world of difference, but to such simple folk it must have seemed that there was one law for some, but not for them! As they saw it the great and the good of the locality were manipulating the rules simply to deprive them of their just desserts.

It was a view shared by the common people living on the coast throughout the United Kingdom. As they understood it provided a ship had been abandoned by its crew they had a right to glean from it what they could. One frequently hears stories, whether true or not, of crew members found injured but alive onboard wrecked vessels who were quietly killed off so that the wreck could truly be declared 'abandoned'. No such tales, I hasten to add, ever attached themselves to Kenfig, but the population did somehow acquire the reputation of being 'wreckers', i.e. deliberately luring vessels to destruction on their shore. Let me say here and now that to date I have never ever found the slightest hint that such was the case. Looters many of them may have been, but ones who were content to profit only from what fate and another's misfortune happened to throw their way. In no instance has there ever been any suggestion that directly or indirectly they had a hand in a vessel's destruction.

The Loss of the Good Ship *Mary of Tenerife* The earliest wreck at Kenfig of which we have a detailed account is that of a sloop called

Mary lost here in 1739. Earlier wrecks are sometimes hinted at from time to time in the Margam accounts which mention items of wreckage recovered from the shore, though the names of the unfortunate vessels from which they came are not recorded. The *Mary* was different because a 'protest' made by the master and his two

surviving crew members still survives thanks to the fact that for some reason the Borough Recorder (Thomas Griffith) made a copy of the original document in the Borough's minute book.

A 'protest' was a sworn statement made before a local magistrate by the surviving crew as soon as possible after the loss of a vessel describing the circumstances by which it had come about. Naturally they took this early opportunity to 'protest' their innocence of any blame or responsibility for the loss of the vessel, which is how these documents got their name. In the case of the *Mary* the master, John Davies, and his two crew members made their statement on the day of the wreck to the Portreeve William Lewis in his capacity as a magistrate for Newcastle Hundred.

Sloops were small single-masted vessels that were the original 'coasters' trading between other British ports and the continent. The *Mary's* last voyage started at Teneriffe in the Canary Islands where she was loaded with 71½ 'pipes' of wine destined for a Bristol merchant. Setting off on 1st February she reached the approaches to the Bristol Channel seventeen days later.

According to the testimony of the captain and crew at mid day on the 18th they 'spoke' with a schooner outward bound from Bristol and were given a bearing for the island of Lundy about twenty or so miles ahead. On this basis they set course to pass between the island and Hartland Point on the English side of the Channel, and when evening fell reduced sail to just the main jib expecting to find themselves in the vicinity of the shoals known as The English Land by day-break.

At about four o'clock in the morning they were suddenly aroused by the mate, Joseph Kent who had the watch on deck, crying out that there was land ahead. Arriving on deck it was immediately apparent that the vessel was in trouble for ahead of them a line of breakers stretched right and left as far as they could see in the darkness. Desperately they tried to set sail and turn the little ship away from danger though it was apparent to at least one crew member that this was a forlorn hope and he chose to dive overboard in a vain attempt to swim ashore. This was the last they saw of him, and within a minute or so the *Mary* herself was trapped in the breakers.

In an attempt to prevent the ship being driven further ashore and turning turtle they cut away her mast but to no avail. The pounding surf stove in the ship's boat and shattered the decking filling the vessel with water. As it rolled helplessly in the surf the breakers continued their work of destruction – "stove in the stern and stove in all the cabbin so that the poore master lost all his substance and papers".

The master and his crew clung to the disintegrating wreck as best they could but about eight o'clock the mate Joseph Kent lost his hold and was swept away. The others managed to survive for another four hours or so before swimming to the beach with the aid of bits and pieces of wreckage. Only then did they discover that they had come ashore on the coast of Wales, "within two hundred yards or thereabouts of the mouth of a small river called Kenffigg River".

Joseph Kent's body was recovered and buried at Mawdlam church the following day, but there was apparently no trace of the other (unnamed) seaman who had dived overboard even before the vessel had struck. As for the fate of the ship's cargo that likewise is not mentioned, but it is a fair bet that however quickly the authorities moved to salvage those kegs of wine, many casks ended up in the homes of the local inhabitants!

The wreck of *le Vainquerer* **1753** which was a French merchant ship which foundered at Sker on the night of 12th December. I have yet to research the story of this wreck for myself, so these notes are based on the work of Leslie Evans 1956 book *Sker House.*

The crew of *le Vainquerer* consisted of ten seamen and the master, and it carried a cargo of oranges, figs, lemons and timber. When she stranded on Sker Point the master and two of his men were drowned but the other eight managed to make it ashore. Like so many wrecks in our area *Le Vainquerer* came to grief due to faulty navigation and was wildly off her intended course from Lisbon in Portugal to the port of Le Havre in France.

From the details of a subsequent enquiry held by Sir Herbert Mackworth of The Gnoll, Neath, we know that as news of the wreck spread through the hinterland a large crowd gathered to salvage what they could for themselves. Not only did they target the cargo but also the ship's rigging and timbers; even setting fire to some parts of the stricken vessel to get the copper nails from the timbers. Neither did the body of the Captain escape their attention when it was washed ashore. Seventeen golden Portuguese coins and his watch were taken from the pockets of the corpse and even the silver buckles were hacked from off his shoes. The watch was later recovered when it was taken for repair to a local watchmaker.

At this time Isaac Williams was Chief Constable for the Hundred of Newcastle, and during the course of the enquiry allegations were made by a witness named Griffith Peregrin of Swansea that he too had participated in pilfering the ship's cargo. Williams, he alleged, employed men to remove goods from the vessel and take them to the barns and courtyard of his house. Isaac for his part maintained that his actions had been designed to salvage as much of the cargo as was possible in order that it could be returned to the ship's owners. Initially, he said, his men had stacked the goods on the shore near the wreck but even though he placed a guard over them some was still spirited away by the looters. Removal of the goods to the safety of his house was, he maintained, the only practical alternative. Another witness named Edward Savours supported his testimony and no action was taken against him, but this was not the end of his troubles.

Seventeen local people had been arrested and charged with offences arising out of the plundering, and it was widely believed that Isaac had a hand in identifying them as the culprits. For some time afterwards, it is said, he went round the district in some fear of his life. Of the Petty Constables brought in by the authorities to search houses in the district all but one shirked their duty, and he too was subjected to threats against his life. A bailiff appointed to serve notices on the accused was so intimidated by his reception that he refused to return to the area a second time even after a promised payment of £50!

The Wreck of the *Friends' Endeavour* 1758 The skiff called *Friends' Endeavour* was a small craft, only rated at eleven tons, that put to sea from Port Eynon in Gower on 7th February 1758. Aboard were Thomas Smith, the master, and a crewman named Moses Jenkin. Their cargo consisting of "oisters and coqules" belonging to a consortium of local fishermen and intended for the fish-market at Bristol (B/K 11).

The two claimed that they reached "The English Land" between Porlock and Lynmouth about "five of ye clock at night", and in making his formal 'protest' Smith describes their subsequent progress in some detail. Whether the pair were drunk, hopelessly lost, or just bad navigators the little vessel clearly did not head in anything like the direction he claimed!

Thomas Smith who had been keeping watch on deck "went downe to ye cabben and desired the s'd Moses Jenkin to stand up in ye healme for fear that ye wind shift" and they would have to trim the sails. When the two got back on deck, they claimed, "we were in ye breakers"!

Unlike the seamen aboard the *Mary of Teneriffe* this pair were lucky. Their vessel was far smaller, and although the sea broke over the little vessel, it was "by good providence" driven "directly ashore" about six o'clock in the morning. The two earnestly declared to Richard Jenkins that the wreck had not occurred "by any neglect nor want of care in them or either of them". Looking out through the windows of the Town Hall towards Port Eynon they must have realised just how feeble a protest this really was, and been painfully aware also that it was unlikely to satisfy the irate fishermen from their village when they got home!

The _Industry_: The Margam accounts for the year 1767 (D/D Ma 21) records that on 17th March a sloop called _Industry_ had been wrecked on Margam Sands, though little else is known about the incident.

The Wreck of the _Planters Velvard_ The details concerning the wreck of the _Planters Velvard_ in 1770 are included by John David in his booklet _Porthcawl and its Coastline (2004: 5)_ in which he states that it struck the shore at Porthcawl Point (where the breakwater stands today). John's knowledge of local shipwrecks far exceeds my own, but in this instance I believe his statement is incorrect for all the evidence I have come across indicates that the vessel came to grief on Kenfig Sands near Sker Point.

Planters Velvard was a Dutch merchantman on passage from Surinam in the Dutch East Indies to Amsterdam. As was so often the case in those days (before the invention of a reliable chronometer) her captain set a course that was too far north and entered the Bristol Channel in the belief that it was the English Channel. There were 45 passengers and crew aboard and the vessel was carrying a mixed cargo of sugar, cotton, cocoa and coffee.

William Thomas noted in his diary (Denning, 1995) on 5th July that this wreck had occurred about five weeks earlier, and that most of the fifteen casualties were passengers and included just one or two of the crew at most. Rumour (for such must have been the origin of his information) claimed that most of the passengers were wealthy and included "a gentlewoman drowned with her fortune of about 200 dollars". "Much wealth", he comments wryly, "Went to the bottom of the sea". He follows this with the enigmatic statement that "Them of Bridgend kept as much as came to shore, except what thievery about, to the owners", which perhaps means that whilst there were looters about most local people handed what they saved for return to the ship's owners. Against this has to be set a report from the customs officer who attempted to save the ship and its cargo that "the country people are quite outrageous, and threaten our lives". The Reverend William Gilpin (1783: 76-9) who was sight-seeing in Wales at the time saw the wreck on Kenfig sands and records how initially "the populace came down in large bodies to pillage the wreck, which the officers of the customs, and the gentlemen of the country assembled to protect". A running fight developed and the authorities succeeded in recovering eight horses loaded with coffee from the looters.

Amongst the casualties of the shipwreck were three brothers surnamed Jackert who had been sent home to Holland by their father to be educated. They lie buried together in the churchyard at Newton, but the gravestone marking their last resting place sank and was eventually lost beneath grass and weeds. Following up clues from some old church documents John David was able to locate the site of the grave in 2002 and their memorial has now been restored to public view.

William Gilpin, who witnessed the remains of the unfortunate vessel on Kenfig Sands, was amongst the first of many tourists who began visiting Wales in increasing numbers as the century progressed. Joanna Martin (1995: 9) expresses the view that the 'discovery' of the beauties of Wales by English tourists (almost exclusively drawn from the ranks of the nobility and gentry) began with a tour of the country undertaken by H P Wyndham in 1774, four years after Gilpin's visit. During the six weeks he spent in the Principality, Wyndham says that he did not encounter a similar party of his countrymen, but his published *Tour of Wales* soon drew their attention to the scenery and history of the country.

With the French Revolution in 1789 and the subsequent war with France, the 'European Tour' that had previously been so popular with the upper classes became impracticable, and many were inspired by Wyndham's account to follow his example. From time to time we will meet some of them who turned up at Kenfig to view the sights and, like Gilpin, left a record of what they saw.

Gilpin was also an artist, and as such, it has to be said, was not impressed by the countryside between Aberavon and Kenfig (which he mistakenly refers to as Pyle). Margam Burrows he found "quite offensive to the eye", and though the hills inland were forested, its woodlands he thought lacked "variety of breaks [which] like the members of architecture, gave a lightness and elegance to their forms". These hills were, he said, "mere uniform lumps of matter; and were everywhere overspread with one heavy, uninterrupted bush".

As can be imagined he was even less impressed with Kenfig "which stands on a bleak coast - the spirit of the country is totally lost". His own spirits were however lifted by the artistic possibilities of the wreck of the *Planters Velvard* where the authorities were engaged in recovering the ship's cargo – "a busy scene composed of multitudes of men, carts, horses and horsemen." He then treats the reader to a discourse on the difficulty of composing a picture including a crowd scene before concluding, "The subject before us is as well adapted, as any species of crowd can be, to exhibit the beauties of composition. Horses, carts, and men make a good assemblage; and this variety in the parts appear to great advantage from the simplicity of a winding shore; and of a stranded ship (a large, dark object) heeling on one side, in a corner of the piece". In lieu of one day discovering a sketch or painting by Gilpin himself depicting the scene, this eye-witness account is the best I can offer.

The Wreck of the *Ballmer* I have two dates for this particular wreck! John David (2004) in *Porthcawl and its Coastline* says that it happened on 14th December, 1792; whilst Yvonne Carr (1995: 11) in *Wrecks Around & About Kenfig* dates it to the following New Year's Day. The latter adds that the vessel was on passage from Lisbon to London with a cargo of oranges, so its captain was yet another of those that blithely headed straight into the coast of South Wales in the belief that he was sailing up the English Channel.

The vessel was of a type known as a brigantine or 'brig', and its name sounds as though it might have been French, but other than this very little is known of its story other than the fact that its final resting place on Kenfig Sands enabled the burgesses to make some money from the subsequent salvage work. In a minute dated 11th January 1793 a note

BRIGANTINE. A small light vessel, vhich can both row and sail well, being idapted either for fighting or for chase

was made of "the service of the Town Hall, and the damage it receives" through being used for housing "cable, sail, rigging and other valuable articles" from the wreck. For this the Corporation received the sum of two guineas (£2.10) per week "while the goods remain in the Town Hall".

Two years later, incidentally, on the 10th January 1794 they also received the sum of three guineas (£3.15) for "Trespass made on the Burgesses' land by hauling timber (being the cargo of the ship *Perseverance*) over the same". The account submitted by the Portreeve, Daniel Rees, later that year adds the information that this too was a brig that was bound for London from the Bay of Honduras and that the timber in question was mahogany.

Appendix to this Chapter: [This long and tedious tale has little to do with Kenfig or its people, but is included here as an amusing diversion! Ed.]

The Strange Voyage of the Kenfig *FALCON*

It is strange but true that not long after the wreck of the *Mary* work began building another sloop in the unlikely setting of Kenfig Burrows. It was the brainchild of our old friend Morgan Waters, late of Marlas farm. Perhaps it was the wreck that had gave him the germ of the idea, and maybe he utilised some of the timber recovered from that ill-fated vessel. Either way he saw this as an ideal opportunity to force his way into the ranks of the merchant class and Leslie Evans found evidence that timber for the vessel's construction was being purchased from the Margam estate in 1740. (Evans, 1960)

What Morgan Waters actually knew about ship construction and navigation would probably not have filled a matchbox, so he took as his partner, a mariner named Evan Evan of Newton who would be the master of the new vessel. It was not long however before Morgan's dreams of entering the world of merchant ship-owners began to disintegrate. He was already up to his eyes in debt with the Margam estate for arrears of rent for Marlas Farm to which was now added the cost of the timber he had purchased to build the vessel that was eventually launched sometime in 1741.

By December of that year the Margam agent for young Thomas Mansel was pressing him for payment and seeking to take possession of the sloop which had been named the *Falcon*. Waters claimed that he had already transferred a half share to his partner Evan Evan for £50, so the agent promptly demanded that he hand over this sum to the estate and transfer to them ownership of the other half. The idea seems to have been that Mansel would retain possession of Morgan's half share until his debts were paid off out of the profits (less expenses) made by the vessel (PM 1537).

This document is dated the 10th December at about which time the *Falcon* sailed out of Tenby with a cargo consisting of 450 barrels of coal; two casks of ale, and a cask of beeswax. Nothing further was then heard of it until 20th May following, when two ragged and travel-stained men presented themselves at the gate of Margam House asking to speak with Lord Mansel.

These were Samuel Hughes and William Humphries who, together with Evan Evan had constituted the crew of the vessel when she set off on that curious voyage. Unfortunately they were unable to give the exact date on which the *Falcon* sailed, only that it was "some day in the beginning of December" which "might be about a ffortnight before Christmas". It would seem therefore that at the time both they and the master were probably unaware of Morgan's transfer of his share in the vessel to Talbot. Having listened to their story Mansel's staff at Margam called in a local Magistrate named Anthony Powell who took from them a statement made under oath which forms the basis of this account (PM 1544).

Ostensibly when she left Tenby the *Falcon* was bound for the Port of London and had obtained clearance from HM Customs for this voyage, but as it progressed there is a strong suspicion that this was not the actual destination that Evan Evan intended. The government of the day, and indeed for centuries before, had placed an embargo upon trade in most produce with other countries deemed to be 'hostile' to Britain – which invariably included both

France and Spain. Heavy export duties were consequently imposed upon goods carried to such destinations the exports from which were likewise very scarce and consequently valuable commodities. Wily mariners therefore often obtained permits to sail from one British port to another and then got blown (or so they subsequently claimed) by storms and contrary winds to the shores of these forbidden destinations. Once there, of course, they disposed of whatever cargo they happened to be carrying and returned home laden with goods which (because of their rarity) earned huge profits on the home market.

The *Falcon* did indeed fail to round Land's End and enter the English Channel, but in truth on this occasion the weather does seem to have been adverse. The two sailors described how a south-easterly gale carried them onto the west coast of Ireland where they eventually took shelter at Crookhaven near Cork after a voyage of five days. Here they remained eight or nine days before setting off again with the aid of a westerly wind that would have been ideal for their stated purpose. Instead, however, just twenty-four hours later they put into the port of Sligo on Ireland's Atlantic coast! A westerly wind would have made reaching Spain difficult, but they were now ideally placed to make such a trip once the weather moderated!

At Sligo, Evan sold off about 90 barrels of coal and the beeswax, but there was a complication in that anchored in the harbour was a British man-of war called *Superb*. By this time the magistrate Powell and the others listening to the seamen's tale were probably themselves becoming sceptical as to Evan's intended destination. When therefore they learnt that the master had disposed of the two barrels of beer to the officers of the warship they began questioning the men even more closely suspecting that the cargo had been used to bribe the Navy men into turning a blind eye to the *Falcon's* activities. On this point however the pair could not say whether the transaction was a sale or a 'gift'.

The vessel remained at Sligo for about a fortnight, but loaded no cargo whatsoever, and when Evan Evan finally set sail on 1st February it was with the declared intention of reaching the Isles of Scilly. Navigation in these days was still largely a case of 'by guess and by God', so there was of course a distinct possibility that, even without trying, he might 'miss' these islands altogether and finish up on the coasts of France. Northern Spain or even Portugal. Either the master's navigation really was woeful or they again met adverse weather, for the next landfall the little vessel actually made was The Lizard peninsular in Cornwall! Here Evan seems to have taken shelter for some fourteen hours to take stock of the situation before setting off once more – this time heading up the English Channel towards the Dover Straits. Perhaps Evan Evan had decided that having been tossed hither and thither by the storms of an Atlantic Winter his original destination of London was not such a bad option after all!

Whether this was indeed the case we shall never know, for as the *Falcon* battled onwards up the Channel a strong NNE wind carried her across to the coast of France and deposited her on a sandy beach on the north-eastern side of the Somme estuary. Despite their efforts to refloat her at high tide it was clear the little vessel was stuck fast. Thinking her to be a total loss they sought assistance from some of the local inhabitants and brought ashore all their provisions and personal belongings before setting off to the town of Abbeyville some twelve miles inland. Here they duly made their 'protest' to the Chief Magistrate in similar form to the one made by the crew of the *Mary* to the Kenfig Portreeve.

At this point Evan Evan sent the two crewmen back to the vessel telling them he was going to St Valery, a small port on the opposite side of the estuary, to secure assistance to salvage her. He did not exactly hurry himself! It was eight days before they saw him again during which time they took up residence back in the *Falcon* which, other than the fact that it was firmly aground, was otherwise little the worse for wear.

When eventually their master showed up he brought with him two carpenters who were unable to complete their examination of the hull due to the state of the tide and the depth to which it had sunk in the sand. It was then another nine days before they saw the master again! This time he did indeed return with a pilot and eight men to try and free the ship, but one is left wondering whether he had been secretly hoping that his vessel would be finished off by some winter storm. Seventeen days had now elapsed since the *Falcon* had first struck the beach!

With this added assistance the *Falcon* was freed from the sand and then sailed across to St Valery under her own power. Here a more thorough examination was carried out but she had in fact suffered remarkably little damage. The jib sail had been torn to shreds, but the damage to the remainder of the canvas and rigging was trifling and, in the view of the two seamen, could easily have been repaired using the remains of the jib. As for the hull the damage was repaired by a single carpenter over the next two days after which "she was sound and tite and had no leak".

Two days after the vessel had been brought to safety Evan Evan again left, telling his crew that he was going to London. When he returned about a week later he told the men that he had there raised a hundred guineas on the vessel's insurance and taken it to his father in Glamorgan. He further claimed that he was now under orders from the insurers to sell the ship as a 'total loss'! Ignorant and illiterate seamen they may have been, but even they could smell a rat when it was a scam this blatant! Once the repair to the *Falcon's* hull had been made they themselves were in no doubt that in all respects she was a seaworthy vessel that "might safely sail to England".

According to the practice of the day a notice was duly fixed to the ship's mast which, so the men were informed, stated that the vessel was to be sold. "A drum was beat for five days about the town" to give notice of the event and on the sixth day the sale took place. Several people attended, and some of them entered bids, but when the auctioneer's gavel eventually fell the vessel had been sold to none other than the ship's master (and part-owner) – Evan Evan himself. He now not only had the insurance money – he was sole owner of the *Falcon* as well!

Once more the wily little master left St Valery promising to return the following Monday (March 1st) with the money to pay for his purchase. It was the last the two crewmen saw of him. Eventually, on the 8th of May, they went to see a Mr Phillip Bollinger who was the agent for the insurers in the port of St Vallery. The two had heard the master say (having presumably acquired the knowledge on his previous visit to Wales) that half the vessel was owned by Thomas Lord Mansel. The agent therefore advised them to return to Britain, seek out Mansel, and tell him what had taken place. In the meantime he would write to the insurers and make sure that vessel did not leave harbour.

As we are aware Thomas Lord Mansel spent most of his short life with his mother at Charlton, but to the crewmen he was the 'Baron of Margam', and after a journey of twelve days, that is where they eventually arrived. Whether they were rewarded for their efforts, and what became of the first and (so far as I know) last ship ever to be launched from Kenfig Dunes, I cannot tell you. As alas is so often the case in local history, our little story ends in mid-air.

Chapter 6
Some Kenfig Curiosities

Because of the nature of my coverage of the period 1700-1750 it is inevitable that several items relating to Kenfig and district during the period have been omitted from my narrative. In the belief that they may be of interest, and show something of the life of the ordinary Kenfig-folk I have therefore included them here in a chapter of their own.

Cleaning the Mill Leat, 1725. "For ale given to the tenants that helped to cleanse Lanvihangel mill pound ….. 5s" (PM 2185). Although I have not come across such a clause in leases relating to property in either of the Kenfig manors, cleaning out the mill leat at Llanmihangel as and when required was apparently a 'duty' imposed upon certain Margam tenants. This must have been a wet, mucky task that cannot have been very popular with those required to undertake it, so it is rather nice to note that the Margam steward on this occasion rewarded their efforts with a little liquid refreshment!

The Earthquake. Sometime during 1726 local inhabitants were shaken (quite literally) by an earthquake that struck the area and is mentioned in a passing reference to the event in the Margam accounts for the following year (PM 2184). This records payment to three tilers and their assistants for repairing damage caused to the roof of Margam House. No other details are known, but the number of workmen involved suggests that the damage was fairly extensive.

Repairing the Tithe Barn. Jenkin Lawrence is a curious character who probably lived in North Cornelly. He is first mentioned in 1712 and died in 1764. Born Jenkin Humphrey, for some reason he changed his name in the mid 1720s, a not unusual occurrence during this period when the use of patronyms was going out of fashion in favour of surnames. In 1722 he combined with a Kenfig burgess (Evan John, the blacksmith from Heol Las) to lease the tithes, tithe barn, and some land adjoining it from the Margam estate for five years (PM 5347) in a similar manner to the Lyddon consortium a few years earlier.

The barn complex was obviously falling into some disrepair, and in 1724 the two had to make repairs to the gate leading into the yard. On this occasion timber for the work was provided by the estate though the normal rule was that tenants made such repairs themselves and then claimed back the cost. Quite serious problems had also developed in the roof of the barn, and the two apparently balked at the sort of expense involved. When their five year tenure came to an end therefore they apparently declined to renew the agreement unless the estate gave them some financial or practical assistance.

In the straightened circumstances of the time Margam had no success persuading anyone else to take on the property on the old terms so accordingly, in April 1729, was forced to conclude a new agreement with Lawrence and John (PM 1514). By this the pair undertook to repair the barn's thatch with reed supplied by the estate, promising that any left over would be returned to the Lord of the Manor. Their annual rent was also reduced by £5 and it was accepted that thereafter responsibility for maintaining the property would remain with the landlord. The couple were even given a ladder to carry out the work 'which we promise to keep drye and leave the same upon the premises'. A small example of how the adverse conditions of early 18th century Kenfig could sometimes work in favour of its residents.

A Question of Reputation. For somebody like myself looking back at the past and its characters with a great deal of affection, it is sometimes easy to lose sight of the fact that these were people who had all the weaknesses and failings that we have today. A case of slander involving Gwenllian William of Cornelly heard at the Llandaff Consistory Court in 1731 (LL/CC/G 609 a-e & 610) is therefore a good antidote to this even though it does not actually relate to Kenfig.

It does, however, involve Jenkin Humphrey (under his alternative name of Jenkin Lawrence) whom we met in the last item, in connection with the Tithe Barn, and also Elizabeth the daughter of Richard Yorwerth who had recently (9th October 1730) married a Phillip Thomas. (At the time of the incident Elizabeth and Phillip lived in the parish of Pyle (probably at North Cornelly) but by the time of the hearing had moved to Margam after which I lose all trace of them. The suit arose out of a violent quarrel in the village of Cornelly (whether North or South is not stated, but probably the former). During this argument, which evidently became very heated, Gwenllian was accused by Elizabeth and a man known as Rees Evan of being a prostitute. They further alleged that Jenkin Lawrence was her 'pimp' who was employing her in this capacity.

These allegations were made in front of a sixteen-year-old lad named Jenkin Lawrence who was presumably the son of Jenkin senior. Young Jenkin subsequently gave evidence on Gwenllian's behalf at the hearing as did nineteen-year-old Jennet Thomas, both confirming the allegations made by her. Nest Morgan, (Possibly Nest Howell (1681-1748), a member of a family that later farmed at Stormy and who baptised children by her husband David Morgan in 1714 & 1723 (PPR)) a widow aged fifty was also called to give evidence but was more wary. She confirmed what Rees Evan is alleged to have said, but perhaps had no wish to get on the wrong side of Elizabeth Thomas and the Yorwerth family. When giving evidence against her Nest claimed she did not hear her say anything as she herself was then "a considerable distance from them". She nevertheless conceded that Jenkin and Jennet "stood nearer to the said Elizabeth ... & might hear what was spoken by each of ye said parties".

As is usually the case with these records we do not know the outcome of the hearing. It nevertheless serves as a timely reminder (if one is needed) that relationships between those characters who appear in our story was not necessarily sweetness and light!

Heating the Town Hall. In the 1990s the fireplace that formerly stood at the eastern end of the Town Hall was carefully blocked off and plastered over to improve the appearance of the room. With the advent of central heating it had long been superfluous to requirements, but was probably an original feature of the building. It was certainly there in the early 1730s when the Portreeve of the day paid Thomas John, a local carpenter and burgess, "for a large stone to putt before ye ffire place; and ye putting of it; & haleing it from Margam Mountain".

Getting the Measure of Things. Documents of this period are full of unfamiliar words used to describe quantities and other various units of measure as we noted when analysing the exports from the Port of

Newton in 1672. It was not however just a question of the terminology used, which the people of the time would have understood even if we don't. There was also the fact that in different parts of the country a unit of measure that was nominally the same as that used elsewhere could actually differ quite considerably. The problem is rather neatly outlined in a document (PM 2714) concerning the processing of tithe corn collected from the parish of Pyle & Kenfig in 1742. In it quantities are given in either 'Bridgend measure', 'Neath measure' or 'Winsister (Winchester) measure'. This is one of the first appearances of the last named which eventually became accepted as the Imperial Standard throughout the country.

Keeping the Hedges Trimmed. A constant source of complaint by juries at Courts Leet was the state of the hedgerows adjoining roads in Kenfig Lower, particularly on those like Heol Fach and Heol y Lane which were all quite narrow. Overgrown and unkempt hedgerows dislodged loads carried by wagons on these highways causing loss of both time and some of the contents. In an effort to alleviate the problem in 1743 the burgesses made a ruling that all hedges adjoining highways in the Borough were to be kept trimmed to within three foot of the top of the field bank. It did little to improve the situation but it is nice to know exactly what standard they thought to be acceptable!

Punishing Offenders. At the Court Leet held in May 1743 the jury noted "the stocks to be out of repair, and to be repaired by the Burgesses". As has already been mentioned (p 44) the accounts of the Portreeve Edward Harris show that he actually had a new set of stocks made and that these were then placed in the churchyard at Mawdlam. Nevertheless I have so far not come across any record of them actually being used, and certainly the manorial and Borough courts held in the Town Hall would not have been able to sentence offenders to be placed in them. Perhaps therefore they were never actually used and just a treasured relic from the days when the Petty Session courts for the Hundred were held at Kenfig before being moved to Newcastle in the time of Henry VIII.

At the same time there is also a record in the Borough minutes that a room beneath the stairs giving access to the Town Hall was, or had been, a lock-up or gaol. This gave the local constable somewhere to temporarily confine offenders he had arrested, but could also have been used to hold local malefactors sentenced elsewhere to a term in the stocks and returned to Kenfig for this punishment to be meted out.

In his accounts Edward Harris, the Portreeve claimed expenses for replacing the Borough stocks in Mawdlam churchyard, though it is debatable if these were actually still used for their original purpose. He includes payments for haulage and the iron fittings, and on his own account one shilling for marking up the timber. However there is no claim for the actual carpentry work involved, and the implication is that he made them himself free of charge.

The Pound It was the responsibility of the Kenfig Hayward to seize any animals found straying in the lower borough and place them in the common pound adjoining the Corporation House. Here they would remain for a time until claimed by their owners (who paid a fine for their recovery) or otherwise disposed of. Technically unclaimed strays became the property of the Lord of the Manor and at Stormy, for example, were eventually removed to Margam. In Kenfig Lower, however, it was apparently one of the perquisites of the Portreeve that he himself might retain such livestock on payment of the appropriate fine to the Lord. So it is that in 1726 there is an entry for the payment of three shillings from Portreeve Howell Jenkin "for three strayed sheep taken up within ye s'd Burrough ……. according to the custome" (PM 2188), just one of many examples that could be cited. Since the fines represented only a fraction of the true value of the animals, this was indeed a valuable little perk of the office.

The pound was a strongly built compound with stone walls and a padlock on the gate, and removing livestock without payment of the fine was an offence called 'pound breach'. This, nevertheless, did not prevent certain people attempting to illegally free their livestock in this manner. "We do present Evan John David", one manorial jury reported in May 1737 (B/K 11), "for Pound Breach in breaking open the wall of ye Common Pound and taking out his cattell contrary to law". He was not alone, and over the years the walls and gate of the pound were constantly in need of repairs over and above those caused by the wear and tear of normal usage.

Evan John David was, incidentally, a burgess who probably farmed at Penymynydd, so he would have been allowed as of right to pasture livestock on the common where the Hayward (William Harry of Corporation House) presumably discovered his cattle. Owners who turned their animals out onto this land were nevertheless supposed to mark them with their own individual sign in tar or pitch ('Pitch marks') so that they could easily be identified. Evan had presumably been grazing this herd on his own land without any thought of turning them onto the common, so they were unmarked. When they broke out of their pasture the Hayward consequently took them to be strays, which technically they were. Evan in turn may well have believed that he was within his rights to release his property when it had been (in his view) illegally impounded.

Again, Edward Harris's accounts indicate a claim for replacing the door of the common pound. The charges for the timber, iron fittings and haulage of the door are duly noted, but nothing for actually making the item or fitting it other than "sixpence for ale to Samuel Lydon and his aprentis for asissting of me in hanging the doer of ye said pound".

It is rather a nice touch as Samuel was, of course, himself a carpenter who had only just returned to the Borough after his sojourn on Stormy Down. Later on Edward Harris frequently employed him to carry out repair work to Borough property. Another item relates to a payment to Edmund Harry, his wife and his daughter at The Corporation House for various tasks including carrying water "& atending of ye mason" employed in repairing the wall of the pound. The daughter would have been Gwenllian who, at the very most could only have been six years of age. We can therefore imagine Harris being amused by her carrying out the little tasks she was given with all the solemn concentration of a child of that age, and quietly slipping her a penny or two for herself.

Laying Down the Laws: Hayfields and Pastures Most years the work of the Kenfig Portreeve was purely routine and not particularly interesting. He oversaw the collection of rates and taxes; ensured that the Town Hall and other Borough property was kept in proper repair; and rubber-stamped such mundane transactions as the transfer of parcels of hay and fern between burgesses. Every now and then, however, there came a time when hard and difficult decisions had to be made and the majesty and power inherent in the ancient office displayed. Such a time arrived for Edward Harris on 18th January 1751. (B/K 11).

As was common practice he gave notice that on that day the burgesses were to assemble at a Hall Day where they were to consider two problems that had probably been awaiting his decision for some time.

Hayfields The first concerned the 'hay ground' in the enclosure at Waun Cimla and the failure or reluctance on the part of certain burgesses to keep the fencing on their parcels in good repair. Complaints about this make monotonously frequent appearances in the Borough minute books as do the subsequent (and evidently inadequate) measures taken to ensure the work was done. The normal action was for the Portreeve (or the Constable of the Castle) to allow the plot-holder a certain period of time to repair the fence subject to a fine. If the work was not done then (in theory!) the fine was imposed and a fresh order made. The normal response to such orders was, however – nothing! Repairs were apparently not done; the fine not imposed; and the same people are reported for the state of the fences at some future court as though nothing had happened.

Perhaps, at bottom, the problem lay with the jury whose job it was to report the state of the fences in the first place. The 'offenders' in question were often their family, friends or neighbours. They knew nothing would happen the first time a property was reported, but once the repairs had been ordered and a penalty imposed, reporting the failure of the miscreant to comply with the order would result in them being fined that sum of money. They therefore seem to have chosen to believe that the work had been done and report it again as though it was a new complaint. It was rather like the case of the manorial courts at Higher Kenfig in the 17th century where (if the records are to be believed) property seems to have miraculously fallen into disrepair on a change of owner. The new tenant was a stranger whereas his predecessor had been a neighbour of long-standing whose failure to maintain his property to the highest standards the jurors had simply chosen to ignore.

The sole purpose of the fences at Waun Cimla seems to have been to mark the division between the 29 plots into which it was divided, for there is no indication that any of the burgesses pastured livestock there. Had that been the case then the internal fences would probably have been raised on banks and reinforced by ditches to make the barriers more effective, but there are no traces of such boundaries on the ground there today.

Some burgesses may have argued that so long as there were a few posts to mark the line of demarcation with the adjoining plots, what was the point in having to fork out for a complete fence? But, Edward Harris may have retorted, the Ordinances stated that each holder was to fence his or her plot, and the law is the law. Furthermore, there was nothing (other than the inconvenient distance of Waun Cimla from Kenfig) to stop plot holders pasturing livestock there if they so wished. If one chose to do so in the future then, without proper fencing their cattle or sheep could trespass across the entire enclosure!

Whatever the reason Harris determined that now was the time to settle this problem once and for all. Having discussed the matter with his council and listened to their advice he ruled that in future the Portreeve and his Eight Elected Burgesses would make an annual inspection of the enclosure at Waun Cimla sometime prior to 24th March. The holders of any plots of hay where the fences were in disrepair were to be allowed a reasonable amount of time to carry out remedial work as previously but if they failed then the Portreeve was given wide powers to ensure the work was done. Firstly he, and those acting on his behalf, could enter on the land and carry out the repairs themselves. Then, to pay for the work, the plot would be rented to another burgesses for as long as it took to recoup the cost. It was a draconian measure but it had the desired effect for complaints about the fences at Waun Cimla are conspicuous by their absence from the minute books for a considerable time afterwards.

Pastures The second matter upon which Edward Harris was required to rule concerned the pasturing of livestock on the Borough common. Every burgess had, since the earliest days of the Borough, been permitted to pasture upon it as much livestock as he owned. Animals found grazing there that belonged to anyone who was not a burgess would be seized, impounded by the Hayward as strays, and the owner would have to pay a fine to obtain their release.

Some of Edward's fellow burgesses had now come up with a dodge whereby they turned outsiders' stock onto the common alongside their own claiming 'an interest' in these animals because they received a fee from the owners for looking after them. This practice Harris now declared illegal, and he ruled that any burgess found doing so would forfeit their own right of common and be disfranchised – i.e. would lose his status as a burgess.

There was one exception which was the Portreeve himself. 'Ah!', I thought when I first read this - 'One law for the rich, etc, etc!' In truth, however, this exception was probably made simply to allow Portreeves to issue permits to outsiders permitting them use of the common pasture in return for an annual fee paid to the Corporation, as the records show was occasionally to have been the case from time to time.

Pont Y Morfa How many people I wonder know that there was once a bridge across the River Kenfig a little downstream from Kenfig castle? I am not talking here about the temporary one erected to carry stone for building the extension to the harbour at Port Talbot in the 1970s, but an even earlier structure. Known as Pont y Morfa it was a footbridge that was probably used by the residents of the two Morfa Farms standing on the north side of the river to reach Kenfig across the dunes. Not only did this enable them in their capacity as burgesses to attend meetings at the Town Hall dry-shod, but also gave them easy access to the two public houses here without having to make the long detour to Pont Felin Newydd further upstream.

Although it is difficult to see any other reason for the bridge, its maintenance was nevertheless the responsibility of the Borough and appears for the first time in the minute books in the record of a Court Leet held on 13th October 1751. Here the jury reported "the bridge leading from Kenfigg to Margam Moors to be out of repair, and to be repaired by the inhabitants of this Borough". Mention of subsequent repairs to the structure appear from time to time throughout the 18th century, but it is not shown on any 19th century maps of the area and had presumably gone out of use by the time they were made.

Spars, Sand, Shells & Shipwrecks. A group of documents comprising the accounts of the Margam estate during the 1750s make particularly interesting reading because the entries in them are unusually detailed as illustrated by the following extracts, not all of which relate specifically to Kenfig but are nevertheless interesting in their own right.

There is, for example, an early example of nature conservancy in the recorded payment of the sum of £2. 1s. 0d. to a Mr John Roberts "for 19 deal spars delivered towards making ladders for the use of sundry tenants". The entry goes on to explain that this was "to save and preserve the destruction of the finest young oak trees usually cut for such purposes" (D/DP 26).

Another payment of £1 15s 0d was made to "Richard Henry and Mary Jenkin" for "work done with their cart, and in carrying of sand from Kenfigg to Margam in order to make mortar towards building the garden walls"(D/DP 24). This is the only reference I have come across to Kenfig sand being used for construction work at this time and it has always been my understanding that it is actually unsuitable for the purpose.

The problem is that having been moved about by the wind for so long the individual grains of Kenfig sand have been rounded off, and so lack the jagged edges of 'sharp' sand from rivers and beaches. As such they are not an effective bonding agent in mortar and cement, nor do they provide good drainage required in potting compost. Nevertheless Graham John, a resident of Kenfig and a founder-member of the Kenfig Society tells me that in the 1930s he well remembers sand being extracted from the dunes on a commercial basis with the aid of a horse-drawn tramway. It is only relatively recently too that sand and gravel extraction has ceased in Newton dunes.

The accounts also tell us that sometime towards the end of October 1752 an unfortunate sailing vessel seems to have come to grief in Swansea Bay, probably on Scarweather sandbank. On 13th October the estate repaid Isaac Williams of Sker House fourteen shillings that he had paid to Edmund Harry, licensee of The Corporation House, and others for salvaging "a piece of wreck mahogany which came ashore on Kenfig Sands" (D/DP 24). Mahogany was (and still is for that matter) a valuable timber, but having apparently not been able to find a suitable use for it, the estate sold it back to Isaac a fortnight later for the same amount (D/DP 18). Perhaps it still exists somewhere in the fabric of the old house at Sker today! In June the following year (1753) there is a hint in the accounts that another shipping disaster had occurred in Swansea Bay when William Henry of Ty'n Cellar and others discovered a ship's mast and bowsprit washed up on Margam Sands. (D/DP 39).

Rather more bizarre is another entry from the same source that records £2. 3s. 0d was paid out, part of which was to be shared amongst "sundry persons for shells gathered on Kenfigg, Margam, Aberavon and Swansea Sands for the use of John Talbot Esqr". The residue was spent "for boxes to put them in to be sent to Lacock". Despite his efforts to get the estate back on its feet Thomas Talbot spent little time at Margam, preferring instead his mansion at Lacock Abbey where he was perhaps planning to create a rural grotto in the grounds that would be decorated with these sea-shells from Swansea Bay.

A General Election Outing No doubt the General Election held in April 1754 caused quite a stir amongst the Kenfig burgesses if only because elections in those days were actually quite rare events. Between 1734 and 1820, for example, there were only four contested elections in Glamorgan for the seat of 'County Member' (Grant, 1978: 10). The Kenfig Burgesses were however casting their votes for Glamorgan's second MP to represent the boroughs of the county, though Raymond Grant's book on the history of Parliamentary Representation in Glamorgan gives no details of this particular contest. Normally such things were arranged by the gentry of the County who, like the Mansels of Margam, controlled the votes of their tenants, determined who should be the one and only candidate amongst themselves. Bad democracy maybe, but as Grant shrewdly notes, a good way of avoiding the huge expenses involved in a contested campaign!

Herbert Mackworth was the sitting MP for the County Boroughs at this time, an office he had held since 1739, but clearly somebody stood against him which forced this election. A ballot was held that he evidently won. His candidacy was supported by the Talbots, and the Margam accounts (D/DP 52) record the payment of £1. 17s. 0d to Edward Harris as the Kenfig Portreeve for "what he paid for the expenses of the Burgesses to and from Mr Mackworth's election at Cardiff". There they had probably been wined, dined and otherwise courted by the agents of the prospective candidates before voting for whoever Harris told them to vote for and arriving back home late that night having enjoyed what was for most of them a rare excursion to 'foreign parts'!

The Rabbit Wars A brief entry in the minute book for the 1754 Spring Court Leet marks the start of what was to prove a continuing theme in Kenfig's history over the next century. (For some reason, probably the election, this was not held until 21st June.) It says simply that the jury had presented "the rabets on the burgesses' land in default of the Hayward". They repeated it again at the Leet held on 11th October, and these mark the opening salvoes in a struggle that I have termed, tongue in cheek, as 'The Rabbit Wars'.

The problem lay in the dunes that formed the burgesses' common at Kenfig which, by the middle of the 18th century, were becoming overrun with rabbits. These pests had been introduced to Britain by the Normans and brought to Kenfig in medieval times with the creation of the warren known as The Conyger. This, it will be recalled, had been situated within the original dune system immediately adjoining the coast and its presence played no small part in causing the destabilising of the dunes and subsequent sand encroachment.

In 1754 this warren was still there, stretching from the Kenfig estuary on the north right down to the border with Sker on the south where there was another warren forming part of that manor. Both the Earls of Pembroke and the Mansels of Margam in their capacity as Lords of the Manor had never exploited the warren commercially themselves but rather leased it out to tenants along with the demesne lands. Originally the rent had been 'thirty couples of rabbits' per year, but by the middle of the 18th century this had been commuted to a cash payment. When the demesne was broken up after 1744 the tenancy of the warren remained with the portion attached to Pool Farmhouse of which a William John was the tenant in 1754.

Over the years other, smaller warrens were also established on the fringes of the dunes. The one at Sker has already been mentioned, but there was another on the north side of The Plwryn that was held with that cottage and a very small one a little further north again adjoining Portland. The tithe map of 1846 also indicates the existence of a fifth warren lying between The Angel Inn and Mawdlam Cross, but how long that had been in existence prior to this I have been unable to ascertain.

Those who operated these warrens encouraged the rabbits to breed there, making a regular cull of their numbers for sale both as meat and for their skins. The trouble was that there was nothing to prevent the conies spreading elsewhere throughout the common, and by the 1750s there was a very real danger of the entire area becoming one vast warren. The rabbits created burrows in which the burgesses' livestock could catch and break a leg, and they also competed for the dune-land's sparse grazing. Worse still this expansion had brought them to the fringes of the cultivated lands of the manor, and the pasture and crops in the burgesses' fields and gardens were beginning to suffer. The burgesses could do nothing about those areas of their common designated as warrens, but were furious about the manner in which the conies now spread unchecked across Kenfig Down and the North or Windmill Hill common.

Initially, as these entries in the minute books show, they blamed the Hayward who may well have protested that culling rabbits on the common was not one of his many duties. His protest seems to have been partially accepted, and in the accounts

RABBITS IN 2012 ON KENFIG DUNES
(GAYNOR BALL)

of the Portreeve, Edward Harris, we find that he actually employed a man to go round the common filling in rabbit holes to encourage them to return from whence they came.

Edward Evan was paid three shillings for undertaking this work for three weeks, but when Edmund Harry performed the task for a whole year in 1751 the cost was 11s 9d. Richard Matthew undertook the job for the years 1752 and 1753 and was paid a total of £1. 3s. 6d. Paltry sums in today's terms maybe, but over 20% of the annual income from the Borough Rate! Whilst the measures seem to have achieved a certain success this was a problem that just refused to go away, and the efforts of the Kenfig Corporation to find a solution repeatedly resurfaces throughout our history hereafter.

The Circulating Schools In Part II of *Kenfig Folk* I illustrated the positive impact made upon local education by the short-lived Welsh Trust School held at the Town Hall during the 1670s. This I did by comparing the number of local men and women living in the borough capable of signing their names against those who could only make their mark. As I explained then, this is not a truly accurate means of assessing the impact of such education but proves some indicator that it was taking place.

The accompanying table shows how, as the former pupils of that school died out so the literacy of the inhabitants tended to decline, indicating that it was probably not replaced. From a high of 73.7% capable of signing documents in 1720, it sank to less than 60% for the period 1750 –1800. Yet, there were schools here, and the statistics actually illustrate a flaw in my system in that schools were held in the borough in the forties and fifties, but ones where the pupils were taught to read – but not to write.

These were the Welsh Circulating schools that were the brainchild of an Anglican clergyman named Griffith Jones (1683-1761) whose name will always be associated with his parish at Llanddowror to which he was appointed in 1716. Here he started his first school in 1731-2 and the movement spread rapidly across Wales. Funds were short, so they were set up only at places where there was a local sponsor and - lacking money to hire premises - classes were usually held on church premises or even in empty houses.

PERSONS USING SIGNATURES AT KENFIG 1710-1850

Year	Total Sample	Adult Males			Adult Females	
		Sign	Mark	% Sign	Sign	Mark
1710	56	35	15	70	1	5
1720	62	42	15	72	0	5
1730	76	45	22	67	1	8
1740	78	47	20	70	2	9
1750	73	38	26	59	3	6
1760	63	31	23	57	1	8
1770	79	39	30	57	1	9

1780	78	40	30	57	1	7
1790	79	42	30	58	0	7
1800	83	46	30	61	0	7
1810	78	48	30	62	0	2
1820	82	57	25	70	0	1
1830	73	50	23	69	0	1
1840	63	45	18	71	0	3
1850	37	30	7	81	0	3

The schools offered what was very much a crash course in teaching people to read. A teacher was supplied for about three months during the winter when agricultural areas had very little work on so people had more free time to attend on a regular basis. The Bible and the Book of Common Prayer served as the text-books, and classes were held for adults as well as children.

So far as I can discover the earliest such school in our district was one at Tythegston held during the winter of 1739-40 which attracted 66 pupils. (Glamorgan, 1974: 460-). This figure reflects only the number of children educated and the Reverend Jones estimated that for every child attending at least two adults also received education. The historian E.D. Evans (1993: 101-2) estimates that (even on the basis of a one-to-one ratio) at least 300,000 people attended these schools during the period 1737 to 1761 which is roughly three-quarters of the entire population of Wales at that time! Small wonder therefore that they were considered both then and now to be a significant landmark in the history of Welsh education.

During the 1740s schools were held at Margam, Newton Nottage, Tythegston and Cefn Cribwr, then one was tried at Kenfig in the winter of 1746-7. The location is not given, but with just a dozen juvenile pupils it can scarcely have been rated a success. In 1754 a fresh attempt was made, presumably under the auspices of the Kenfig Corporation for it was held in the Town Hall. With the backing of the burgesses this proved far more popular, and the number of junior pupils that received education was put at 32. The same number is recorded when it returned again the following winter (1755/6), and 34 attended when one was held two years later during the winter of 1757/8.

Chapter 7

Richard Jenkins:
The Last Great Portreeve 1756-1761

Although a shadow of its medieval self, Kenfig Borough in the 16th & 17th centuries nevertheless was, or appears to have been, a vibrant and confident organisation prepared to act whenever the interests of its inhabitants were threatened. With the benefit of hindsight we can see that the traumas of the first half of the Eighteenth Century must have hit the organisation hard and dealt it a blow from which it never recovered its former confidence and poise. Perhaps too many of the older families had died out or moved away; maybe memories of the first Borough were now so distant as to be meaningless; but after 1750 things generally started to decay, and slowly but steadily the organisation began sliding downhill.

Hitherto the discipline imposed by successive Portreeves had welded the burgesses into a surprisingly effective organisation operating for the benefit of the community as a whole. The enclosure of Waun Cimla; the sedge planting and the introduction of the Welsh Trust Schools are just three instances that spring readily to mind. On a national scale the status of the Borough of Kenfig had been negligible – derisory even – but as these decisions illustrate, locally it had played a hugely important role in the lives of its inhabitants.

As the second half of the century wore on, the decline in the Borough's status, even within its own community, becomes increasing apparent. It is almost as though the burgesses themselves were more interested in what they, individually or collectively, could get out of the organisation rather than the wider concept of ruling the community for the benefit of all. In an era where an increasingly articulate middle class was pressing for Government reform at all levels, the absurdity of archaic institutions such as the Borough of Kenfig in the modern world was becoming ever more apparent. Amongst many outsiders therefore the formerly proud Borough of Kenfig and its burgesses were fast becoming objects of derision.

Yet it might just have been different, for in the 1750s one man did attempt to re-establish at Kenfig the old values and the former pride that had animated the earlier burgesses. He failed, and with his failure the gradual and ultimately irreversible decline of the Borough was set in motion.

The Autumn Leet of 1756 (B/K 11) Normally Edward Harris as the retiring Portreeve would have sat alongside the Constable of the Castle at the Autumn Leet of 8th October 1756, and his absence indicates that he was either dead or dying at the time. In accordance with hallowed tradition the 'electors' at this sitting therefore put forward three candidates to succeed him in the office.

Jenkin John was perhaps the oldest of the three having been first mentioned in 1711 and was by now probably well into his sixties. Married to Mary, one of the daughters of Noah Lyddon he had built up a sizeable farm in Kenfig Lower though to date I have been unable to discover where he actually lived. Since 1746 he had been an unsuccessful nominee for this office every year except 1755.

Richard John was by comparison a newcomer who had only arrived in the district in 1748 and was married to Mary Hawke of New Mill. The daughter of Richard Hawke and his wife Ann Richard, Mary was a 'life' on their lease taken out on the holding in 1717 when she was aged about six (D/D Ma 140 (Lease Survey)). Her father died in 1723, and her widowed mother apparently ran the farm herself until her own death about the year 1747 when the tenancy passed to Mary and her husband. As the new tenant of a 'burgage property' Richard was duly admitted as a burgess the following year. Aged about 37 in 1756 Richard was a man of some education who frequently finds mention as the Borough Recorder in records after 1760.

Aged 35 **Richard Jenkins** was the youngest of the three and the tenant of Marlas Farm. Even though this was no longer part of the Margam estate there is nevertheless a certain inevitability that he would be selected, for socially he stood head and shoulders above the other two. Originally from Neath he had married Mary (PPR) the daughter of David Pralph (the head of a notable family in that town) in November 1748. Probably through some connection with Bussy Mansel, David had been the tenant of Marlas farm since about the year 1741, though the 'David Pralph' who appears in local records at this time (and was created a burgess in that year) is most likely his son. Following Mary's marriage David senior transferred the tenancy to her and her new husband which enabled Richard to secure a lease of his own from Louise Barbara Mansel in 1754 (PM 6417)

In contemporary documents Richard is invariably accorded the title 'Mr' or 'gent'. He was the Glamorgan High Sheriff in 1750 and played a leading role in setting the local parish charity on a firm footing with the purchase of land at Heol Broom. As a burgess of Kenfig he had already shown an active interest in its affairs and on several occasions sat in council as one of the Eight Elected Burgesses.

So it was that in 1756 Richard was selected as the new Portreeve in the traditional manner, but the record shows a fundamental change in the way in which the other officers that were to serve with him were chosen. Hitherto the practice had been for the 'Electors' to nominate three persons for each post – six in the case of the two Aletasters, and for the Margam Steward to make the final choice. At this Leet, and at every subsequent one until Richard was replaced in 1761, only one person was nominated for the posts of Sergeant and Hayward and two for the two offices of Aletaster.

Someone (and the indications are that it was most likely Richard himself) had clearly taken the time and trouble to read the town's charter of 1397 (Grey, 1909: 108-) very carefully indeed! It was this document that laid down the annual procedure whereby the Portreeve was selected. Three nominees or 'bailiffs' selected by the burgesses were to be brought before the Sheriff or his deputy the Constable of the Castle, and they then chose one to be 'Bailiff for the Borough' – the Port-reeve. That was clear enough, and the practice had been faithfully adhered to ever since.

Concerning the office of Sergeant the charter actually states that the burgesses were to nominate two of their number of whom the 'Provost' or Portreeve was to select one to serve for the coming year. There is no mention whatsoever of the Sheriff or Constable having any hand in the selection process at all, and in the case of the two Aletasters the document simply says that two persons were to be selected to serve in the office without any details of a selection process.

Once selected both Aletasters and Sergeant were then sworn-in before the Sheriff or the Constable of the Castle, and this passive role was the only part the latter were specifically authorised by the charter to take in their election. No mention is made in the charter of how the Hayward or the Petty Constable were selected, but as these were manorial offices, the manner of their appointment depended upon the custom and practice of the manor rather than that of the Borough.

Somewhere down the centuries the original selection process had been altered so that the procedure for appointing all the Borough officers, Constable and Hayward included, was the same as that for the Portreeve. The burgesses made the nominations – the Constable of the Castle the final selection. Now, and for the period of Richard's Portreeveship only, the burgesses alone selected those who would be their Sergeant, Hayward and Aletasters. Only for the Portreeve and Petty Constable was the previous procedure retained. In the case of the first this was because it was in accordance with the terms of the charter; and for the latter because it was standard practice in all the other manors of Newcastle Hundred. Technically the Hayward, as a manorial officer, should also have been chosen in like manner, but for some reason was not.

The practice of making these appointments at the Autumn Leet Court for the Manor of Kenfig Borough was also continued, though in theory this was a manorial body that included the sub-manors of North and South Cornelly as well as the lower Borough. None of the Borough officers had any authority in either of these manors which appointed their own Petty Constables.

As to what authority the Borough officers enjoyed outside Kenfig Lower is indeed open to debate, especially in relation to Higher Kenfig. As manorial officers the Petty Constable and Hayward would have had none since it was a separate manor. But what of the others? All burgesses swore to accept the authority of the Portreeve, so he must have been able to exercise a certain measure of control over those who lived north of the river. Perhaps as his executive officer the Sergeant enjoyed some limited authority there as well, but the Aletasters seem to have had none.

This alteration in the selection procedure apparent for the first time at the Autumn Leet of 1756 suggests that Richard Jenkins had forced Margam to recognise the fact that under the terms of the Borough Charter their steward (in his capacity of Constable of the Castle) actually enjoyed only a very limited role in the annual election of officers. What the Lord and his steward made of it all we can only imagine, but there was little they could do about it in the face of the terms contained in the Kenfig charter. Legally Richard Jenkins and the burgesses were within their rights, and no doubt many of the latter greatly enjoyed this re-assertion of the burgesses' ancient freedom. Others will not have been so certain.

Whilst Margam and Kenfig had had their differences in the past, by and large the two had normally rubbed along well enough. Was it, some burgesses may have argued, really worth antagonising the Borough's principal landlord for something that was little more than a gesture? Richard Jenkins, they may have muttered darkly, didn't have to worry about the consequences, for although he rented some land from the Talbots his main holding belonged to the Briton Ferry estate. Nevertheless Jenkins was their new Portreeve and had demonstrated his intention to re-establish the dignity and prestige of their ancient organisation. His re-introduction of the 'correct' procedure for appointing the Borough's officers however proved to be just a foretaste of what was to come.

The new Portreeve's first year in office nevertheless seems to have passed quietly enough, but by the following autumn he began to show his mettle by ordering a Hall Day (B/K 11) to be held on 23rd September. Its stated purpose was "to establish and confirm the ancient ordinances of ye s'd Towne and Borrough according to ye custom". This seems to imply that the practice had been going on since time immemorial, but there is actually no previous mention of the practice in the minute books. Possibly therefore this was something that Jenkins himself claimed to have 're-introduced'.

After this date entries relating to such inspections of the Ordinances regularly occur from time to time, though they are equally brief. What actually happened at such sittings is never stated, but presumably the Borough Ordinances were read out to the assembled burgesses and then formally confirmed by the Eight Elected. It is a truism of modern legal practice that 'ignorance of the law is no excuse', but it seems that the Kenfig burgesses had less excuse than most in this respect!

Less than a month later, on 14th October, Jenkins called another Hall Day (B/K 11), this time with the object of conducting a review of the parcels of fern on Kenfig Common. This ascertained that no less than twelve now lay vacant and the Corporation formally re-possessed them so they could be re-allocated and by the end of the year five had been assigned to new owners.

'Hall Days' were meetings of the burgesses held to discuss business relating solely to the affairs of the Borough. Previously such sittings noted in the minute books are very few and far between, but under Richard Jenkins they become increasingly frequent. Hitherto most routine business such as the formal approval of transfers of parcels of hay and fern had been done at the monthly Courts Baron which, unlike the Courts Leet, were presided over by the Portreeve rather than the Constable of the Castle. They were nevertheless manorial courts held for the Manor of Kenfig Borough which meant that those burgesses who were tenants of Higher Kenfig were not required to attend. Furthermore, amongst those who were required to be present were persons who were not burgesses such as the resiants and out-dwelling tenants.

What Jenkins was now doing was ensuring that ALL Borough business would in future be dealt with at Hall Days where only burgesses were present. As many will have been quick to point out, this also increased the number of courts they had to attend during the course of a year. As with the manorial courts attendance at Hall Days was probably not optional and failure to put in an appearance would have resulted in a fine.

The Autumn Leet of 1757 (B/K 11) At the Autumn Leet Richard Jenkins was re-appointed as Portreeve and the council demanded that Sarah, the widow of Edward Harris, produce her late husband's outstanding accounts for his final period of office. This, however, was a demand she chose to ignore and the burgesses would have to badger her for some considerable time yet before she eventually complied!

Also noted at the court was the death of **Evan Edward**, a burgess and a freeholder in Kenfig Lower who was aged about 43. A blacksmith by trade he appears several times in Edward Harris's accounts for supplying such items as hinges and other metal fittings for a cupboard in the Corporation House and the Borough stocks; mending a padlock and making a key for the same. He and his wife Mary Evan had a son named Evan Evan who, at this time was only about eight years old, so his mother now became a 'female burgess' keeping the position open until he became of age.

At the same court the burgesses again attempted to place responsibility for controlling the increasing nuisance caused by the rabbits on their Hayward, **Edmund Harry**. Rabbits apart the manner in which he discharged this duty was clearly appreciated by the burgesses for he held this office on no less than nine occasions. Nevertheless, as he probably pointed out, he was the licensee of The Corporation House and ran a smallholding. Whilst in the past he had indeed been employed by Edward Harris to stop up rabbit holes on the common, he probably argued that to undertake such work as part of the normal duties of the Hayward was too much to expect. Certainly the point seems not to have been lost on Portreeve Richard Jenkins though for the moment he too could offer no immediate alternative solution to the problem. Employing somebody to block up rabbit holes as Harris had occasionally done was an expense the Borough could not really afford, but at the same time tackling the issue of the rabbits was now clearly becoming a major issue that had to be faced.

Property Transfers and Other Matters (B/K 11) On 10th April 1758 Richard Jenkins called a Hall Day to discuss certain Borough matters. These included the acceptance of his accounts for the first year of his office which in itself must have come as something of a shock – Edward Harris had only ever presented his once, and the Corporation was still pestering his widow to produce the remainder!

Unfortunately the record of the meeting was not entered in the minutes, but we know from the agenda that it included repairs to the common pound and the appointment of a new Sergeant-at-Mace. This was because at the Autumn Leet Edmund Harry had been selected for this post as well as that of Hayward. The Constable of the Castle, who had confirmed these appointments was obviously quite happy with this arrangement but Richard Jenkins clearly was not!

Richard's attempt to improve the Borough is again apparent in the minutes of the Spring Leet that year. Previous Recorders had noted the transfer of freeholdings reported at such hearings only in the sketchiest of terms. A typical example from the previous year simply notes "the death of Friswith Leyson, a free tenant under the Court, and a relief to the Lord, and Evan Leyson her brother to be tenant in her stead". (A 'Relief' was a payment due to the Lord of the manor on the death of a tenant. It could be the best animal or most valuable item the deceased possessed, or a cash payment in lieu.)

Such brief entries had been the norm since the earliest records in 1729-30, but Richard Jenkins now required that details of such transfers be set out in full and include a full description of the property to which it related. For me, as a local historian, this is a godsend, but I can well imagine the Recorder gnashing his teeth in suppressed fury at the extra amount of work involved!

These expanded entries in the borough minute books show just how much information it could give to us, but after Richard Jenkins' day the Recorders breathed a heartfelt sigh of relief and reverted back to the practice of noting only the barest of details as previously.

The property transfers were not the only items of interest dealt with at this court however. **David John** was reported for "cutting furzes on Kenfigg Down upon the certain place called ye Eithin Man contrary to the ordinance". For this offence he was ordered to pay a fine, though the amount is not stipulated.

There were two men of this name in the Borough at the time, but this was probably David John of Kenfig Farm who was aged about 60. He had not arrived in the Borough until about 1741 at which time he was an unsuccessful nominee for the office of Portreeve. He was then probably sub-leasing the farm from Richard James, but in February 1748 secured a lease (D/D Ma 140) upon it in his own right.

The reason that he had been harvesting the furze or gorse on the common is probably that he had run out of winter fodder for his livestock. Neither the winter nor the spring had been notably harsh, so it seems that David had merely failed to lay in enough hay for his stock or was doing something he had done previously without hindrance. The gorse he had harvested from the common would, chopped up finely, have been mixed with his hay as a winter feed.

It is interesting to note that the Ordinance under which David was prosecuted would have been either No 50 or No 51 dating back to the medieval period. Under the latter he could have sought permission to cut the furze from the Portreeve but had either not done so, or been refused. Richard Jenkins, we can well imagine, was not one to have allowed such a slight to the office he held pass unnoticed! This was, however, the least of David's troubles during the year, for on 27th

December the Parish Registers record the death and burial of his wife Ann.

Another jury presentment was the reported agreement that henceforward "no efected horses shall pasture upon our common" which was obviously an attempt to prevent diseased animals being turned out there to graze alongside everyone else's stock. These items (and also the final one – a declaration that a George Thomas had lived in the Borough for a whole year) were in fact more properly the responsibility of the Hall Day Court. In this instance, and contrary to the usual practice under Richard Jenkin, they seem to have been business carried out at the end of the Court Leet after the Constable of the Castle had stood down from the chair.

The last item reported that day was a declaration noting the death of The Reverend Thomas Talbot. He was only 39 years of age, and his eldest son Thomas Mansel Talbot was only eleven. With memories of what had happened earlier in the century the older burgesses probably shook their heads and predicted a dire ten years ahead until the young lord at last came of age. Fortunately their gloomy prognosis proved largely unfounded.

Burgesses & Residents The Autumn Court Leet for 1758 was held on 12th October 1758 and is rather unusual in that the entry in the Borough Minute Book (B/K 11) concludes with two lists of names, one entitled "Resiants (residents) of the Town and Borrough", and the other "Number of Burgesses at this Leet". Although, like the Suit Roll of 1699 these lists should relate only to such persons residing in Kenfig Lower, they do in fact include others from Higher Kenfig who were presumably present for the annual election of Borough Officers. Why this record was made we are not told, but it does provide us with the most complete list of Kenfig inhabitants since the 1699 suit roll (The full list is given in Part 4 of *Kenfig Folk*).

In all a total of 51 people (all male) are named, thirteen of whom were classed as 'resiants'. This was a term used to describe 'heads of households who were not tenants' and included "sub-tenants, ex-tenants who were still resident within the manor, and some householders who eventually became tenants" (Hey, 1996: 394).

Because of their nature these lists do not include those who were not present at this court. Besides actual absentees these would have included 'female burgesses', resiants from Higher Kenfig, and any others from that manor or the Manor of Kenfig Borough not specifically required to be present. Also omitted (presumably in error) is the Portreeve, Richard Jenkin, who was obviously present as he was re-appointed to the office at this sitting!

Of the 13 residents my records show two could sign their name whilst two could only make their mark. In the case of the burgesses Thomas Julier sometimes signed and on other occasions made his mark! Of the others 14 could sign and 11 could only make their mark.

INFORMATION FROM OTHER SOURCES INDICATE THAT THE 52 NAMED INDIVIDUALS FOLLOWED A VARIETY OF OCCUPATIONS:

Unidentified	17	Shoemakers	2	Blacksmiths	2
Farmers	18	Weavers	2	Publicans	1
Independent Means	1	Tailors	1	Labourers	2
Masons	3	Carpenters	1	Servants	2

A Pair of Scales; a Nest of Weights & Measures On 27th November 1758, and notwithstanding that some Corporation business seems to have already been transacted after the Autumn Leet, Richard Jenkins called his third Hall Day of the year. This was so that Sarah Harris could at last present her late husband's accounts covering the final eleven of his fourteen years in the office of Portreeve. Problems were anticipated – and problems they got!

Proceedings apparently opened with an enquiry into a shortfall in the money that Sarah now handed over to the Corporation as the balance remaining once the expenditure listed in the accounts had been met. From this it seems that the Recorder, in his capacity as the Borough Treasurer, had not received any cash from Portreeve Harris for a very long time prior to the latter's death! What he had received was made the subject of the enquiry at which Edmund Harry of the Corporation House and William John of Pool Farm gave evidence on oath.

If nothing else the hearing that followed reveals the rather farcical state in which the Borough finances were being handled at this time. It will be recalled that the Portreeves annually collected the Borough rent through the Sergeant, paid £2.10s 0d. into the Treasury, and then pocketed the remainder. The enquiry conducted by Richard Jenkins reveals the kind of wheeling and dealing that went on between successive Portreeves to ensure that they didn't lose out financially and, that (so far as the burgesses were concerned) their books were balanced!

William Lewis who had been appointed Portreeve in 1737 and 1738 but disappears from the records about 1740, and you will probably not be surprised to learn that despite repeated requests the accounts for his two years in office were never subsequently produced! He was, however, apparently brought back to the Borough and taken to task over this failure by his successor, Edward Harris who demanded from him the money due to the Borough from his years of office.

Thinking 'on his feet' Lewis demanded "who had the effects of William Harry?" - the former licensee of The Prince of Wales, who had died in 1741. Edmund, who was present, identified himself as William's son and successor, whereupon Lewis declared "You owe me two year's rent for Ty Newydd [The Corporation House]!" Having made that astonishing demand he then declared, "If I had that, and the Burgesses; rent [the rates] I shall not be very short in accounts!" On that thought he turned on Howell Rees (d. 1745) who had been the Serjeant during his second term of office. "What became of ye Burgesses' rent which you collected?" he demanded!

From this it seems clear that Lewis had not bothered to collect either the rent due on The Corporation House, or the Borough rates, and had left poor old Howell Rees holding the baby – or at least the proceeds from his collection. He was, however, an honourable man, who had apparently kept the money safe waiting for Lewis to return and collect it. Honest men, however, can in their own quiet way create huge waves for others less scrupulous, and the direction of the meeting was stood on its head when he declared calmly "What I received I have delivered to Mr Edward Harris the Portreeve"!

Harris, so it seems, was well aware that this little gem was going to surface, and that to date he too had not accounted for receiving this money or paid it in to the Treasury! Like a conjurer pulling a rabbit from a hat he therefore produced a group of objects and placed them on the table. "There is a pair of scales, one nest of weights, and measure to you for them [the rates]" he announced to the assembled burgesses.

Edward Harris, be it remembered, was an important man in the community who, if he did not talk to God at least had the ear of Bussy Mansel. With a scales, weights and measures that were totally superfluous to requirements (they already had a complete set) the burgesses nevertheless declared themselves content, which is why the National Museum now has in its custody two such sets belonging to our former Borough!

With this explanation of the deficit in his predecessor's account Richard Jenkins had to be content, so he then went on to conduct a further examination of the accounts produced by the hapless Sarah. To all appearances everything then proceeded smoothly and they were duly accepted, but hidden amongst the end-papers of the Minute Book is a little note by the Recorder. This states that Harris's accounts had at last been submitted - "Richard Jenkins Esqr being Portreeve, in the year 1758, when those accounts were settled - but not without much trouble and difficulty!"

The 1758 *Life Book* During the course of the year the Margam estate office produced a document entitled *The Life Book* (D/D Ma 140). It contains details of all estate property currently held on lease, the details of the lessors, and the amounts of rate and duty they paid. As such it is an immensely valuable document to local historians since it includes brief details about leases that have often not survived elsewhere in the manuscript collection as well as giving the ages of those whose lives were still current. Unfortunately it is too long and involved to allow me to take you on a tour of the manors of Higher Kenfig and Kenfig Borough as outlined in its pages, but in summary the picture it paints of the Margam property in Kenfig is as follows.

In the Manor of Kenfig Borough 11 holdings are mentioned as held under leases against 23 held 'at will'. In Higher Kenfig, where the estate had been utilising leases to amalgamate smaller holdings into larger farms, the same number of tenancies were held by lease but only six were held at will. Five of the latter were cottages, and the sixth was Llanmihangel Corn Mill.

Of the 22 leases in being in 1758 four (all in Higher Kenfig) dated from before the time that Bussy Mansel first became involved with the estate following the death of Thomas Mansel in 1723. Just five had been issued in the 24 years between then and 1747 when Thomas Talbot began to take an active interest in the estate. One additional Higher Kenfig Lease (to Howell John) had in fact been issued but had been renewed prior to 1758. The remaining 13 all date from 1748 or later. This, in its way, is a fitting comment on those dark years when the estate itself all but collapsed.

Defending the Borough Under Richard Jenkins, meetings of burgesses at Hall Days were now becoming a frequent event, certainly more so than noted in the minute books either before or after. Unfortunately the reluctance of the burgesses to enter details of their business in these documents still persisted, so our knowledge of what went on at such meetings is strictly limited. One held on 20th April 1759 is more informative than most. On this occasion the Portreeve seems to have sat with a Grand Jury rather than the Eight Elected, as the object was to review the Borough boundary between *Croes Siencyn* (pictured on the right) on Marlas Road and a boundary stone at Cae Garw. That done the jury declared that the value of the portion of Llanmihangel Farm lying within their borders was £37.

The entry concerning another Hall Day called for 10th October is less fulsome. It tells us only that Jenkins called the meeting "to subscribe in the behalfe and defence of the Borrough against Edward David & Richard Burnell, both of ye parish of Newton Nottage". Dramatic words indeed, but off-hand I would suspect that this was merely something to do with contesting responsibility for the maintenance of a pauper that the parish of Newton Nottage claimed properly belonged to Kenfig.

The final Hall Day of the year on 14th December is perhaps the most significant. The furore over the rabbit problem was now reaching a crescendo, and Richard Jenkins no doubt pointed out that every year over the past three years he had paid somebody eleven shillings to stop up the rabbit holes on the common. This was over 20% of the annual income from the general rate, and the Borough finances could not afford such a constant drain. If the burgesses wanted the rabbit problem solved, or at least kept in check, then they would have to do the work themselves.

At the meeting "it was appointed by Mr Portreeve that all the burgesses of this Town and Borough ought to appear upon our

Commons called Kenfigg Down and Windmill Hill with their spades, in order to stop the rabat's holes on the burgesses' lands". The chosen day for this to take place was 11ᵗʰ January, early enough in the year for the rabbits to be encouraged to move back to the areas designated as their warrens before the Spring when rabbits do what rabbits do best! The chances were that the day would be cold, and most likely wet. It was not a solution that appealed very much to anyone!

Tackling the Rabbits The year 1760 started with the burgesses and the burgesses' widows turning out with their spades to stop rabbit holes on their common as had been ordained by their Portreeve. After a day spent doing this in the middle of winter, they may have thought that was that – but Richard Jenkins had other ideas. On 8ᵗʰ February he ordered that they turn out again on the 14ᵗʰ of that month. I don't know if they celebrated St Valentine's Day then, but I am certain that there was no love lost between Richard Jenkins and the good burghers of Kenfig thereafter! In fact, I will go so far as to suggest that it was partly because of this Valentine's Day 'treat' that his own days in the office of Portreeve became numbered!

The Fall of Richard Jenkins Richard Jenkins called yet another Hall Day on 2ⁿᵈ June 1760 at which the only item of business to be transacted was the transfer of a parcel of hay at Waun Cimla from Howell Rees to Richard John. In the past such routine matters had been done at the end of manorial court business without the need of additional attendance at a special Hall Day sitting. It can well be imagined the burgesses were not best pleased at having to turn up simply to rubber-stamp such a transaction even without the double-helping of blocking up rabbit burrows in the depths of winter! Revolution was brewing!

On 27ᵗʰ September Richard Jenkins presided over his last Hall Day as Portreeve when a new lease was agreed with Edmund Harry for his tenancy of The Corporation House. This was another innovation for previously such details had not been recorded in the minute books. Along with the premises themselves (here called Ty Newydd) went a stable, the garden and an acre of land which is undoubtedly 'The Prince Field' on the opposite side of the main road. The lease was set to run for 31 years, and the annual rent was agreed at twelve shillings.

I suspect that by now the burgesses were heartily sick and tired of Richard Jenkins, and he of them! Whilst he wanted everything done properly 'according to the book', they were probably yearning for a return of the rather slap-dash ways of the late Edward Harris. Hall Days were being called for business that had normally been done at the termination of manorial courts, and it can well be imagined that his solution to the rabbit problem found little favour with those who went out stopping up rabbit holes in the middle of winter. Jenkins had been their Portreeve for five consecutive years, but at the Autumn Leet his name was not even put forward as one of the nominees.

Perhaps it was their desire for change that forced them to make a small alteration in the nomination procedure for the post of Portreeve that is first apparent at this Autumn Leet of 1761. Previously the names of those to be considered for the various Borough offices were put forward by two (sometimes three) 'electors', but in the circumstances it maybe proved impossible to find two burgesses willing to risk possible retaliation by Jenkins! Now and hereafter all nominations were made by the jury of presentment chosen to sit that day. Whatever the reason Jenkins' name was not one of the three put forward, and his reign as the Kenfig Portreeve was brought to an end.

Also at this court they reverted to the former practice of making several nominations for all the Borough offices and allowing the Constable of the Castle to make the final selection. The Recorder reverted to his former rather slap-dash method of recording business; Hall Days became less frequent, and the Kenfig method of doing things reverted once again to the old comfortable ways of Edward Harris and his predecessors.

Just over two weeks later Richard Jenkins presented the accounts for his last four years in office and thereafter virtually ceased to have anything to do either with the burgesses or their Borough. He did, however, serve as an Assessor on several occasions, but this was only for the purposes of the manorial court.

Chapter 8
The 1760s

To replace Richard Jenkins the burgesses chose one of their number named Richard Williams whose origins are somewhat confused for, although there seems little doubt that he was connected to the Williams family of Sker House, his exact relationship is uncertain. I tend towards the view (expressed by 'Llyfnwy' in his 1869 book *The Cupid*) that he was a younger brother of Isaac Williams the current tenant at this time. Honesty compels me to record however that Richard's descendant Brian Ll James (himself a noted local historian) has some reservations on this score.

Richard Williams was the tenant of Kenfig House Farm on Water Street, and had probably been living there when he married a Mary Williams in 1755. (PPR) At that time he is described as a widower and was probably about 36 years of age. There is also some mention of him holding land at Cornelly, and possibly this may have come to him via his new wife. (PM 9541)

As the brother of Isaac Williams of Sker, Richard would have been uncle to his daughter Elizabeth who was destined to become the legendary 'Maid of Sker'. She would probably have been in her early teens when he was sworn in as Portreeve, for the eldest of Isaac's children, John, was only about fifteen at this time. Their mother Catherine had died on 1st October 1753.

The Rabbit Hole Rate Within a few months of taking up office Richard Williams was confronting problems of his own which, as with his predecessor, stemmed from the proliferation of the rabbit population on Kenfig common. With the finances of the Borough too inadequate to allow him to hire somebody to carry out the task, Williams like Richard Jenkins before him, felt he had no option but to order the burgesses "every one with their spades" to meet on Windmill Hill to stop up the rabbit holes.

He made this announcement on 6th February 1761 at the end of a sitting of the Court Baron, and seems to have faced something of a revolt by the burgesses present. Much as they might object to traipsing round the common with their spades on cold winter days however, they were forced to recognise that the parlous state of the Corporation finances left the Portreeve with no practical alternative. Eventually a compromise was agreed whereby the task of filling in the rabbit holes would be carried out by a burgess named Rees Morgan "for the space of one hool year". To pay his wages a special fund would be set up into which every burgess and burgesses' widow would pay the sum of sixpence.

On hearing this, their former Portreeve Richard Jenkins may well have permitted himself a wry smile, for I suspect his introduction of the digging expeditions on the common had been designed to provoke them into just such a course of action! So it was that the 'Rabbit Hole Rate', levied separately from the general rate, was born, and continued to be levied thereafter whenever people were contracted to carry out such work. At the same time it seems from subsequent entries that it was still open for burgesses to perform the work themselves rather than pay the cash. One also presumes that burgesses whose property lay solely in Higher Kenfig would have been exempt both from performing the duty and payment of the rate. This was after all purely a problem that affected those who owned or occupied property in Kenfig Lower.

Rees Morgan, a burgess, now agreed to undertake this work. Unfortunately his deal with the Corporation seems to have struck problems almost immediately. The snag may have been that the area proved too great for one man to cover or perhaps, after experience of the scale of the task in hand, Rees felt he was being grossly underpaid! Another meeting of the burgesses was therefore convened for 5th June where three burgesses – Edmund Harry of the Corporation House; Evan Jenkin (son of Evan & Elizabeth Jenkin, deceased); and Richard John of New Mill – agreed to undertake the task for the ensuing year for ten shillings apiece. Between them they would be responsible for the North Common whilst Mary Edward (alias Mary Evan the widow of the blacksmith Evan Edward) agreed to carry out the work needed on Kenfig Down for the lesser sum of seven shillings.

In the event employing four persons on the work seems to have been rather more than was necessary, and subsequently the normal practice was to pay just two – one for Kenfig Down and the other for the North or Windmill Hill Common. During some years nobody appears to have been employed, but mention of contracts entered into for such work now become a regular feature of the minutes.

New Burgesses and Wider Qualifications for Entry During the course of 1761 no less than ten persons were proposed and accepted as burgesses, from which it seems that the Corporation was making a determined effort to fill vacancies and bring their numbers up to the maximum. At the same time it is clear that the grounds for admission had also changed from those current during Richard Jenkin's term of office and previously. In the four years of his rule just three new burgesses had been created, and all three seem to have qualified on the grounds that they had become tenants of houses traditionally regarded as burgages.

Whilst the farmhouses of Higher Kenfig had fallen into this category, the cottages there did not. For the most part the latter were occupied by farm labourers or their widows, some renting direct from the Margam estate, others as sub-tenants of particular farms. The reorganisation of the manor under the Talbots had seen many of the smaller original tenant farms at Higher Kenfig go out of existence, amalgamated with others to create larger and more commercially viable holdings. This in turn reduced the number of 'burgages', and since the process seems to have had little impact south of the river, an imbalance had arisen in the proportion of burgesses representing the two elements of which the Borough was composed. It therefore seems the Corporation determined to correct this by allowing suitable cottagers from Higher Kenfig to be admitted to their ranks, and two of those nominated in 1761 seem to fall into this category. One was a labourer named David Rees and the other a blacksmith called David Thomas, but a further examination of the other eight candidates reveals there was also a further widening of the grounds upon which residents of the Borough could claim admission.

Marriage to the daughter of a burgess could now in itself be claimed as grounds for qualification. This is the stated reason for the nomination of four of the prospective new burgesses - John Richard,

Thomas Henry, John Phillip and Hopkin David. Hitherto such grounds had been claimed only by somebody whose wife was the sole representative of the family of a burgess still living at Kenfig. Such would have been the case if, for example, the spinster Jennet John mentioned earlier had ever married. Such, however, does not appear to be the case with at least some of these nominees.

In the case of **John Richard** I know that he had married an Ann John the previous year, but unfortunately I have been unable to trace her family. **Hopkin David** had married Catherine the daughter of Evan John (who may have been the tenant of Penymynydd Farm) back in 1757, and his father-in-law was still alive in 1761, though he died just two years later. **Thomas Henry** had been married to Alice the daughter of William John of Pool Farm for even longer - since 1754 in fact - whilst **John Phillip**'s marriage to Ann the daughter of Thomas Rees (of the Rees/Thomas family) had taken place in 1759. Both men are listed simply as 'resiants' in 1758, and in both cases their wives' fathers were still alive in 1761 and had sons of their own, some of whom were already burgesses.

It seems clear therefore that, although not mentioned in the Borough Minutes, another new qualification for admission to the office of burgess had been introduced, and one that in turn eventually opened the way for burgesses to have their sons admitted during their own lifetime. This had happened from time to time in the past, but almost invariably it was because the son had left home (usually on marriage) and taken up residence in a property holding burgage status.

Edmund Harry of the Corporation House seems to have been the first to explore the possibilities of this altered situation when his eldest son David was put forward for consideration in 1763. Edmund's own status as a burgess is not specifically stated to be the grounds for his son's qualification, but the fact is that David, a cordwainer by trade, was aged 27, unmarried, and apparently living at home with his parents. Although duly admitted, there is no mention of his participating in Borough affairs, and he seems to have taken his place as a 'burgess in waiting' pending the death of his father. Several such can be identified in the records over the following years. Although resident within Kenfig Borough they played no active role until in due course they succeeded their father when he died. Unfortunately for David he died just two years after his admission whilst his father was still alive.

From this time onward nomination for admission on grounds of hereditary right or marriage to a burgess's daughter appear with increasing frequency. Marriage is given as the grounds for the admission of John Harris in 1766 and Thomas Evan (1768), whilst John William (1766) was the son of a burgess still living. Being a burgess's son is also the stated reason for the admission of John Robert and Edward Evan (both sworn in 1765) though in their case they were replacing fathers who had recently deceased. Nevertheless, Francis Yorwerth, John Hopkin and Rees Daniel were all nominated for admission in 1770 and served as officers of the Borough whilst their fathers were still living

For the present the ancient qualification based upon pre-determined 'burgages' still continued, but from now on its use steadily waned as burgesses pressed to have their sons admitted during their own lifetime, though (as indicated above) not all immediately took on an active role. By the time the Borough was abolished in 1886 it seems that all claimants to the office of burgess relied solely on hereditary grounds to support their candidature, and the old 'burgage' qualification had vanished completely.

It is probably significant that this rush of qualifications based upon the new criteria immediately followed Richard Jenkins's term in the office of Portreeve. The three new burgesses he admitted during his four years in power all seem to have qualified in the traditional manner, through tenancy of a 'burgage'. Here, or so it appears, we have another issue over which he and his burgesses had been at variance. Whilst he had stuck rigidly to the traditional criteria of the past, they for their part had been concerned that this was no longer effective in maintaining their numbers to the maximum 57/58 permitted.

Burlake Bridge At the Autumn Leet, held in September 1763, the jurors made the rather surprising presentation that Pont y Bwrlac was out of repair. This was a little bridge that carried Water Street across the Bwrlac Brook (now by the entrance to the industrial estate) and was in Higher Kenfig - an area of the Borough over which they had no jurisdiction. They may, however, have taken the view that it was on an important road connecting the two parts of Kenfig Borough, so the Constable of the Castle seems to have agreed, and ordered that it be done within four months or a fine of five shillings be paid.

Pyle & Kenfig Parish in 1763 In 1763, at the request of the Bishop, every parish in the Diocese of Llandaff made a return setting out the answers to a questionnaire. It was not the first time this had been done, but it is the first such 'visitation' that has survived intact, and has been published in full by the South Wales Record Society (Guy, 1991). It reveals that the parish of Pyle & Kenfig did not have a vicar of its own, but was administered by the incumbent at Margam who at this time was the Reverend John Williams who submitted the report. The Reverend Williams tells us that there were 67 families within the parish served by "two chapels about a mile asunder in very good repair". Services were held at each alternately with one (sometimes two) on Sundays when a sermon was preached. These were supplemented with others conducted on Wednesdays and Fridays during Lent, and at every Feast and Festival such as Christmas and Easter. In all there were about a hundred people in the parish entitled to take communion "of whom about eighty usually receive".

There were, he reported, no dissenting congregations, confirming that the Nonconformist community that had formerly met at Kenfig Farm had not survived the demise of the Aylward family. This is not to say that there were no dissenters living in the parish – there almost certainly were – but as yet they were not sufficiently numerous or organised to form themselves into a regular church and acquire their own meeting house.

Although Reverend Williams confirms there was no public school in the area there was apparently one run by the church, presumably at Pyle. About twenty children attended who "are taught to read and write, are carefully instructed in the principles and doctrine of the Church of England, and brought duly to church".

The Epidemic of 1764 The year 1764 was notable for an epidemic of some sort that struck the parish of Pyle & Kenfig in August and continued until the end of November. The available records give no clue as to its nature, and my current research is too restricted to indicate whether it was purely local or more widespread. All I can say with certainty at this time is that the appalling death rate apparent within the parish finds no echo in the records of its neighbour at Tythegston.

Over the previous five years, the average number of burials recorded in the parish registers is 6.2 per annum with the highest number being nine (in 1759). During the whole of 1764 no less that 33 burials are recorded, 27 of them taking place between 8th August and 29th November. Although Kenfig escaped comparatively lightly, several of its inhabitants were among the dead whilst many others were people who had a connection with the Borough and have previously figured in our narrative in the past.

All in all, and despite the death of several of its leading residents, the Borough of Kenfig seems to have escaped the ravages of this epidemic fairly lightly. At the same time the register may record the burial of Kenfig folk (particularly children) whom I have not been able to identify, and as yet my research has not extended sufficiently into Higher Kenfig for me to speak of victims there. It was also frequently the case that some people who had emigrated to Kenfig subsequently chose to be buried with other members of their family at their place of origin so that there is no record of their burial locally.

The Washing Pound Edward Evan, a burgess (he was admitted in 1766) was a blacksmith, and appears in the Portreeve's accounts for 1766-8 providing fittings for the 'Washing Pound'. This feature was situated at the northern end of Kenfig Pool, and had been built by the burgesses to provide a facility that enabled them to wash their flocks prior to shearing. The earliest mention of this facility - "ye po[u]nd att Kenfygg Pool" - occurs in the accounts submitted by Richard Jenkin for his last years as Portreeve, so it was something presumably installed either by him or his predecessor Edward Harris. It subsequently appears frequently in Borough records and was apparently situated at the northern end of the lake though I have noted no traces of it there today.

The Last Circulating Schools. By 1766 some time had elapsed since the last occasion that one of the Welsh Circulating Schools had visited Kenfig. The Reverend Griffith Jones of Llanddowror had died in 1761, but the circulating schools he instituted still continued for a little while longer. Two final visits to "Cenffyg Village" are recorded during the winter of 1766-7, the one attracting 24 pupils and the other 30. After this it would seem that all formal education within the Borough ceased once more.

Out-Burgesses: At the Spring Leet in 1767 the names of twelve individuals were put forward as suitable candidates to be burgesses. All were 'out-dwellers' with the possible exception of one, and the entry seems to mark the start of a deliberate campaign by the Talbots to boost the number of 'out-burgesses' they controlled at Kenfig for the purpose of voting at General Elections. Although this was a practice that had certainly gone on in the past, the numbers involved previously seem to have been quite small. Now batches of such burgesses were regularly admitted from time to time, particularly when an election was in the offing. The Talbots paid a fee for each individual admitted, part of which went to the Recorder. As this influx became a flood it is difficult not to see the increase of this practice as a further step in the disintegration of the Borough.

Several of those in the list did actually have some connection with Kenfig. **Lewis Thomas,** 'gent' of Blaen Maelwg Farm, Margam for example, had acquired a lease to Yorwerth's Land in Higher Kenfig in 1748. His wife, Eleanor Lewis, was related to Lewis Howell of St George-super-Ely, which is undoubtedly why the death of their son Richard in 1762 rated a mention in the diary of William Thomas from nearby Michaelston (Denning, 1995: 36).

Lewis Leyson of Bryn y Fro, Llangynwyd, another of these 'out-burgesses', was a Kenfig freeholder that we have already met with in this history. Of the twelve the only one that was probably an in-dweller was **Richard Lewis** who was aged about thirty. He and several others were reported for the state of their hedges on Heol y Lane later that year, and he was appointed Sergeant-at-Mace in 1769. When two years later he married Gwenllian Harry (one of the daughters of Edmund Harry of Corporation House) he is however described as 'of Margam' indicating that he was then living in Higher Kenfig. Nevertheless, from 1771 onwards he became quite active in the affairs of the Corporation.

Chapter 9
The Portreeves and The Talbots 1760-1781

Richard Yorwerth, Portreeve As Richard Williams's term as the Borough's Portreeve came to an end at the Autumn Leet of 1768, he hoped to continue. Although he was one of the three candidates whose names were placed before the Constable of the Castle, on this occasion the latter chose Richard Yorwerth of Pool Farm to fill the post for the ensuing year.

The deposed Portreeve, Richard William, submitted his accounts to the Corporation in November, and these are noteworthy for one particular entry which shows that during his term in office the roof of the Town Hall had been repaired with Cornish tiles. That in itself is quite unremarkable for this material had been used for the purpose before and would be again. Richard, however, claimed an additional expense to cover the cost of hauling these tiles to Kenfig *from the River Afan*. This, so far as I am currently aware, is the first mention of a harbour operating in the mouth of the River Afan which at this time flowed into Swansea Bay at Taibach. John Leland in 1538 (Smith, 1906) did indeed mention a "haven for ships" here at that time, as does Rhys Merrick in 1578 (James, 1983). This seems to have subsequently decayed as in the second half of the 17th century and the early part of the 18th Margam was shipping in goods purchased at Bristol either via Newton, Porthcawl or Neath - rather odd if the Afan port was in use at the time.

Previously the Margam estate had shipped its goods in or out through either Newton or Neath. Now the energetic Thomas Mansel Talbot had evidently created the precursor of the great harbour at Aberavon today, probably to service industrial developments near Taibach that were implemented at about this time. In 1789 a traveller known only by his initials 'C.C.' passed this way and noted (Hopkins, 1965; 132) a "copper-works with an uniform row of tenements for the workmen on the left side of the road, and another row, on the slope of a hill, at some distance to the right". Four years later Sir Richard Colt Hoare (Thompson, 1983) noted "extensive forges and a new village".

Kenfig Pool & The Jack Fish By 1769 Thomas Mansel Talbot had reached the magic age of 21 and taken full charge of his own affairs. His interest in hunting and fishing had not diminished, and he probably still made frequent expeditions to Kenfig to enjoy the facilities the Pool offered in this respect. The wildfowl here were undoubtedly plentiful, but the fishing was rather limited. In 1661 the Survey made of the manor of Kenfig Borough stated that the only quarry its waters offered in this respect were "eels and roaches". Now that he was in charge of his own affairs Talbot lost no time, and no little expense, in creating better and more varied sport for his rod and line.

The Margam estate accounts (D/D Ma 22) tell us that during 1769 Talbot organised the restocking of Kenfig Pool with 'jack fish' (pike) brought from as far away as Llangorse Lake near Brecon. Details of four of the six journeys it required to transfer these fish are given. Tin containers had been specially made for the purpose, and were presumably carried in panniers slung across the backs of horses. The route they followed from Llangorse was across the Brecon Beacons to Pont-Nedd-Fechan, and most of the fish that survived the journey went

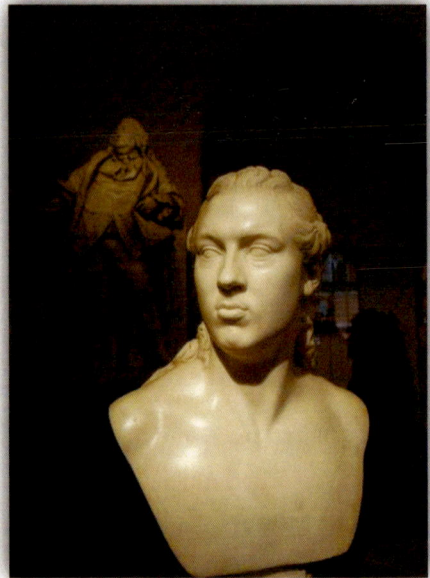

BUST OF THOMAS MANSEL TALBOT
PHOTO CREDIT: SOFTLY, SOFTLY /
FOTER.COM / CC BY-NC

into the pool, though some were also used to stock the lakes in Margam Park. On the last trip of all a party from Kenfig led by Rees Rees of Kenfig House met the hauliers at Pont-Nedd-Fechan and brought the fish the rest of the way. On this occasion, we are told, seven fish survived the arduous trip.

As you can imagine, it was an incredibly expensive operation. Purchasing the fish plus payments to the haulage contractor John Jones "for his own trouble, servants, horse hire, etc" for these four journeys came to £20 and other payments would have been made to Rees Rees and his party as well as the cost of making and repairing the containers. Not content with this Talbot also paid a George Bartlet to make a similar trip to Hensol castle to collect perch from the fishponds there which were again used to stock Kenfig Pool.

Initially those pike put in the Margam lakes struggled to find enough prey to survive, so William John (presumably the son of the late tenant of Pool Farm) was paid to catch roach at Kenfig Pool and transfer them there. He was also paid to make a flood gate on the lake at Kenfig whereby its water level could be controlled.

Clearly Thomas Talbot was not going to all this trouble and expense creating his own version of a coarse fisherman's paradise at Kenfig to share it with the burgesses! Whilst they may have believed back in 1661 that they had successfully secured the fishing rights for themselves, a hundred years on their successors were left in no doubt that (whatever the rights and wrongs of it might be) these now belonged to the Talbots. So far as I can see they mounted no subsequent challenge to recover their rights. You win some; you lose some, and sooner or later (they may have reasoned) the wheel of fortune would spin their way and they in turn would get their own opportunity to score a point at the expense of their Lord of the Manor!

Ty'n y Towyn and The Angel At the 1769 Spring Leet the Court noted that Daniel Rees had now purchased "Tun y Mawdlam and Tun y Tywin, with thirteen acres of freehold land" from Edmond Thomas, gent. Ty'n y Towyn was a farmhouse which stood, and in a much altered form, still stands, behind The Angel Inn to the east of Mawdlam church. Its name (The House in the Sands) is a vivid indication of just how close the advancing dunes had come to overrunning the village prior to their dramatic halt at the end of the 17th century.

The earlier history of this farm is obscure, as are the origins of Edmond Thomas himself. At this point in time I tend to believe that he was a grandson of Thomas Edmund (d 1692) of Old Park Farm, Margam by a son named Henry, but the evidence for this is rather flimsy. Current research leads me to believe that Ty'n y Towyn and Ty'n y Mawdlam made up most if not all of the property he acquired from Evan and Catherine Lyddon, but this is by no means certain.

I am also pretty certain that the 'Ty'n Mawdlam', included in this sale was in fact The Angel Inn which was certainly part of the property transferred to Margam with Ty'n y Towyn when the estate bought the latter in the 19th century. Who the licensee was at this time I cannot discover, and perhaps it was not even in use as an alehouse. This is the first year in which the annual renewal of alehouse licences are recorded in the minute books, but the only one mentioned is The Corporation House. In order to secure it, the current tenant Edmund Harry, had to enter into a bond or recognisance of £10 and find two sureties prepared to put up £5 each. If he then breached the conditions subject to which his licence had been granted these bonds would be forfeited. The entry in the minute book (B/K 11) sets out the conditions as follows:

> That Edmond Harry of Kenfigg, ale housekeeper, shall keep good lodging for travelers, sufficient meat; wholesome drink, viz ale & small drink, for men & women, upon all occasions, & fodder to be provided for horses. To serve His Majesty's subjects and to sell a quart of ale for four pence & a quart of small drink from halfe a penny, & not to suffer any to continue tipling & drinking in his house upon the Lord's Day, nor upon any other day nor night above the hours limited & alowed according to law. And likewise not to suffer no unlawfull game or games as cards [or] dice to be played in his said house.

Sker & Richard Jenkin The tenancy of Sker House following the death of Isaac William in December 1766 has hitherto been something of a mystery. His eldest son, John, was aged about 21 at that time, and may possibly have remained there for a few years, but in 1771 he took out a lease on Newlands Farm in Higher Kenfig and was probably already living there at that time.

It therefore seems that in 1770 Sker was vacant, and at this point we renew our acquaintance with our old friend Richard Jenkin of Marlas of whom we have heard little since the termination of his years of office as Portreeve in 1660. In truth there is little to tell. The sole references to him that I have come across in local records during this period are confined to the annual entries in the Margam rentals and an occasional presentment at the manor court concerning the state of his hedgerows.

On learning that Sker had fallen vacant he was swiftly off the mark to secure a lease upon it from John Curre. This included a cottage called Castell-y-Morluck as well as the house and farm, along with two additional closes called Cae'r Berllan and Cae Ffynnon (PM 9380). 'Castell-y-Morluck' is, presumably, is the house shown on the OS Map as Castle Morgraig which lies between Sker House and The Rest. Nothing stands above ground today, and the name has led people to speculate that perhaps it was originally the site of some sort of fortification. I have never searched the location myself, but some who have claim to have found the footings of walls of great thickness, and at least one has advanced the theory that these may actually be the remains of a watchtower dating from the Roman period

In the event taking this lease seems to have been one of those things that 'seemed a good idea at the time' but subsequently proved not to be case. Certainly Richard's tenancy was not of any great duration and by 1775 the house and its land were in the occupation of Morgan Howells whom we shall meet with in due course.

The Pool on Heol Las The Borough minutes often throw up brief snippets of information, unimportant in themselves, but which together help to create a more detailed picture of the land of Kenfig in the past. One such entry was made at the Spring Leet in 1770 (B/K 11) which tells us that there was formerly a pool on Heol Las "between the churchyard and Cross y Green". It was known as Winters Hill Pool, which perhaps indicates that it stood somewhere in the vicinity of the field of that name and near the present footbridge across the M4 Motorway — the original field of this name however did extended as far as Heol y Broom. It was said to be in disrepair, "and ought to be repaired by Jenkin Lewis" who was given until the next court to do the work or else pay a fine of ten shillings.

I know very little about Jenkin, or why he should be held responsible for the maintenance of this pond that apparently formed part of the highway. He does not even seem to have been a burgess. This is the last reference I have to either him or the pool itself which does not subsequently appear on any of the early 19th century maps of the area.

More Improvements at The Pool; a Treat for The Tenants; and Rough Justice for a Beggar. Several other small incidents during the year 1771 are of interest and well worth a brief mention in passing.

In June the Margam accounts (D/D Ma 24) record payment of 19s 2d to a man named John Jenkin "for his journey with two men and four horses to Hensol for fish to be put in Kenfig Pool". Other entries include the cost of hauling the Margam boat from the pool for repair together with "pitch, tram oil and nails, etc" needed for this work. Repairs to this boat subsequently feature regularly in the accounts.

Many Margam tenants also got a rather agreeable surprise this year, for another payment in the records is for malt and hops to brew ale "for the use of the tenants when they pay their rents". Why this should have been done at this time is a mystery, for the only notable event in the Talbot household was the death of Ann the sister of Thomas which, since he was clearly very fond of her, was scarcely a cause for celebration.

On 12th June Richard Jenkins of Marlas, in his capacity as a local magistrate, signed a warrant committing a widow named Mary Lewis to The House of Correction (the gaol!) at Cowbridge to await trial at Cardiff Quarter Sessions. Her offence was that she "was this day found wandering and begging" and since she was a vagrant who had no local connections he and the Overseers of the Poor took this preventative action so that she would not seek to become a charge by seeking relief from their Parish (Q/S R 1771C 70).

During the course of 1772 major repair work was carried out (at Margam's expense) to the doors of the Tithe Barn on Heol Las, much of the iron-work, such as hinges and nails, being supplied by Richard Yorwerth. The estate accounts also indicate the existence of a lime kiln at Croes y Green, lime from which was carried "from thence to Margam by sundry tenants" which also shows that at least some 'carriage duties' included in the tenancies of certain holdings were still being performed in kind.

A New Portreeve The major event of 1772 was, however, the failure of Richard Yorwerth to secure a further term in the office of Portreeve. His name, together with that of his predecessor Richard Williams, was indeed submitted to the Constable of the Castle by his fellow burgesses, but the latter's choice fell on the third person nominated – the comparative newcomer Daniel Rees. Although he had been living at

Llanmihangel in 1767 it is possible that by this time he had moved to the farmhouse at Ty'n y Towyn which he purchased in 1769. Daniel, as things turned out, was to be the last Kenfig Portreeve to hold this office for more than two whole years in succession.

Daniel Rees: The Last 'Significant' Portreeve: Significant not because Daniel Rees (who now succeeded Richard Yorwerth) did anything particularly notable or praiseworthy whilst holding this office, but only because he was the last person to hold it for a term of several consecutive years. After his day the Borough rules relating to the Portreeveship were altered so that under normal circumstances nobody could hold the post for two years running. As usual there is no mention of the momentous decision in the Borough minutes – so far as records are concerned it just happened!

Waun Cimla Fencing When Daniel took office as the new Portreeve the first problem awaiting his attention was the thorny old question of maintaining fences at Waun Cimla which was now starting to reappear after an absence of many years. Quite evidently he and his council had carried out their annual inspection required by the ruling of 1751, and found these to be wanting, so at a Hall Day on the 5th February 1773 the plot holders were given until 25th March to have the work carried out. Rees and his Council also declared that in the case of any that failed to comply, then the repairs "shall be ordered to be done immediately by the Portrieve at the expence of the owner or owners thereof"(B/K 11). There was at this point in time, still no shying away from grasping the nettle apparent here - the ordinance introduced by the late Edward Harris was still being rigorously applied to the full!

A New 'Seat' for Local Government! A particularly interesting entry in the Borough Minute books was added after the sitting of the Courts of Pleas and Baron on 5th March 1773. It is interesting because it records the making of "one new seat in the Town Hall" from "44 foot of deal board". In a reference to the same work the Portreeve's accounts amplify this statement by saying that the work entailed "making a new seat and mending the old seat".

This seat is undoubtedly the old wooden settle that occupies the wall at the western end of the Town Hall today which, together with the great table, is mentioned in the accounts of former Portreeve Edward Harris covering the years 1745-56. It was here the Portreeve sat at the centre of the great table presiding over various courts and other meetings, yielding his position only when the Constable of the Castle was present for the two annual Courts Leet. To enhance the majesty and prestige of these two worthies as they sat facing those assembled before the table, there were two strategically placed windows. Positioned either side of the central chimney-breast these illuminated the faces of those present whilst creating an area of shadow at the centre of the bench that lay between them. Here sat the Portreeve and/or the Constable, their forms and features obscured by shadow which would have been even more intense in the evenings with the setting sun shining directly through the windows. A simple device, but an effective one to enhance the mystery and the majesty of their office!

In the shadow those in front of the table would have been able to make out a coat of arms emblazoned on the wall above the head of the presiding officer, whilst ranged on either side of him (them) along the settle were presumably the officers of the Borough from the Recorder right down to the Petty Constable. It must have been an impressive, not to say daunting sight to those appearing before the court – as indeed it was intended to be!

Town Hall Interior Today The new seat was made by two carpenters who were both local men. John Owen is frequently mentioned in the minute books carrying out repairs to both the Town Hall and the Corporation House, and had been the Sergeant-at-Mace in 1771, though other than this I know very little about him. Thomas Yorwerth was the son of Richard and Ann of Pool Farm, and was aged about 25. He is mentioned as a carpenter in 1769 at which time he was living at Pyle, and perhaps in recognition of this work on the seat he was nominated as a burgess at the Spring Leet and subsequently admitted. Being an 'out-dweller', however, he took no part in Borough affairs thereafter, and this is actually the last mention that I have so far found of him.

The total cost of their labour and the timber came to £4.8s.3d which was paid directly from the treasury rather than by the Portreeve who nevertheless included it in his accounts. This possibly indicates that the old seat had totally collapsed and the new one was required as a matter of urgency at a time when the recently installed Portreeve had no funds at his disposal pending the collection of the Borough rates. His accounts show that he also paid the men an additional 14s.8d in connection with the work, though no reason is given.

The Angel Inn The minute books now routinely showed the annual renewal of alehouse licences for premises in the Borough every September, and in 1773 comes the first mention of the grant of such a licence in respect of The Angel Inn (though the name of the premises is not actually given). The tenant was a widow named Mary Evan, daughter of a former burgess named Edward Evan who died between 1739 and 1744. Mary was one of seven children and was now about 60 years of age, but of her former husband I know only that his second name was Andrew.

Despite her age Mary was to continue running these premises for over 25 years though initially she seems to have had one or two problems! In 1774 she sued two burgesses for debt and then two years later was in her turn the subject of a similar complaint by another. After this the dust seems to have settled and the remainder of her tenancy, except for its longevity, was largely uneventful.

The Portreeve's Accounts and the Recorder's 'Perks of Office' In 1774 Richard Yorwerth submitted the accounts for his term in the office of Portreeve up to Michaelmas 1772. This included payment for several small repairs that were carried out to the Town Hall of which the major one was re-pointing the 'slopehouse' (lean-to?). The hall had been whitewashed, and the carpet that graced its floor had been washed.

Later the same year Daniel Rees, the current Portreeve, submitted his own accounts for his first year of office in which a great deal of work had been carried out on the stable attached to the Corporation House. This had actually been partially rebuilt and the thatched roof replaced by tiles. Further work was done whitewashing the building, and there were some minor repairs to the washing pound. In all Daniel spent almost £7 during his first year of office – nearly three times the annual income from the general rate. Fortunately the Treasury was in a position to meet the deficit.

The highlight of 1774 however was a blazing row between Rees Rees and the Corporation arising from the large number of out-burgesses admitted the previous year (four more were nominated during 1774). Rees was in all probability the Recorder at this time (a post he held on several occasions) and in that capacity had apparently visited "several Gentlemen sworn as Burgesses in this Borough" to deliver the necessary paperwork relating to their admission.

Several of these had given him "sums or sum of money ... over and above his fee" which the Corporation felt he should not have accepted as they already allowed him money for "his troubles and expences in waiting upon those Gentlemen out of Court". They therefore demanded that he pay these 'tips' into the Borough coffers, something that he was clearly unwilling to do since he considered them one of the perks of his office. Willingly or unwillingly, he nevertheless seems to have eventually complied, for we hear no more of the matter other than a formal reminder during the Autumn Leet that he had not yet presented his accounts for approval.

A Grisly Discovery at Marlas By virtue of his office, the Kenfig Portreeve was also the Coroner for the Borough, though this incident is the first occasion that the fact is acknowledged in the minute books. Indeed, it was to be many years before Recorders again entered the details of inquests in these books as a matter of course. Besides being the first such record, the report of this particular inquest held on 6th January 1775 is more detailed than most. At the court the jury were required to consider evidence relating to the discovery of the body of a newly-born child found at Marlas Farm, the home of Richard Jenkins, on the preceding 14th December.

Jennet John and Elizabeth Matthew were probably servants at the house, and the latter claimed in evidence that she had been suspicious for some time that Jennet (who was unmarried) was carrying a child. On the day in question she realised from the other's physical condition that her suspicions were correct and challenged her that she had recently given birth. Acting upon what Jennet told her she then went to a storeroom where she found the body of a new-born female child wrapped in Jennet's flannel petticoat. She alerted the household and presumably Daniel Rees as Portreeve and Coroner was notified.

Having viewed the pathetic remains Rees then seems to have taken it upon himself to summon others to join him at the house. These included Margaret Harry (née Jones) of the Corporation House who, besides being the licensee was also the local midwife. With her came a

Mary Powell and having thoroughly examined the remains and ascertained that they bore no signs of violence, they cleaned and 'dressed' the little body. Both were quite satisfied that the infant had been still-born and informed Rees accordingly

Daniel Rees seems to have been an intelligent and prudent man - probably a compassionate one as well. He would have known that the evidence of the two women was all that stood between young Jennet and a charge of murder. Most, if not all of Kenfig would be quite happy to accept the word of their local midwife, especially when supported by somebody like Mary Powell who herself had given birth to at least eight children. Any conclusions reached by his inquest would however be reviewed at the Court of Quarter Sessions and, he probably wondered, would 'the nobs' there be prepared to accept these two as 'expert witnesses'? What, moreover, if some of the local rumour–mongers (and there are always one or two of those!) began spreading malicious tattle? How 'convenient' the death had been for young Jane; and wasn't Mrs Jones perhaps 'getting-on a bit' to still be delivering babies yet alone pronouncing 'cause of death'?

You know the sort of thing. It goes on now, and it went on then, but with one very big difference. Today we have a professional Police Force backed by some of the finest medical and scientific facilities available in order to determine how and why a person dies suddenly. Back in Daniel's day he had – well not a lot! If such rumours grew out of control, then there was a distinct possibility that young Jane would end up in prison awaiting trial. I come across several instances of this in the court records of the period - the accused brought before the jury purely on the basis of allegations that had circulated in the locality after the death. When placed before a judge and jury these turned out to have no basis in fact, the prosecution's case collapsed, and the accused walked free.

There was therefore a distinct possibility that, in addition to the physical and mental distress of giving birth to an illegitimate and still-born child, young Jennet could find herself facing the ordeal of being remanded to the horrors of Cardiff gaol followed by the trauma of standing trial for her life. Daniel Rees, or so it seems, was determined to spare her this and in addition to the action he had already taken, took certain additional steps which he believed would not only satisfy the higher court, but also put a stop to any malicious local gossip.

Firstly he summoned five local men and asked them to make a thorough examination of the baby's body for marks of violence, and when they too found nothing, had them to repeat this on oath at the Inquest. Secondly he also had the body examined by an 'expert witness' in the person of a Mr Alexander who is described as a "surgeon and man-midwife". He too subsequently gave evidence to the effect that in his opinion the child was undoubtedly 'still-born'.

It was, I think, rather more trouble than many Coroners would have gone to in those days over a mere 'still-birth', but thanks to Daniel Rees's thoroughness the verdict of the jury at the inquest was a mere formality.

Who the unfortunate Jennet was I do not know, but it is unlikely that she was Jennet John the 'female burgess' and spinster sister of Jenkin John of Pwllygath Farm for she was about 54 years of age at this time! Ironically it seems that Elizabeth Matthew did not learn from her friend's misfortune as eleven years later she herself gave birth to an illegitimate child by a man named John Thomas. (PPR)

Defaulters In February 1775 the Borough contracted with William Harry, son of the late licensee of the Corporation House, to "stop up rabbit holes" on the North Common, and with David Yorwerth for Kenfig Down. To William was also given the task of collecting the Rabbit Hole Rate (for which he received an extra two shillings) and, having deducted the money due to David and himself, there were six shillings left over which he paid into the Treasury.

Nevertheless the account he submitted to the Corporation shows that his collection was about four shillings short because certain burgesses refused or neglected to pay. It was, it seems a case of 'the same ones every time', so Daniel Rees named and shamed them at the next Court Baron, ordering each to pay arrears amounting to ten shillings and sixpence. If they failed to do so, he declared, then the outstanding amount would "be levied on their goods and chattels by the Hayward, or [they were] to be disfranchised at the next Baron Court".(B/K 11) Apparently all paid up, for the next Court Baron came and went without incident.

Morgan Howell and a prize turnip Shortly before the year 1775 a powerful new character appeared on the local scene in the form of

Morgan Howell who moved into Sker House with his family. He was the 'father of the maid' remembered by old Lena Rees in her conversation with Thomas Morgan ('Llyfnwy', 1876) who mistakenly believed she was referring to Isaac, the father of Elizabeth Williams. Lena recalled that Morgan arrived at Sker with "a *pedwaran* (a quarter of a bushel) of guineas" that were all subsequently spent on the property. Although only six or seven years of age in 1775 Lena may well

LLYFNWY (CIRCA 1890)

have been privy to such information because later in life she was employed by Morgan as a servant at Sker House, and no doubt too, Morgan's apparent affluence would have been the subject of much local gossip at the time he took up residence.

Where Morgan Howell came from with such wealth is one of those annoying little puzzles that neither I nor his descendants have so far been able to work out. Wherever it was it is likely that his body was returned there for burial for there is no record of an interment locally for either him or his eldest son Owen.

The first mention of him being at Sker comes in 1775, recording that he won the prize for the best crop of turnips grown that year awarded by the Glamorgan Agricultural Society (Evans, 1960: 56). Believe it or not the cultivation of the humble turnip was at this time considered a sign of agricultural excellence. It was a relatively new crop that was being grown to good effect in England but had gained little favour with Welsh farmers who as a result were considered rather backward by their contemporaries across the border. At the turn of the century in Pyle Inn, James Marment the innkeeper liked to brag to his important guests that he had been the first to introduce cultivation of the turnip to this area (Thompson, 1983: 210) but, as the entry in the Agricultural Society records shows, any kudos in this respect actually belongs to Morgan.

Amongst the family that arrived with him at Sker was Morgan's little daughter Martha, aged about four. In time she would weave her own legend at Sker which, thanks to Llyfnwy's error, became incorporated into the story of her predecessor Elizabeth Williams.

Martha's story, so far as I and her descendants can ascertain is one that seems to be solidly based on fact, and from it we learn that Morgan was a staunch Nonconformist, and also a stern un-bending sort of man - a fore-runner of the typical Victorian fathers of the future. Perhaps not surprisingly therefore he seems to have struck up a close friendship with the ageing Richard Jenkins of Marlas, and was one of the signatories to the latter's will made in 1777.

Twilight for the Portreeves

For over six hundred years the Portreeves of Kenfig had guided the fortunes of their town and borough through good times and ill, having been specifically equipped by their fellow burgesses with the necessary legal powers to enable them to do so. Despite the fact that few could claim the social status of a 'gentleman', within the confines of their borough, and for the duration of their term of office, they were accorded a status on a par with the local gentry whose own social status resulted merely from an accident of birth. The Portreeve was their undisputed ruler, and though custom and practice required that he consulted with his council of Eight Elected Burgesses before making any decisions, the final say was his and his alone.

Back in 1750, Edward Harris of Llanmihangel Mill, Portreeve, had risen to his position of power from being nothing more than a lowly carpenter. The health of his patron Bussy Mansel might be failing fast, but his own authority within the Borough was unchallenged and would remain so until his death in 1756. At that time, Kenfig's Portreeves still enjoyed to the full the ancient authority handed down to them from their medieval forebears, but it seems that beneath the surface changes were in the offing.

Measures designed to curtail the Portreeve's powers were not actually introduced until the 1770s and, as usual, the Borough's minute books are silent about the implementation of the new practice, far less contain any hint during the preceding years that such changes were in the offing. All that can be said is that the appointment of Rees Rees as the Portreeve at the Autumn Leet in 1775 marks a radical change in the way in which the three nominees for this office were chosen. Such changes cannot have been made on a mere whim, but there is no record of any prior discussions about the matter or even a hint that such was even under consideration.

This major alteration was that no Kenfig Portreeve was subsequently nominated to be continued in office for a second consecutive term, although an exception was made where their first term came about through having to replace a Portreeve that died in office. Hitherto there had been no bar on the current holder's name being put forward year after year and as we have noted, Edward Harris held the office for fourteen years consecutively. After 1775, with the one exception already noted, the name of the current Portreeve was never put forward to the Constable as a candidate for the office.

Thanks to the silence of the Borough records we have no real inkling as to why this change was made. One possibility that occurred to me was that the burgesses were attempting to prevent the Talbots exerting undue influence over them through the Portreeve as I have speculated may have been the case with Edward Harris. Against this it has to be pointed out that Harris's immediate successor, Richard Jenkins (who held office for four years) was the tenant of Marlas Farm. Thanks to Bussy Mansel's sleight of hand this now belonged to the Briton Ferry estate, so it seems resisting political pressure from Margam when choosing a new Portreeve was not a problem.

Another possible explanation is that the burgesses were seeking to shackle the hitherto unfettered authority of their Portreeves. A twelvemonth in office allowed the new incumbent to do little more than 'warm the seat'. By the time he got round to consider introducing any contentious measures, his period of office was over. Maybe therefore, without actually stripping the Portreeve of his powers, the burgesses had made it easier for them to control his actions. In this connection another significant change apparent from the minute books occurs in 1761 when responsibility for making nominations for the various offices was removed from the hands of the two Electors and vested in those of the burgesses as a whole. If a sufficiently large number favoured a particular course of action it was now a simple matter to ensure that the names of three of their number were put forward as the candidates. If the chosen candidate subsequently failed to 'deliver the goods', then twelvemonths later they could simply try again.

Such a radical change in the Borough's organisation presupposes that, perhaps as early as the time of Edward Harris, there was amongst the burgesses an element that was already actively seeking change in the way the borough was run. If, as I have suggested, they were also thereby attempting to ensure for themselves a greater say in its affairs then this, in its way, is quite remarkable. The latter part of the 18th century was a time when agitation to secure rights for the common man was starting to appear across Europe. In Britain it saw the rise of the Chartist movement, and across the channel this spilled over into the violence of the French Revolution. Quite amazingly therefore it seems that here at Kenfig the burgesses may, quietly and unspectacularly, have already introduced measures aimed at making their own organisation a more democratic form of local government!

This, of course, is only speculation on my part, but the fact remains that whatever the actual intent behind these changes, the eventual result was to effectively reduce the autocratic authority of the Portreeves and by the end of the century give the burgesses themselves a greater say in the ordering of borough affairs. Whereas previous decisions affecting the Borough had been made by "The Portreeve and the Eight Elected", minute book entries in the mid 1790s speak of such declarations being made by "The Eight" or by "The Jury". In certain instances they even appear to be directing the actions of the Portreeve in respect of certain matters. A major change in the way the Borough organisation had taken place.

New Restrictions on the Portreeves At the Autumn Leet of 1775 Daniel Rees was not even nominated for the office of Portreeve, giving the first indication that the new criteria for choosing candidates for this office had been introduced. As usual there is nothing in the minutes to show that such alterations had been made, or why, but the fact is that Daniel Rees was the last person to serve in this office for more than two full consecutive years. Hereafter the retiring Portreeve was never nominated for continuation in the post unless he had been originally appointed to fill a vacancy left by the death of a serving Portreeve.

Perhaps the idea was that the burgesses should share the job amongst themselves and all enjoy the perks of the office from time to time. Maybe they didn't like having the same person lording it over them year after year. Probably (as I tend to believe) they wanted to effectively remove power from the hands of the Portreeve and secure it for themselves as a body. Whatever the reason, the new order now took effect and continued so long as the Borough itself existed.

From time to time future Portreeves did take decisive action in the manner of their predecessors, but twelve months in the office was no time at all to carry through a programme of reform, change or improvement, albeit that they probably still had the legal right to do so. In practice they increasingly become mere figureheads in the Borough organisation. Some were so old when appointed that they died in office. Others were illiterate and/or simple labourers who had merely been burgesses for a very long time and were apparently being rewarded for their longevity.

I suppose, living in a democratic age as we do, we should applaud this early example of a transfer of power to 'the people', but in practice it didn't work quite like that. Each and every burgess was alert to the fact that there were little perks to be had in the Borough organisation, and were constantly on the look-out for anything that might be to their own advantage. When, as we will see in due course, opportunities arose to handle large amounts of money that could be devoted either to the use of the Borough, or to line their collective pockets - it was no contest! It might be impossible to get turkeys to vote for Christmas – but they'll peck your fingers off for a handful of corn!

The new Portreeve appointed to replace Daniel Rees was **Rees Rees** of Kenfig House who was about 57 years of age and has already made several appearances in this history. By this time he had firmly established himself in the community, and made his home into the centre of a sizeable farm that was still being expanded. Twelvemonths later, his term of office over, he stood down and was not even nominated to be continued in office. A new phase in the Borough's long history had begun.

The Portreeve appointed to succeed Rees Rees after his year in office was **Hopkin David** whose age is unknown but who was probably well into his forties. He had come to Kenfig in 1757 from Cadoxton, Neath, on his marriage to Catherine the daughter of a burgess named Evan John, and was one of those we noted who were admitted as burgesses in 1761 on the basis of such marriages.

His father-in-law died in 1763, and his widow two years later, after which Hopkin and Catherine were given possession of the family plots of hay and fern. Hopkin may, or may not be the man of this name who was one of a group of individuals charged with assaulting Edward Howells, the licensee of *The Tap* at Pyle, back in 1759. (GGS:Wales 4 618/3)

If so then he seems to have settled down somewhat since then. Able to sign his name he appears as a witness to several wills of burgesses, which in itself tends to indicated that he was well respected and trusted locally, as do his appearances both as an assessor at Courts Leet and a collector of the Land Tax.

The Borough Mace This was the only occasion that Hopkin David ever held the office of Portreeve, but it is interesting to note that whilst he held the office of Sergeant during 1777-8 a payment was made to him for cleaning the Borough mace. Traditionally the Sergeant was the only person permitted to handle the mace, but this is the earliest reference I have come across that such a symbol of the Borough's authority actually existed.

It is evidently the mace now on display at the National Museum in St Fagans, though a replica is also kept in the possession of the Trustees of the Borough at Kenfig. The fact that this is the first mention of it in the records suggests that it had not long been in the possession of the Corporation. For a description of the mace itself I can do no better than quote the one given by Leslie Evans (1960: 44)

> The mace, a replica of which is to be seen in the Prince of Wales Inn, was of silver. It is exceptionally small, being 37 cms long, and is the work of Gabriel Sleath, who made it about 1714, the year of the accession of George I. The maker's initials appear on it, as does the name 'Kenfigg Borough', incised on the stem. Within the cup-shaped head is a disc bearing the Royal Arms in relief, and the arches of a crown, springing from a coronet around the head, are surmounted by an orb and cross.

It has been suggested that the miniature nature of this mace is perhaps due to the fact that it was originally made by Sleath as a 'sample' of his work, and in the context of the time when it was fashioned this is quite plausible. The death of Queen Anne having left the throne vacant, in 1714 the country turned to George the Elector of Hanover to be their new king. Supporters of the exiled and hated King James II launched an uprising which, although it achieved some limited success in Scotland, was quickly crushed. Nevertheless, the silversmith Gabriel Sleath, may well have anticipated a steady call on his services by Borough Corporations and others eager to express their loyalty to the new order by replacing their existing mace with one bearing the new monarch's coat of arms. The Kenfig mace may well therefore have started life as a sample made to show prospective customers the sort of finished article he could produce.

Such being the case the Borough of Kenfig is unlikely to have acquired the mace for some time after it was actually made when it became either superfluous to the needs of the maker or his firm went out of business. If they actually purchased it themselves, then they probably did so prior to 1730, for there is no record of the transaction in the minutes or the Portreeve's accounts after that date. On the other hand it may have been presented to Kenfig by a wealthy patron such as the Mansels and Talbots of Margam, or even a wealthy burgess like John Thomas or Edward Harris who may have acquired it at a bargain price. The account of Richard Jones (alias John) for his year in the office of Portreeve (1784-5) indicates that mace was engraved with the name of Borough during his term of office which tends to suggest that it had not long been in their possession. As to how it was actually come by, the Borough minutes themselves contain no clue.

Waun Cimla Fences The earliest sign of the effect of the transfer of power from the hands of the Portreeve to the Burgesses as a whole is a change in the attitude to those who failed to keep their fences at Waun Cimla in repair. Like his predecessors Hopkin David in company with Eight Elected Burgesses made the annual inspection at Waun Cimla, and in May 1777 reported that they had found the fences of ten plot-holders to be in need of repair. These were ordered to do the necessary work within six days or pay a fine of five shillings "to be levied on their goods & chattels by David Yeorwarth the Hayward".

Despite the aggressive wording, this was actually a return to the method of enforcement that Edward Harris's order of 1751 was brought in to replace. It was probably not a coincidence that with the change of the rules under which the Portreeve was appointed, and the perceptible shift of power to the Burgesses as a whole, the old and failed method was reinstated. Presumably the provisions of the order of 1751 were unpopular with many of the burgesses because it FORCED them to have the work carried out, whereas they knew full well that the threat implicit under the previous regime was rarely carried out until the defects had been reported on several occasions. And so it became. Complaints of fences at the enclosure being in bad repair once more become a frequent feature of the minutes, but despite this no attempt was made to return to the enforcement measures introduced in 1751.

"Whome She Goeth Bigg With" As has been mentioned in an earlier chapter it is but rarely that the work of the Borough's Overseers of the Poor find a mention in surviving contemporary records. One problem they were always on the lookout for was that of illegitimate children who, together with their mothers, could easily become a charge on the parish rates. They were not being moralistic, it was simply that they took what steps they could to identify the father so that he could be made responsible for the maintenance of his offspring. Through some whim of the Recorder (who did not normally note such items) one example occurs in the Minute Books in 1777.

Elizabeth was the daughter of William John and the granddaughter of the man of that name who had kept Pool Farm until his death in 1766. I have no record of her birth or baptism, but her sister Ann had been baptised in 1747, so she would most likely have been in her twenties. The day came when it was apparent to everyone that Elizabeth, who was unmarried, was heavily pregnant, and mindful of his duty the Overseer of the Poor brought her before the Portreeve as the local magistrate. There she swore on oath that

> David Yeorwarth, the son of Richard Yeorwarth, ... is the true father of
> the child or children whom she goeth bigg with.

Having secured that admission the Overseer's duty was done for, when the child was born, its maintenance would become the responsibility of David who, at this time, was 32 years of age and also unmarried himself.

The son of Richard Yorwerth of Pool Farm, David is variously described as a labourer or a tailor, and later in 1777 the Parish Registers tell us that Elizabeth gave birth to their daughter whom she christened Jemima on 21st July. Sadly the child's life was tragically short for the same source records that she was buried on 14th July the following year.

This however was not to be the end of the story, and it could be that here, in David and Elizabeth, we have another unsung Kenfig romance, for in 1783 the registers show that the two baptised another illegitimate daughter they named Elizabeth. I can find no record of the child after this date, so possibly she too died in infancy. In 1784 David is named as the father of a son baptised that year, although in this case the mother is not named. The year after this Elizabeth became the second wife of John Beynon of Cornelly, and in 1788 David married a woman named Martha.

Undoubtedly there's a story here somewhere, but what it is the records at my disposal are too limited to tell. After a liaison that lasted seven years or more, and the birth of two and possibly three children, why did the couple never marry? Both were adults, so parental interference should not have been a factor. Which of them jilted the other? We will probably never know, so I must leave it to you and your own imagination to reconstruct the story of their romance as suits your fancy.

A Change of Landlords at Sker The year 1777 also saw the death at Bath of John Curre who was the landlord of Morgan Howells at Sker. He left no heir, and by his last Will and Testament gave some of his land (including Clemenston in Glamorgan) to his brother William. Sker, and other land in Gwent, he bequeathed to his servant Joseph Lloyd (Evans, 1956: 36). This news undoubtedly evoked no little interest at Margam House where Thomas Mansel Talbot had long expressed an interest in adding Sker to his Glamorgan estate (Martin, 1995: 58). For the moment, however, the house and its land still remained beyond his grasp.

The New Portreeve 1777-8 The man chosen to succeed Hopkin David as Portreeve at the Autumn Leet of 1777 was a burgess named **Evan Jenkin**, who is something of a problem character in my research since there were three persons with this name living in the district at this time. The one I believe him to be was 42 years old and the son of yet another Evan Jenkin who lived in Higher Kenfig and died between 1739 and 1744.

His mother, Elizabeth Jenkin, survived until 1759 and through her he became tenant of part of Ynys y Pandy on which his father had secured a lease in 1723. On his mother's death Evan was admitted as a burgess, and continued as tenant of Ynys y Pandy until 1773 when the holding was included in the lease to Hopkin Llewelyn on Llanmihangel Mill. Where he actually lived is still a mystery, but there is a possibility that he may have become Llewelyn's tenant at the mill. Other evidence suggests that he was a shoemaker and that he was sufficiently educated to sign his name (though towards the end of his life he only made his mark).

Evan was certainly an active individual in the affairs of the Borough even before his admission as Portreeve. In 1761 he had been contracted to stop up rabbit holes on the Common, and was one of those the Portreeve Rees Daniel called to view the body of the still-born child found at Marlas Farm. In 1776 he went surety for the renewal of Margaret Jones's alehouse licence in respect of the Corporation House. In being selected as the Portreeve, Evan Jenkin completed a clean sweep of the Borough Offices, having served in every capacity from Petty Constable upwards at least once.

The Kenfig Coat of Arms Was there ever a Coat of Arms for Kenfig Borough? I mentioned in the previous chapter that a coat of arms is believed to have appeared above the seats in the Town Hall occupied by the Portreeve and Constable of the Castle. This is the most likely location for one that is mentioned about this time with certain indications that the arms displayed may have been those of the Borough of Kenfig.

This was something that several members of the Kenfig Society, particularly (as I recall) the late Haydn Reynolds and Rennie Davies, spent some time exploring in the early days of our group. Haydn, I remember, even contacted the Royal Society of Heralds, but none of their enquiries met with any success.

Two references in particular had alerted us to the possibility that such an insignia, hitherto unsuspected, may actually have existed. The first was in a poem by Mary A Richards ('*Mair Tir Iarll*') in which she speaks of her thoughts on contemplating the Borough Coat of Arms. Initially we tended to dismiss this as an error (or poetic licence) for the Borough seal. What made us all think again was an item in the minutes of the Autumn Court Leet held in October 1779.

There the jury 'presented' the fact that the Hayward, Edward Evan, had failed to pay into the treasury the sum of three shillings received from Edmund Thomas and Thomas Lewis for trespass on Waun Cimla. In all probability this was no more than an agreed sum for them to enter into the enclosure for some purpose of their own such as surveying, prospecting for minerals, or even to obtain access to adjoining property.

The Constable of the Castle, as the presiding officer, ordered that this money be paid to the Portreeve "and that the s'd sum shal be applyed towards redoing the arms of the said Borough and mannor in the Guild Hall." So *Mair Tir Iarll* was vindicated after all!

It seems highly likely that the arms were in the form of a mural painted on the wall, and the most likely place for them to have been displayed would be in the area between the two windows in the west wall. Unfortunately at some time in the relatively recent past (probably towards the end of the 19th century) a wall-safe has been inserted into the masonry at this point. So even if the arms survive beneath layers of paint and lime-wash (as has sometimes happened to wall paintings in medieval churches), much of it will have been destroyed. Nevertheless perhaps this possibility can be borne in mind in the event of future work ever being carried out here or elsewhere in the hall.

At the same court **Rees Thomas**, aged 49 and the current head of the Rees/Thomas family, was chosen to be Portreeve for the coming year. Normally he signed records with his mark suggesting illiteracy, but on the very first occasion, back in 1765, he appears to have written his name. It seems that not having much opportunity to write, he had simply forgotten how to!

This year too, a Rees Thomas "of the Parish of Pyle & Kenfig, yeoman" appeared before the Court of Great Sessions (GGS: 4 Wales 624/3) to answer a charge of assaulting one Thomas Harris, a gentleman. Whether or not this was Rees Thomas of Kenfig is impossible to say, but if so it seems to have had no detrimental effect upon his candidature!

A Mock Election On 31st March 1780 a strange event took place at the Town Hall. Present were the Constable of the Castle, the Portreeve (Rees Thomas) and some sixty-three burgesses - a mixture of 'out-dwellers' and 'in-dwellers'. Also present was Sir Herbert Mackworth of Neath, the sitting MP for the Glamorgan Boroughs. There then followed a curious ceremony whereby two burgesses named David Yorwerth and William Esias stood in "an election for a gift that Sir Herbert Mackworth did please to beestow".

The nature of the 'gift' is not stated, but not surprisingly 1780 was an election year, and so what took place was evidently some gimmick designed to rally Sir Herbert's support in the Borough itself.

How the two 'candidates' had been selected we are not told, but it seems they were actually related by marriage.

David Yorwerth is the grandson of David and Barbara Yorwerth and has previously appeared in our history. Back in 1758 he had married Eleanor Esaias of Margam who was presumably a relative of his opponent, William. The latter had been admitted as a burgess back in 1767, but although nominated as an Ale-taster at that time there is no record of any other involvement with the Borough afterwards. I assume that he had therefore left Kenfig and in 1780 was an 'out-burgess'.

This mock election proved a close-run thing in which David Yorwerth polled 30 votes against Esaias's 31, so that the prize (whatever it was) went to the latter. No doubt Sir Herbert also took the opportunity to deliver an address to his potential supporters, and probably paid for much of the liquid refreshments they undoubtedly consumed as well!

Rents, Rates, and Taxes The year closed with the appointment of **John Williams** as the Portreeve. There were two active burgesses of this name, but the use of 'Williams' as opposed to 'William' indicates that it is the surveyor John Williams of Newlands Farm that is the one in question.

The year 1781 closed with the wreck of the merchant ship *Caterina* at Sker Point on 28th December, a major event in the locality to which I have devoted the whole of the following chapter. For the burgesses themselves the year had also started with something of a bang with a blazing row at a Hall Day called by the new Portreeve on 16th February. I suspect in fact that the whole thing may have erupted because Williams, like the Portreeves of yore, attempted to force through certain measures that he personally wished to see implemented.

It will be recalled that difficulty had already been experienced collecting the Rabbit Hole Rate from certain individuals living in the Borough, but it seems that this was symptomatic of a far more widespread malaise. Officers of the Borough were also experiencing difficulty in getting certain burgesses and 'Burgessis widows' to pay the various rents and rates due to the Borough itself and also the rates and taxes it collected on behalf of local and national government.

Sitting with his eight Elected Burgesses, John Williams put forward his preferred option for dealing with the problem whereby anyone who refused to pay "after being demanded of him or them, he or shee shall at the next Court Day bee discomined and disfranchised. "

Hitherto in Kenfig's history this council of eight had been there only to advise the Portreeve, and there is no better illustration of the change in this relationship that was taking place than that four of them took strong exception to the introduction of such draconian measures. There was still no question of a ballot on the matter, and technically it was still possible for John Williams to push the measure through without his council's agreement, but in a defiant display of their growing authority the four objectors simply got up from their seats and walked out! This meant that Williams did not have a council of eight as custom and practice demanded, so the meeting broke up in confusion.

A week later at the monthly Court Baron, John Williams tried again. The same eight were called forward to form the council, but the four rebels – David Yorwerth senior and junior; Evan Jenkin; and John Loveluck, simply refused to answer when their names were called. This time however their Portreeve was prepared. Summoning Daniel Rees and Edward Evan to act as Assessors he fined the rebels a shilling each, and declared the measure implemented anyway! One of the four may have been the Borough Recorder at this time, or else that individual may also have joined the rebellion, for the record of both these meetings seem to have been written into the minute book by Williams himself.

This, or so it would seem, was the first trial of strength between a Portreeve attempting to wield the traditional authority of his office against the growing power of the burgesses as a body, and it seems that Williams had his way. In later minutes there are indeed instances where burgesses who fell into arrears with the rates were disfranchised after being given due warning, and John Williams' personal standing does not seem to have suffered from the incident either. Although nobody could now become the Portreeve for consecutive years there was nothing to prevent them being nominated on some future occasion, and in all John was to serve no less than seven terms in the office!

Chapter 10

'Desperate Banditti':
The Wreck of the *Caterina*

Desperate Banditti The wreck of the Venetian merchant ship *Caterina* at Sker in the closing days of 1781 is perhaps the best recorded of all the early local shipwrecks thanks to a file of documents from Gnoll Estate (D/D Gn E/204). It was put together by Sir Herbert Mackworth of Gnoll who became involved in the attempt to salvage the wreck and its cargo and to a lesser degree in the subsequent apprehension of those involved in looting it.

The population of Kenfig had an ill-founded reputation for being smugglers, wreckers, and looters of wrecks, thanks largely to an Edward Donovan (1805) who visited the area in 1804 and branded them "A desperate banditti of lurking fellows". There is absolutely no evidence to support the allegation that the people of Kenfig deliberately lured vessels ashore for the purpose of looting them, but it has to be admitted that some were almost certainly guilty of looting wrecks that occurred by accident or mischance. According to Leslie Evans (1960: 76) an old Welsh *triban*

> makes reference to a boat called the **Marina** which was stranded at Sker, and tersely adds that its cargo of cotton was worth four thousand pounds to the men of Pyle.

So far as is known no ship of this name ever came to grief on these rocks, and the verse is almost certainly a reference to the *Caterina* whose cargo indeed consisted mainly of bales of cotton.

The story of her final voyage is told in a document (D/D Gn E/204/34) headed 'Relation' and penned by her captain, Vicenzo Tommasi. In places too, some of the words and phrases used by Tommasi are probably not grammatically correct – 'broken French' as opposed to 'broken English'. One or two phrases and words therefore defied the translators' best efforts, but they were nevertheless able to reduce Tommasi's statement to a coherent account of the final stages of his voyage. To the best of my knowledge, this has until recently defied all attempts to decipher it. On the basis that some of the words appeared to be French I enlisted the aid of a young couple who were respectively an English teacher who teaches French and his partner, a French teacher who teaches English. Neither could make head nor tail of it, nor could a French University professor whose aid they enlisted. I therefore take no credit in finally working the thing out. That belongs to Carl Smith (Author of *Mumbles Lifeboat* (1989) and *Gower Coast Shipwrecks* (1993)) and his friends Mr & Mrs Ogg, and I am deeply indebted to Carl for making their research available and allowing me to use it. Carl was quick to point out that almost his sole and only contribution to unravelling the puzzle was the acquisition of an old French book giving the meanings of nautical terms which enabled him to work out the odd phrase here and there. The main work of translation was done by Mrs Patricia Ogg with the assistance of her husband Graeme. Both are professional interpreters, and Mrs Ogg is fluent in fourteen European languages, but cracking the "*Relation*" still took them some three months! The difficulty lay in the fact that although the language used in the document is indeed French, it was written by an Italian who could probably speak the language well enough, but was not fluent at writing it. He therefore wrote everything phonetically as an 18th century Italian would. In addition of course, the French language would be archaic to the same extent that the English of the period is to us, using words and phrases that have long since fallen out of general usage.

It started at noon on Christmas Day 1781. At this time the **Caterina** was somewhere in that part of the Atlantic sometimes known as the Western Approaches and heading towards the British Isles. She had loaded at Livorno (Leghorn) in Italy with a cargo that was principally cotton, but also included wine, brandy, some crates of coral (then regarded as almost a semi-precious stone), blocks of marble, currants, soap, and other goods destined for London. Aboard were twenty-one people - Tommasi and his crew consisting of three officers, a 'lieutenant mate', boatswain, 12 crewmen, the ship's boy and the captain's personal servant. The twenty-first was the joker in the pack, a man named John Halerow whom the captain had employed as "pilot and linguist".

Halerow was an Englishman, and from the known details of the voyage it is supposed that he must have been taken on by Tommasi long before the vessel entered the Western Approaches, and probably at Leghorn itself. It also becomes clear as the narrative of the voyage develops that although Halerow may have had some knowledge of navigation, he had probably never actually sailed up the English Channel in his life!

Both Captain and Pilot were able to obtain separate sightings of the sun at noon on Christmas Day that more or less corresponded, and these enabled them to fix their approximate position on the chart. This was in the days before a reliable chronometer had been invented, and whilst it was relatively easy to estimate how far east or west the ship's position was, it was never possible to be entirely certain just how far north or south she lay. Like many other vessels before her, *Caterina* was actually too far north, and heading towards the Bristol rather than the English Channel.

The first disagreement between Captain and Pilot occurred at 6 p.m. that evening. Their vessel had made good progress all day but the wind was becoming stronger and the ship was taking water. Halerow therefore advised the captain to take in sail and reduce speed, complaining "Sir, you are wearing out the masts after such a good voyage!" Tommasi, however was concerned that to do so now would cause the ship to "drop to leeward in [the] heavy seas" and announced his intention to "keep all the sails set until midnight".

At ten o'clock Halerow's prognostication proved true when the force of the wind carried away the storm jib and tore the centre of the mainsail. A chastened Tommasi ordered running repairs to be made and sail reduced.

By 8 a.m. on Boxing Day morning the wind had greatly moderated and the weather become foggy. At about eleven the Captain announced his intention of taking soundings with the lead to determine the depth of the ocean, but his Pilot suggested they delay. "Sir" he explained "we English do it after we have sighted some birds which is a sign that it will be possible to find the depth with the lead".

Due to the fog and overcast they were unable to obtain a sighting on the sun at midday, but about an hour later they spotted a bird indicating that land was possibly not too far distant and commenced taking soundings with the lead. This showed that the ocean at this point was 54 fathoms deep and that the bottom was composed of sand and shell. On the basis of this Halerow declared

The ship has not drifted more than half a point [from its course]. In my opinion we are closer to the coast of France than in the middle of the Channel because the water is white, whereas on the English side it is black.

Armed with this the information the Captain calculated their revised position on his chart and amended their course accordingly, further to the north. Captain Tommasi was in fact suffering from some injury to his chest (which he does not elaborate upon or offer as an excuse) but which was sufficiently severe to confine him to his bed for much of the time. It was therefore the Pilot who was in charge on deck at 3 am on the morning of the 27th December when an island was sighted ahead and to starboard (right). He altered course northwards and sent a messenger to inform Tommasi that they were passing to the north of the Isle of Wight.

When the Captain came on deck and saw the island he was flabbergasted! He may never have sailed the English Channel before, but he had at least studied his charts! "If that is the isle which you say it is", he told Halerow, "the ship would have gone aground!" From its size and shape he thought it could only be Guernsey in the Channel Isles, and the Pilot could only agree! In making such a simple error it is clear that not only had he undoubtedly never seen the Isle of Wight before, but was probably unable to read a chart either! What they had sighted may have been part of the North Cornish coastline looming out of the darkness, or even the Isle of Lundy at the entrance to the Bristol Channel – a tiny speck of rock in the ocean and just a fragment of the Isle of Wight. In fact this incident leads one to suspect that John Halerow was an impostor who possessed some charts and navigation instruments but only the sketchiest knowledge of how to use them!

About six o'clock the light strengthened and ahead in the distance they could see land stretching across their course from east to west. Some of the crew claimed to recognise it as the coast of England in the vicinity of Plymouth. The Pilot climbed the mizzen mast for a better view, and an hour later returned on deck to report to Tommasi. "Sir," he announced, "the land you can see to the North-West is Portland, and I could see the tower of the fort which stands there". Satisfied with this Tommasi set a fresh course of East-South-East to enter (as he thought) the English Channel.

At 11 am they sighted some small islands, and the Pilot claimed he could identify The Needles rocks at the southern tip of the Isle of Wight about six miles ahead. At 4 pm the weather cleared sufficiently for them to take sightings, but Tommasi does not say what these were, probably because they bore so little relation to the position of the vessel as they conceived it to be from the Pilot's sightings along the coast! Nevertheless, elements of doubt were creeping in, and Tommasi hadn't forgotten Halerow's massive blunder over the Isle of Wight earlier that morning.

Some sort of argument seems to have broken out between the two and eventually Halerow turned to Tomasi with the chart of the English Channel in his hand.

> Sir, do you believe that we are at present nine miles south of the Isle of Wight? If you think it is right, during the night we will sail East-South-East since, in this way, we will pass at a great distance from the coast.

Faced with his Pilot's assurance that the coast they were following was indeed that of Southern England, the Captain could only conclude that his sighting was incorrect, and whilst admittedly nervous about the hazards of navigating these waters, agreed to such a course of action. As the sea was calm he ordered that all sails should be set until such time that they were well clear of the notorious sand banks off the coast at Portsmouth. Four hours later, in the pitch darkness, they ran firmly aground!

Still believing he was in the English Channel and that he had run onto the very banks he had been seeking to avoid, Tommasi ordered a cannon to be fired to notify the authorities at Portsmouth that there was a vessel in distress, and dropped anchor. The tide was evidently low, and the sands on which they had grounded exposed, so some of the crew were landed upon it in the ship's boat. When they returned it was with the unwelcome news that the ship was indeed aground on a sand bank and not a beach.

An hour later the cable of the anchor dropped by Tommasi to prevent his ship being driven further onto the bank by the tide, parted as did the hawsers of two other anchors he subsequently lowered. In heavy seas the ship was steadily being driven higher and higher onto the sand with every prospect of being rolled onto its side by the incoming tide, or even turned over completely. The crew certainly had seen enough and, without orders, launched the longboat and started abandoning ship. Tommasi, however, was all for staying, proposing that they reduce the ship's top-heaviness by cutting away her masts. Injured as he was he nevertheless attempted to do just this by taking an axe to the rigging supporting the main mast, but his crew would have none of it. From the relative safety of the longboat they called on him to join them, suggesting that they remain near the vessel until first light and see how things stood then. Reluctantly he agreed.

They assisted him down into the boat and then anchored a short distance away to await the dawn, but the sea was rising and their position soon became precarious. The *Caterina's* mainmast toppled over, and a large wave broke over the longboat. In the darkness, and with little idea where they were, they cut away their anchor and headed for where they believed the shore to be. They were lucky, for the course they set took them directly towards Sker Point. They could have struck the reef in any of a number of places where the rocks (which were being pounded by waves) extended well out into the sea, but instead were wrecked at a spot where a relatively short scramble got them, soaking wet but otherwise unharmed, onto dry land.

From here they made their way inland until they arrived at a house where the occupants gave them food and shelter. Only then did they discover that they were not on the south coast of England, but at Sker House in South Wales!

"With Weapons in Our Hands" At dawn the following morning (Friday 28th) the crew went back to the rocks on which they had landed and, to their great surprise

> found the ship in the middle of the rocks, entirely out of the water and in a position that we could recover everything, but not the ship.

The next sentence of the Captain's account foiled our intrepid translators. As far as they could make out it seems to indicate that some gold (perhaps money in the form of coins) was recovered, after which the Captain set his men to clearing the main hatchway preparatory to removing the rest of the cargo. His ship was evidently a total loss, but his cargo, he was confident, could be recovered quite easily.

By now a small crowd of bystanders had gathered around the vessel, some no doubt just to watch what was going on; others bent upon plunder and plainly put out that the ship had not been abandoned. They therefore began trying to intimidate the crew "kicking the sailors and hitting them with sticks". The crew were not without means of defending themselves and their vessel, for besides the cannon on board, an inventory of items later salvaged from the *Caterina* includes 12 pistols, 6 cutlasses, 8 muskets, and 3 blunderbusses (D/D Gn E/204/35).

By midday the crowd had grown quite large and Tommasi, deciding that discretion was the better part of valour, abandoned his attempt to salvage the cargo. He determined nevertheless to try and save some of the most valuable items.

> We had to force our way to the cabin to rescue the boxes of coral and, with weapons in our hands we managed to get out three.

With that accomplished they carried these to Sker house and took refuge there with Morgan Howells. In salvaging these items, however, Tommasi was forced to abandon his own possessions (including the ship's log) which were all lost. At his request Sir Herbert Mackworth subsequently gave him a written testimonial acknowledging the part he played in rescuing the valuable coral in the face of such a hostile mob (D/D Gn E/204/37).

Tommasi begged Morgan Howells to send for the local 'governor', a term that rather confused the latter since, as he explained to the Captain, there was no such person. Instead he agreed to send a message to somebody Tommasi describes only as "the Master of that Land".

Shortly afterwards a 'Mr Ginches' arrived with three men on horseback. This is probably a Mr Jeffries the Customs Controller from the Port of Swansea into whose custody the Captain entrusted the boxes of coral (D/D Gn E/204/37). He quickly sized up the situation

> and told me that he could do nothing against so many people and I would have to defend myself with my own weapons. I said I would not do that.

For the rest of the day therefore the mob had free rein to plunder the *Caterina* unhindered.

The following morning (Saturday 29th) a "Mr Guilem arrived, and soon after Mr Lessen". The names are probably Tommasi's attempt to render 'Llewelyn' and 'Leyson'. Who the latter was I am not certain, but in the Gnoll file he is subsequently mentioned arresting several of those alleged to have been involved in the looting. His companion was almost certainly Hopkin Llewelyn, the Margam Agent, though in this capacity he had no authority here for the manor of Sker still belonged to John Curre's former servant, Joseph Lloyd. According to the Captain's account these two, like Jeffries the previous day, admitted that they could do nothing in view of the size of the crowd, and he says that after advising him to go to Swansea to make his 'protest', they left.

A deposition taken from David Jones of Aberdulais (D/D Gn E/204/15) suggests however that the pair also visited the wreck. Jones arrived at Sker rocks on the afternoon of the 29th. Here he says that he

> heard Mr Hopkin Llewellyn of Margam, who stood by ye side of the ship, say that if ye people would let ye men belonging to ye ship have their victuals & cloaths they might take ye rest, or words to that effect.

News of the vessel aground at Sker Point had by now spread to all parts of Glamorgan. As Tommasi and the Pilot John Halerow made their way to Swansea to make their official 'protest' they found "the whole road full of people, women and children and horses, carrying cotton".

The Authorities Make their Move By dawn on New Year's Eve the authorities had still made no move to protect the wreck and its contents. Looters crawled all over it helping themselves to whatever took their fancy. Indeed, in the absence of any attempt to prevent them from helping themselves, and with Hopkin Llewelyn's assurance, many believed that they were acting quite legally, an attitude that is reflected in several of the documents in the Gnoll collection.

As late as the 16th January, Aaron Bowen of Llangynwyd was writing to Mackworth to enter a complaint on behalf of David John of that parish claiming that he had been *robbed* of cotton he had taken from the wreck! This was alleged to have taken place as John was making his way home past the **New House** (evidently **Ty Newydd** – The Prince of Wales). Here, he claimed, he was set upon by two men named Evan David and John Leyson who forcibly took away the cotton he was carrying. Bowen also names a witness who was prepared to say on oath that he afterwards saw the same two men spinning cotton in the house, and requested Mackworth to obtain redress!

Of the two men who robbed David John, I have no record of anyone bearing either name connected with Kenfig at this time, though they may of course have been labourers employed locally at this time.

David Jones of Aberdulais near Neath (who heard Llewelyn make his declaration to the mob) is similarly quite open about his subsequent removal of cotton from the stranded vessel in a statement he made to Sir Herbert Mackworth (D/D Gn E/204/15). Having heard what Llewelyn said he

> went into ye ship Caterina, then stranded on ye rocks, & from thence [took] some cotton in a bag or wallet which he carried to ye forge at Aberavon & there left it.

On Sunday he returned to Sker again, and this time took a small bag of cotton he found on the rocks and "a handful" from inside the ship.

Monday morning he was back again, but this time discovered "ye King's Officers" were in position guarding the remains of the ship and cargo. He claims that he then remained there until nightfall 'assisting' them, then "returned home & went no more".

It had taken three whole days for the authorities to take effective action since the *Caterina* had been cast away! The problems faced by the Customs & Excise men in responding swiftly to the situation that developed at Sker are however neatly outlined in a report by Sir Herbert Mackworth included in the Gnoll file (D/D Gn E/204/20). He was seeking to establish a 'Protecting Fellowship' – an armed and mounted force of volunteers – and the events at Sker (where he had now taken charge of the salvage operation) prompted him to put his thoughts into writing.

SIR HERBERT MACKWORTH
LOW RELIEF POLYCHROME WAX PORTRAIT BY SAMUEL PERCY 1779
VICTORIA AND ALBERT MUSEUM, LONDON

His report outlines the complete lack of any armed rapid-response force available to the civil authority in the County that could be used to prevent and disperse "ye assembling together of riotous & lawless mobs for ye purpose of plundering ships & other wicked intentions". Although the events at Sker were foremost in his mind when he wrote, he also pointed out that no such force existed to protect the coasts of Swansea Bay from the depredations by French raiders during the course of the current war. Indeed, he pointed out that enemy privateers engaged in preying on merchant shipping in the Bristol Channel regularly anchored in Mumbles Roads with impunity.

Nothing came of Mackworth's attempts to create an organisation such as he envisaged, and the delay in taking any effective measures against the mob that had taken control of the **Caterina** had probably been occasioned by efforts to raise a sufficient force to accomplish the task. The body that eventually turned up at Sker was the Swansea Volunteers, a militia force that numbered some sixty men, but it had taken time to gather these together and issue them with arms and equipment. Then, of course, they had to get to Sker, their rate of travel limited by the fact that less than half were mounted and the rest marched on foot.

Mackworth's final accounts for the operation include payments for cartridges, ball, powder and flints showing that the mob in possession of the wreck did not yield their prize without a fight, and inevitably there were casualties. William Thomas noted in his diary (Denning, 1995: 310) that "three people came to their death by the late riots about the wreck of the **Catarina**". It also goes without saying that many others suffered injury even though Thomas makes no mention of them. As there are no entries of burials in the Pyle & Kenfig Parish Registers at this time it seems that, whoever they were, these fatalities were not local people.

Another person who seems to have been particularly active in defence of the wreck at this stage was the sheriff, Charles Bowen, later reimbursed the sum of 7s.10d for "powder and shot" presumably expended in support of the Volunteers. He lived at Merthyr Mawr, not in the fine mansion that stands outside the village today, but rather in the rather less pretentious old house that is now Home Farm.

Whilst helpless to achieve very much at the scene of the wreck in the initial stages, he had on his own initiative already taken steps to do what he could to start bringing the looters to justice. We know this from a letter penned by a William Rees to Bowen's gardener on the Sunday after the wreck(D/D Gn E/204/1). Having learnt what was happening at Sker Bowen sent two men in the charge of this gardener, Rees Jenkin, to set up a road-block at New Bridge (The Dipping Bridge) which at this time was on the main highway from Cardiff to Neath. Here they stopped and searched all traffic coming from the direction of Sker, and seem to have achieved a measure of success.

Rees's letter to Jenkin complains that the three had stopped one of his tenants named Rees Phillip from Goston (modern Treos) and forcibly relieved him of three hemp bags. He admitted that the bags contained cotton from the wreck, but dismissed this as of no consequence

> as I find every body were permitted to take the cotton without molestation. Be that matter as it may, you and your colleagues will have an action brought against you for the bags unless they are forthwith delivered up with the cotton contained therein.

The writer cannot have been unaware that Jenkin and his men were working on behalf of the Sheriff, and for all his bluster must have been equally aware that this complaint was going nowhere!

Back at Sker those overseeing the salvage operation seem to have set up their headquarters in Sker House, for there are records of payments to Morgan Howells for the "use of the house and buildings" and "trespass and damage". Other payments to him included providing stabling facility for horses, "meat and drink" and sending a cart for bread, but what story, I wonder, surrounds the payment of compensation to Morgan for "loss of pigs"?!

In all Morgan received over £43 in compensation, and as Mackworth noted this sum did not include any provision for his "time and trouble". Nevertheless the relationship between Morgan and his guests seems to have been a rather uneasy one that can scarcely have been made any easier by the fact that on the Sunday a John Curre also suddenly appeared on the scene. This may perhaps have been the son of William, brother of Morgan's former landlord, the recently deceased John Curre. By the latter's last will and testament William Curre had been bequeathed the manors of Itton and Clemenston. John Curre junior was a Glamorgan magistrate, but Bowen and Mackworth for their part apparently suspected (possibly because of the family's connection with Sker) that he and Morgan Howell were up to something involving appropriation of part of the *Caterina's* cargo!

On the Monday the first arrests were made, and raids carried out on several local houses in the hope of finding stolen property. Amongst those accused was a Kenfig man named William Harry, also known as William Henry, on the basis of evidence volunteered by Elias Jenkins who was a Kenfig freeholder (though he seems never to have lived here). Harry, blissfully unaware of this, was meantime working with his horse and cart as part of a team Mackworth had put together to haul the remaining cargo from the wreck to a place of safety. Whilst he was busily working away in the confident expectation of a lucrative remuneration, his house was raided and cotton recovered(D/D Gn E/204/43).

William was soon in custody along with eleven others, and it is interesting that he indeed was the only Kenfig man amongst them (D/D Gn E/204/14). His companions in misfortune included men from as far away as Llantrisant, Llanharry, Penmark, St Brides Major and Neath! Some were bailed, but William Harry was amongst a group kept in custody overnight to appear before magistrates the following morning. John Curre was supposed to be one of the latter, but early on Tuesday morning the sheriff received a brief note from him pleading that "the fatigue of yesterday has made me so ill that I cannot possibly attend today" and asking that the committal hearings went ahead without him. Mackworth and Bowen's suspicions regarding him deepened still further.

At least four prisoners were committed in custody to stand trial for their part in the looting, William Harry amongst them. Throughout Glamorgan however feelings were running high over this action, and whilst the Mackworth papers do not give any reason, this was undoubtedly because people believed that those rifling the wreck had been given permission to do so by Hopkin Llewelyn. Henry Knight of Tythegston, who was probably one of the justices that had sat in the committal hearing, therefore elected to accompany the prisoners and escort at least as far as Cowbridge (D/D Gn E/204/17).

With him he carried a letter from Mackworth to the Bailiffs of Cowbridge Borough (who were the chief authority there in lieu of a Portreeve or mayor) ordering them to provide the prisoner escort for the second leg of the journey to the gaol at Cardiff. The Bailiffs, however, were not so keen! There had, they informed Knight, already been 'incidents' in their town and their information was that a determined attempt would be made to rescue the prisoners on the road to Cardiff. In view of the sort of numbers reportedly involved they claimed that they were unable to provide an escort in sufficient numbers to deter or prevent such a rescue attempt.

The escort that had accompanied Knight and the prisoners from Kenfig had probably done so on foot and consequently were themselves tired and in no fit condition to continue the journey or thwart a determined attack. He therefore resorted to subterfuge. Instead of continuing on to Cardiff he lodged his prisoners at Cowbridge gaol, thereby hopefully wrong-footing any mob reportedly lying in ambush on the road ahead. They, he hoped, would disperse believing that the party would recommence their journey at first light the following day. Instead he secretly hired carriages for his men and their prisoners, and they set off again in the middle of the night whilst it was still dark.

His ruse was apparently successful. Those who had gathered to waylay the party (if indeed they were not merely a figment of the Cowbridge bailiffs' overheated imagination) had dispersed to their homes with the intention of regrouping at daylight. Nevertheless the journey was not without incident, for near Cardiff the escort recovered a horse carrying two hundredweight of cotton! What had happened to those accompanying it Knight does not say, but presumably they fled when challenged, and in the circumstances he was happy to allow them to escape.

On 3rd January Mackworth ordered the publication of a pamphlet offering a "handsome reward" for anybody giving information leading to the recovery of property stolen from the *Caterina*, or the arrest and conviction of anyone who had been involved in the looting. He and Charles Bowen also set up some sort of trap for John Curre which is alluded to in a letter from Bowen dated 5th January(D/D Gn E/204/18).

> I this moment rec'ed a letter from Mr Bruce informing me Mr Curre was seized with the gout in the foot, & that he was so ill he sh'd be obliged to keep his room. Consequently our scheme is frustrated for this day.

Whilst John Curre may have proved too wily a bird for them (if indeed he was anything other than completely innocent!) so Mackworth made one last attempt to nail Morgan Howells on 7th January. Those organising the salvage of the ship had probably moved out of Sker House by now, so Sir Herbert reasoned that Howells would see this as a good opportunity to bring any loot he had secreted in the area back to Sker. Bluff and double bluff! He therefore issued a search warrant in respect of Sker House and its outbuildings, but to his disgust nothing incriminating was discovered. It is perhaps significant that in the Gnoll

Papers this warrant is listed separately from those made out for raids on houses in Kenfig.

Cotton from the **Caterina** travelled far and wide throughout Glamorgan and beyond. In his letter reporting John Curre's indisposition Charles Bowen told Mackworth that

> The people at Bridgend have been carrying their cotton away to hiding places these two or three days past to prevent a search.

At the same time he also announced that he had employed a "ship cryer" to publish news throughout that town advertising the forthcoming sale of the wreck itself, and sent details to other parts of the country as well.

A pamphlet (D/D Gn E/204/38) published by the agents acting on behalf of the owners at Neath on 23rd January, speaks of cotton openly offered for sale by shopkeepers at Cowbridge, Llantrisant, and Caerphilly as well as Bridgend. It was these agents, named Thomas Keene and William Brutton who perhaps made the most spectacular arrest of the entire investigation. They pursued a David Howell as far as Tewkesbury before arresting him and another man referred to only as 'Reece'. Having recovered a quantity of cotton they then collected more at Newport in Gwent and Newent in Gloucester which Howell had disposed of during the course of his journey.

The Trial and Its Aftermath The final act in the drama of the **Caterina** was played out in the Assize Court at Hereford, it being considered too risky to bring those arrested before one of the Great Sessions Courts in Glamorgan itself. I understand from Carl Smith (who has seen the record - such as it is of this trial in the Record Office at Kew) that a far greater number were charged with offences arising from the looting than were convicted. No details of the hearing are given, but I would suspect that in the case of those acquitted by the jury the defence made great play of the declaration made by Hopkin Llewelyn and claimed that the defendants genuinely believed they actually had permission from a person in authority to remove goods from the wreck.

Nevertheless when the trial ended on 22nd July four men had been convicted of felony arising from the looting (Denning, 1995: 315) - John Webb of Aberavon or Margam; Evan Thomas of St Brides Major; Thomas John of Llantrisant; and William Harry of Kenfig. In addition a David Llewelyn of Treguff near Llancarfan was convicted of stopping and plundering wagons being used by the authorities to salvage cargo from the wreck. William Thomas in his diary tells us that Llewelyn was sentenced to be transported for seven years to Africa, and that of the others only John Webb was sentenced to be hung. Unfortunately Thomas does not state what sentence was imposed on the other three who included William Harry from Kenfig. A few days after the hearing, Thomas received news that Webb was reprieved, but this information was incorrect, and his diary records that the death sentence was duly carried out at Hereford on 5th September.

For us therefore the question remains, who was William Harry (alias Henry), and what sentence did he serve? Here I am in the annoying position of having a local character stepping out into the spotlight from relative anonymity who is difficult to identify simply because his name was not uncommon in the area. The only information I can glean about him from the Gnoll documents is that he lived at Kenfig which means that he was a resident of the lower Borough.

Brief as it is this is, at least sufficient to eliminate two characters who have already appeared in our history. William Henry of Ty'n Cellar was a farmer who lived in Higher Kenfig in the parish of Margam, whilst William the son of Edmund Harry was living at Tranch in the parish of Tythegston, and had been there since prior to 1776. Clearly therefore neither of them was the William Harry convicted at Hereford.

Another William with an, albeit rather tenuous Kenfig connection was the son of Evan Henry who was briefly a burgess here just prior to 1750. The family then moved to Newton, and it was here that William was baptised in 1754, and where he married in 1784*. There There is therefore nothing to indicate that he returned to live Kenfig even for a brief period. Indeed, he is probably the "William Harry of Newton, a farmer" mentioned on the reverse of a letter by the sheriff Charles Bowen (D/D Gn E/204/18) who, the writer alleged, "has large quantities of cotton at his house".

By process of elimination therefore I have narrowed down the identity of this man to a William Harry, alias Henry, who first appears in local records in 1770 when he married a woman named Ann John by licence on 15th May (PPR). She was probably the daughter of a burgess

---

* Information supplied by family historian Peter Henry of Porthcawl.

for he was nominated for admission the same year and sworn-in on 26th April 1771(B/K 11). He possibly lived on Heol Las at Mawdlam where the boundary between his croft and Winters Mead was stated to be out of repair in 1776, and was one of those reported for being in default with payment of their Rabbit Hole Rates the same year. The year after this he was the defendant in an action for debt brought by a Thomas Henry (alias Harry) (B/K 11).

Borough records between 1777 and 1780 show that William was several times 'presented' over the state of the hedges of fields in his occupancy that were evidently the result of complaints from his neighbours. All in all therefore he does not seem to have been exactly a character out of Kenfig's 'top drawer'!

In 1780 he was a member of the jury at the Autumn Leet court, but his name does not occur again on any Borough jury until 1789. On the face of it this seems to suggest that, having been spared the death penalty he may have been sentenced to a term at a penal settlement in the colonies like David Llewelyn. The Parish baptismal records suggest however that a lesser penalty was in fact imposed.

Altogether this lists seven children baptised by himself and his wife Ann. Mary their daughter baptised on 15th September 1782 could have been conceived about the time of the wreck of the **Caterina** and the christening performed in William's absence. The following year, however, another daughter named Margaret was baptised on 21st August, and this suggests that William may actually have been released from custody before the year 1782 was out.

A possible alternative explanation (which rather appeals to my sense of the romantic!) is that Ann could have gained access to her husband whilst he was in custody either during or shortly after the trial. Given the conditions prevailing in the gaols of the period this would have been quite feasible on payment of a suitable fee to the gaoler. In any case I think we can be certain that William was back at Kenfig at the end of 1786 as his son William was baptised in August the following year. His sentence therefore may have been commuted to one of imprisonment for four years either with 'hard labour' or in 'solitary confinement' which were the sort of sentences being imposed on other criminals at this time.

It is also interesting to speculate that William may not have been convicted because he took cotton from the wreck itself in the initial stages, for had that been the case then, thanks to Hopkin Llewelyn's unauthorised announcement, his case would have been dismissed with the rest. Rather it may have been because he had been pilfering it from the loads he was supposedly assisting the authorities to salvage with his horse and cart! Although William appeared on the jury of two manorial courts in 1789, this is the last certain mention of him in connection with Kenfig, though he was apparently still alive in 1802 when the parish registers record the burial of his five year old daughter Jennet.

Banditti? The Gnoll records relating to the looting of the *Caterina* do a lot to place the reputation of the people of Kenfig in context. Of the three people shot dead at the riot that developed with the arrival of the troops at Sker, none appear to have lived in the parish of Pyle & Kenfig, for no burials are recorded in the Parish Registers at this time. Of the five persons convicted, only one came from the Borough, and the role of the local population in the looting is further diminished by a closer look at the facts contained in the documents in the Gnoll collection. In all 67 people are mentioned as being suspected in some way or other of plundering the wreck – principally because Mackworth subsequently issued warrants for their homes to be searched. Of these only 18 were subsequently arrested, and of these William Harry was the only person from this locality.

Convicted	Arrests	Suspects	From (Area)	Details & No of Suspects
1	4	16	Aberavon & Margam	Aberavon (2) Taibach (6) Margam (8)
1	2	2	Llantrisant	Llantrisant (2)
1	2	2	St Brides Major	St Brides (1) Lampha (1)
1	1	13	Pyle & Kenfig	Kenfig (11) Pyle (1) Cornelly (1)
1	1	1	Llancarvan	
	4	4	Penmark	
	2	5	Neath & District	Aberdulais (1) Cadoxton (2) M'crythan (2)
		11	Llangynwyd / Bettws	Llangynwyd (9) Bettws (2)
		4	Newton Nottage	Newton (2) Sker (2)
		2	Bridgend & Dist	Oldcastle (1) Treos (1)
	2	7	Unidentified	
5	**18**	**67**		

'**Arrests**' include those for whom warrants are known to have been issued.

That old *triban* about **The Marina** should however make us cautious about giving the Kenfig folk and their immediate neighbours a completely clean bill of health – maybe long practice had merely made them more adept at concealing their ill-gotten gains! But there is nevertheless another point in their favour too. On 1st January Mackworth drew up a rough list of those who had been arrested and the names of the witnesses against them. Elias Jenkin, as has already been mentioned, gave evidence against William Harry, Evan Thomas, and Thomas John – all of whom were subsequently convicted. He was a Kenfig freeholder, though he did not live there. Of the other four witnesses who had come forward two, David Yorwerth and John Owen, were both burgesses, and it is Yorwerth's evidence that helped to convict David Llewelyn (incorrectly stated in this particular document to be of Llanharry Parish) for plundering the salvage carts. Moreover, it has to be pointed out that these people came forward with their evidence **before** the printing and publication of the broad-sheet offering a reward.

Unsurprisingly therefore the hard evidence is that Kenfig was **not** a community where everybody was devoted to the looting of wrecks. It was simply an area where wrecks occurred and were looted, and they just happened to live there. Some undoubtedly participated. Many (perhaps the vast majority) did not.

I was reminded of this very strongly during an incident in which I was involved in my capacity as the local Police Sergeant back in the 1980s when a blizzard blocked the M4 motorway stranding over a hundred vehicles. Sure enough an element within our community saw this as a golden opportunity to start looting the stranded cars and lorries. Although few in number we were able not only to halt and deter the looters, but also obtain sufficient evidence to subsequently arrest many of those responsible when communications with the 'outside world' were eventually restored.

These were subsequently convicted of offences at the Bridgend Magistrates' Court (though happily there was no question of death sentences being imposed!), and it is the actions of this small minority that subsequently grabbed the headlines in the media. Little or nothing was said about the far greater number of residents who opened their homes and premises to provide food and shelter for the hundreds of stranded motorists without any thought of reward or recompense. Nor was anything said (for we never revealed their identity) about the people who, disgusted by what was happening, came forward to identify those responsible. Again, like the constables of 1782, we just arrived at the homes of those responsible where recovery of the 'loot' was in itself usually sufficient proof to ensure conviction. Let it be said too, that no violence was ever offered to those of us attempting to protect the stranded vehicles by potential looters even though my total force amounted to just five (unarmed) men and not the sixty soldiers available to Mackworth and Bowen!

"To Ask ye Gentlemen by Fair Words" One sad postscript arising out of the looting of the *Caterina* I have kept until last. It concerns a farmer from Llangynwyd named Aaron Bowen who has already been mentioned briefly in these notes regarding his letter to Sir Herbert Mackworth concerning the robbery of David John near the Prince of Wales. Who he was I do not know, but the penning of such a letter on 16th January when many arrests had already been made for looting the vessel suggests that he was perhaps a rather naive sort of person. He may, nevertheless, have been a magistrate for the letter says that the details of the allegation made by John had been taken under oath. John Lyons (now of Narberth) tells me that he has found a record that a man of this name married a Margaret Bowen by banns at Llangynwyd church in 1760, and is almost certainly the same person. Another of the same name (probably a son) married an Ann William in 1796.

There is also an indication that Aaron may have been amongst those who helped themselves to the cargo, for his name is appended to a list of "Sundry persons who sold the wool cotton to Evan Hopkin" (D/D Gn E/204/3). The amount in question was stated to be 31 lbs, and it is alleged that this transaction took place as late as 29th February. Whether he stood trial on charges arising out of that incident I cannot say, but he certainly stood trial on other matters at the Ship & Castle Inn, Neath, on Monday 18th February 1782.

According to the details set out in summonses issued for service upon witnesses requiring them to appear and testify at this trial (D/D Gn E/204/21) Aaron Bowen faced two charges. The first was for making threats against the Chief Constable of Neath Hundred, and the second was of endeavouring to assemble a body of people to oppose the Magistrates in the execution of their duty when assembled to examine persons guilty of plundering the ship *Caterina*.

In the case of the first there is no evidence concerning such an offence in the trial documents included in the file - which is not to say that the ones containing the relevant material may be missing. Of the second I can only say that this charge is a very strange fish indeed! Perhaps not quite trumped-up, but one that certainly seems to contain some very misleading information!

The trial record shows that the actual location for this meeting of magistrates was at Pyle, and the premises used would undoubtedly have been the coaching inn known as *The White Hart* (now known as *The Tap*; This was not replaced by *Pyle Inn* until 1791/2). In normal circumstances holding this sort of committal proceedings described to determine whether the prosecution evidence was sufficient to warrant sending the accused for trial, was normal practice. In this case, as we have seen, the local population were incensed by the arrests and the authorities were in such fear of a rescue attempt that the trial had been moved to Hereford. Yet (if we are to believe the summonses) they now proposed to hold these committal proceedings, to which some prisoners would have to be brought from Hereford and Cardiff, in a public house at Pyle!

In fact the stated reason for the Pyle meeting seems to have been an out-and-out lie according to evidence given at Bowen's trial by a prosecution witness named Thomas Tyler. He was the Agent for the Copper Works at Margam, and in evidence states quite clearly that this was a

> meeting of ye Justices of ye Peace & Commiss's of ye Land Tax ...
> being ye first meeting after ye wreck of ye ship *Caterina*.

To an unbiased observer therefore it appears very much as though right at the outset the Prosecution was attempting to place Bowen's actions in the worst possible light.

The date of this meeting was 24th January, nearly four weeks after the *Caterina* had foundered. Edward William, the curate at Llangynwyd, claimed that at about ten o'clock the previous evening Aaron Bowen called at his house in the village demanding a penny candle and the key to the church. When the curate asked him for an explanation he said that he and several others intended going to Pyle

> to ask ye Gentlemen whether they would let ye people go free who were with ye wreck, & if so they would engage not to do such things for ye future.

This might sound rather naive, but Bowen would have been speaking in Welsh, and this is how it was translated at the court. What he was probably saying was that they would agree to be 'bound over' in a certain sum to keep the peace – an order frequently used by courts of the period. The signal for this party to assemble was to be the ringing of the church bell.

William also alleged that Bowen went on to say that if the Magistrates refused to agree to their request, then they planned to "go forward & break the gaol" and that he anticipated several hundred people would join the demonstration. The curate claimed that he refused to give Bowen the key but 'believed' that the latter must have subsequently acquired it from one of his children.

Shortly afterwards he heard the church bell being rung, and with creditable bravery went over to the building where he found Aaron Bowen with several other men in the church tower. He ordered them to get out, then immediately left leaving them in possession of the church and (apparently) the key. He claims that his abrupt exit was because he was "very angry with ye people for what they had done", but there seems little doubt that his nerve had failed and he was a frightened man. He was after all alone on a dark night, in the middle of nowhere, and in the presence of a group of very determined men. The group drank a jug of ale they had with them and then left the church for Pyle.

Evan William was the only witness who actually claimed to have heard Aaron Bowen state that he intended to use force if his peaceful protest failed. A Llangynwyd farmer named David John is apparently the same man on whose behalf Bowen had written the letter to Mackworth. He claimed

> that he heard [from] several people, & particularly Rich'd Gibbon, that Aaron Bowen intend'd to mob ye Gentlemen at Pyle if they did not agree to what he w'd have them do.

Now in a modern court of law such evidence would be ruled as inadmissible because it is 'hearsay' – something said when the accused was not present to challenge it. In plain language it was just tittle-tattle or local gossip.

David John, moreover, may well have had an ulterior motive for giving this evidence for there is in the Gnoll papers a petition from various residents of Llangynwyd (including the Vicar) dated 18th February (the day of the trial) affirming his previous good character. This seems to indicate that he too was facing charges – perhaps arising from his own actions at the **Caterina**. Was his statement therefore an attempt to curry favour with the prosecution? Had in fact some deal been struck?

It seems that very few answered Aaron's summons with the church bell, but the group nevertheless set off for Pyle across the mountain, and on the way their leader stopped off at Margam Copper works and attempted to get the workmen there to join them. The Agent for the works, Thomas Tyler, describes how on going into the refinery he found it deserted of workmen, and eventually discovered them, and employees from elsewhere on the site, in conversation with Aaron. They were speaking in Welsh of which Tyler had no knowledge, so he got Jenkin Morgan the Coal Agent of the works to act as his interpreter.

The latter also gave evidence at Aaron's trial and said that at Tyler's request he asked Bowen what he was doing and was told that he wanted the men to "go with him to Pyle before the Gentlemen to ask a favour by fair words, & to know what answer would be given them". On hearing this Tyler ordered him off the premises and warned the men that any who went with him "would be immediately discharged". According to Morgan what he actually said was that for anyone who followed Bowen "it was his marching orders"! Neither they, nor one of the workers who gave evidence, alleged that Bowen said anything to indicate that the protest would be other than a peaceful one. Indeed the fact that most, probably all, the prisoners were in custody at Hereford makes Edward William's allegation that the mob would attempt to 'break the gaol' rather absurd.

It seems then that Aaron, having failed to raise a sufficient body to make the protest meaningful, just went back home, for the words of the charge brought against him accused him only of "endeavouring to assemble a body of people" to protest. In the prevailing climate of outrage against the arrests however, the authorities were determined to make an example of him. Hence the trial with its dubious set of charges and suspect allegations of violence.

In his defence Aaron Bowen produced an impressive list of references as to his character. Charles Llewellyn, an attorney, stated that he had known him for five years,

> and during that time have had many transactions with him and has behaved, to me, as a quiet just and honest person".

Two petitions signed by over forty people claimed

> that his character was in his neighbourhood that of being a diligent & industrious (& until his being lately concern'd in the late wreck) and honest man.

A connection that again seems to indicated that Bowen may have been a local magistrate.

What the result of the trial, or what sentence (if any) was passed on Bowen I have so far failed to discover, but the root cause of his protest – that many of those arrested had been unjustly accused – seems to be vindicated by the fact that so many were in fact acquitted when the case came for trial at the Herefordshire Assize.

Chapter 11
'A Straggling Place'*

After The *Caterina* The year 1782 opened amidst the excitement, the alarms and the raids arising from the wreck of the *Caterina*, but, as the saying goes, 'life must go on' though the problems that concerned most people at Kenfig were, by comparison, fairly trivial ones. On 13th January the Borough Recorder was provided with a brand new and impressive minute book bound in leather and with the title 'Kenfigg Borrough Record' handsomely displayed on the front in gold letters embossed into a red leather inset (B/K 12). Whilst the forces of law and order hauled alleged looters off to prison and Sir Herbert Mackworth fretted over the ultimate disposal of the wreck and cargo, the burgesses worried over the state of the fences at Waun Cimla; and the Margam agent sweated over the compilation of a new 'Life Book'(D/D P 68)

This last was drawn up on the same basis as the ones of 1758 and 1768 in that although all the tenancies in the Margam manors are apparently listed, the object was to show which were held by lease together with brief details. There were 10 such in the manor of Kenfig Borough from a total of 37, whilst in Higher Kenfig there were 11 out of 21. This shows that little had changed from the comparable figures in 1758 (11/34 and 11/17 respectively), but the honeymoon between the Talbots and their tenants seemed to be ending. Only four of these leases had been issued in the 24 years since the previous such survey.

The Turbervilles had gone from Hall some forty years earlier when Dr Thomas Turberville sold the Manor of North Cornelly to the Margam estate. Now the body of the last member of that family, his daughter Christian, returned to the parish of her birth for burial. I know nothing whatsoever about her husband other than that his surname was Savage.

No doubt there was much talk and speculation about the fate of those arrested for their part in the looting of the Venetian ship, but by

---

* This description comes from the 1790 The *Universal British Directory of Trade and Commerce*

and large 1782 was a rather humdrum sort of year except for another event that also involved neighbouring Sker.

Sker House for Sale It is about this time that Sker House and its land came on the market, and Thomas Mansel Talbot, who had been waiting patiently for just such an opportunity, took his chance to add it to the Margam estate. The descendants of Morgan Howells, who was the sitting tenant, tell a story that he too decided to bid for the property so that the subsequent auction turned into a bidding war between him and the Margam agent.

In her ramblings to 'Llyfnwy' (Morgan, 1876) old Lena Rees of Kenfig described how Morgan (whom he mistakenly took to be Isaac Williams) had come to Sker with "a *pedwaran* of guineas" which "were all spent there". Her claim that it was Sker that also helped to part Morgan from his guineas likewise seems to have some basis in truth, but according to Morgan's descendants it was his attempt to outbid the Talbots that eventually brought about his demise. Although eventually out-bid by the Margam Agent, Morgan had pushed the selling price well above what Thomas Talbot himself had expected to pay. He remained the tenant but, his family say that Talbot, as his new landlord, made him pay dearly for his temerity and eventually caused his financial ruin.

This, of course, is mere hearsay, but what is certain is that the following year (1783) Sker was added to the Margam rental for the manor of Kenfig Borough with Howells as its tenant, paying an annual rent of £120.

Threats and Fines As we have already noted there was an increasing laxity apparent amongst the burgesses in general towards keeping the fences at Waun Cimla in repair and paying their rates and taxes. As the 1780s progressed, so this malaise seems to have grown increasingly worse. At the Spring Leet of 1784 a round dozen of them were accused of failing to maintain their boundaries at Waun Cimla, though there is no indication of any action taken against any of them to force compliance. It comes as no surprise therefore to find that the following year two had still not carried out the work and six other plots were found to be in need of repair. On this occasion the miscreants were given two days to do the necessary work or forfeit a fine of 2s.6d., but there is no mention of this being imposed and three out of the eight were amongst six persons 'presented' the following year when they were given nine days to carry out the work under the same penalty.

There seems to have been no cause for complaint in 1786, but the following year the minutes record that the hedge and ditch that formed the boundary of the enclosure on the north, south and western sides was "out of repair", and that "the same ought to be repaired by the 29 proprietors of the said meadow". They were given a week to get the work done or else each one who failed would be fined 3s 4d. No work was done and no fines imposed. Indeed the only action taken against the plot-holders was to again list 28 out of the 29 in November of that year and threaten them with a fine of a shilling per perch of boundary not repaired by 19th December. This seems to have at last stirred the majority into action but four who had consistently and stubbornly refused to carry out the work were then fined at the Spring Leet in 1789.

The fact that the Corporation had at last done something more than merely threaten punishment ensured that for a time the condition of the fences at Waun Cimla gave little cause for complaint. The issue was, however, but one aspect of a certain contempt with which the Borough organisation was regarded by some burgesses. Also at the same Leet court in the Spring of 1784, fourteen were reported for not turning out to stop up rabbit holes in March of that year or paying the appropriate Rabbit Hole Rate in lieu. The following year eight burgesses were reported for failing to pay the Borough's General rate, and although six eventually paid, Rees Evan and John Hopkin failed to do so; this time the Corporation did something more than just threaten, and the pair were solemnly disenfranchised.

Then, at the Autumn Leet held in October 1786 it was Richard Yorwerth, the retiring Sergeant at Mace, who was called to account for "not colecting the Chiefe Rents due to the Lord of the Manor at Michaelmas 1785". The year following this there was a complaint against "Rees Thomas the present Hayward for neglecting his duty on the common". What action (if any) was taken against Yorwerth is not stated. But Thomas was allowed "one month for reformation on pain of being turned out of office".

For a time there was an improvement both in the degree of application shown by the Borough office-holders and prompt payment by its ratepayers, but it did not last long. In 1791 eleven burgesses were given a fortnight to pay their rates or be disfranchised. All seem to have subsequently paid, but the number of burgesses that had to be badgered into paying their rates, and the frequency these instances occur is quite remarkable. Hitherto individuals had indeed been threatened with such action from time to time, but such instances had been very rare. Likewise the Corporation hitherto seems to have had little cause to reprimand any of its officers, and taken together these events seem to indicate a growing disillusionment with the Corporation even within the Borough organisation itself. This general attitude is also perhaps behind the sudden proliferation of unauthorised 'enclosures' being made by some burgesses at this time.

I remember old Mr Mordecai of Pwll-y-Hwyadd Farm once telling me how "We old farmers are all the same Mr Griffiths! If we think we can pinch a bit of waste land here, and another bit there and get away with it, we won't hesitate!" The Borough minute books show that during the 1780s several burgesses had been taking advantage of the Corporation's apparent inertia to do just this and were helping themselves to slices of common land. In 1786 Morgan Howells of Sker (who was not actually a burgess but had nevertheless acquired land within the Borough) was alleged to have made an encroachment on Borough land "at Hewl Laes, opposite the dwelling house of Llewelyn John", and agreed to pay the Corporation a rent upon it "of twopence per annum for ever".

This entry may suggest that there had been a prior agreement between Howells and the Borough in respect of this enclosure, but elsewhere, similar unauthorised events were also taking place. They were probably at the heart of two boundary disputes in which the Manor Court was required to intervene, one in May 1787 when James Marment, licensee of 'The Tap' in Pylc, was accused of filling up with stones a ditch that formed the boundary between his land and that of William John. This was probably on Heol Fach in the vicinity of Cornelly Cross where Marment had interests in a limestone quarry.

The other appears in the minutes in the form of an affidavit taken on oath from a certain John David included in the year 1789 without other explanation. In it David describes how, in the Spring of 1761, he had been employed doing ditching and fencing work for Richard John of New Mill. Unfortunately he does not say where this work was being done, but deposed that he "Was ordered by the said

Richard John to begin about three foot on the east side of a certain oak stand'g on the said hedge".

This seems to relate to an illegal enclosure of land adjoining a road, and certainly by this time the Corporation was becoming increasingly concerned about such matters. At the Court held on 30th December 1791, where eleven burgesses were reported for failing to pay their rates, another eight were also reported for making illegal enclosures within the Borough. No action was taken immediately, but the Corporation had at least served notice that it was aware of what was going on.

Elsewhere on the common other problems were also occurring, of which the perennial problem with the rabbit population was just one. "The rabbits run up and break ground out of bounds" complained the jurors at the Autumn Leet in 1787, but in a new twist to the hoary old complaint placed the blame squarely on the shoulders of John Loveluck. They took the novel view that as the rabbits originated in the Margam warren, and he was its tenant, therefore the pests were his responsibility.

Hopkin Llewelyn the Margam steward was as usual presiding at this sitting, and he agreed, giving Loveluck two months to exterminate the rabbits outside the boundaries of his warren, or pay a fine of twenty shillings. The matter was not raised again, so on the face of it he succeeded in achieving what the combined efforts of the Kenfig burgesses had hitherto failed to do and eliminated the pests on their part of the common. This seems highly unlikely, and the rabbits were soon giving cause for complaint once more, but maybe John's game-keeping skills enabled him to achieve some element of control that led to a significant reduction of the nuisance.

When the Corporation believed it necessary to issue a stern warning to their fellow burgesses about possible breaches of the Borough by-laws, then it is virtually certain that (as with the illegal enclosures) some infraction of the rules was taking place. So when at a Hall Day held on 17th August 1787 the Eight Elected burgesses announced that no parcels of fern on Kenfig ought to be sold to any out-dweller, whether a burgess or not, then we can be sure that somebody had, or was considering, doing just that! The burgesses were reminded that a breach of this law could result in being disenfranchised and also that no ferns were to be cut on the common until after the first day of September.

The latter provision was apparently made in the interests of the plot-holders themselves. It will be remembered that the bracken harvested here was used as supplementary animal fodder, and according to the old farmer from Maesteg who supplied that information, the time when it was harvested was important. September was considered the earliest it should be cut.

Strange Happenings in Pyle Interesting things were happening at Pyle in the late 1780s, though as is so frequently the case it is difficult to discover much beyond the barest detail. Who, for example, was the man murdered there in 1786 by somebody "thrusting a knife to his guts" as graphically described in his diary by William Thomas in January of that year (Denning, 1995: 343). "The murderer (also unnamed) is", he tells us, "com'd to Cardiff's Jail".

Also *en route* to the gaol at about this time was Edward Evan of Pyle, but probably originally from Kenfig. His offence was illegally felling oak trees at Pyle, and the Margam estate reimbursed Lewis Griffith the sum of 6s 2d for obtaining a warrant against him and paying the constable to take him to 'the House of Correction' - the gaol at Cowbridge (D/D Ma 35).

If it is indeed the same Edward Evan that had previously been a Kenfig burgess, then he would have been in his early 70s, having been baptised in 1714, and admitted to the burgesses' ranks sometime prior to 1741 when he was appointed one of the Aletasters. One of those listed as a defaulter for his Rabbit Hole Rate in 1784 he was clearly preparing to leave the Borough at that time, and to this end sold his parcels of hay and fern the following year. A shoemaker by trade he survived his term in prison and died in 1794.

Things come in threes so they say, and thus it is that William Thomas's diary contains details of a third Pyle miscreant who met an untimely end in the February of 1788 (Denning,1995: 364). He and his father were being brought under escort to Cardiff in the custody of the local constable who had arrested them for theft of a barrel containing 60 lbs of butter. Both prisoners and escort were probably on foot, and nearing the end of their journey when the lad thought he saw an opportunity to make his escape. As the party crossed the bridge over the river Taff prior to entering the town he made a break for freedom, successfully eluding his escort and leaping over the bridge parapet. Unfortunately he then drowned in the swirling waters of the river beneath. His body was later recovered and now lies buried in St Mary's churchyard in the city. Again, unfortunately, William Thomas gives no names of the people involved.

In January 1786, and not for the last time in the Borough's history, the serving Portreeve died whilst in office. He was William Morgan who was the owner/occupier of the cottage in Mawdlam known today as 'Sunnyside'. Although he had been a burgess since 1758, there appears to be little about him that merited his translation to the office of Portreeve in the first place, and he was almost certainly illiterate. The man who replaced him however was the Surveyor John Williams of Newlands Farm, who not only served out the residue of Morgan's term of office but then followed this with a term of twelve months on his own behalf as well.

It is also interesting to note that in the period immediately following Morgan's death, responsibility for the day-to-day administration of the Borough was taken by the Recorder, Rees Rees. It was he also who apparently made the appointment of the new Portreeve acting purely on his own initiative, though Williams had been nominated for the office with William Morgan at the Autumn Leet. This practice seems to have been continued by other Recorders when similar vacancies arose later on. Indeed, if the death of the Portreeve occurred only a short time before the Autumn Leet (when a replacement was due to be appointed anyway) Recorders often continued to fulfil the role themselves until the Court hearing.

Griffith Thomas and The Cefn Cribwr Common A new character at Kenfig who enlivens the closing decades of the 18th century is Griffith Thomas who is one of those who suddenly appear on the scene without apparently having any previous local connections. His origins are therefore obscure and actually rather intriguing. The very last reference to him in local documents (Q/D/LTA/NEW/8 1802) before he vanishes as mysteriously as he arrived, specifically accords him the honorific title 'Mr' which suggests that possibly he had suddenly become heir to somebody of higher status, for he had not been accorded such a title previously. Certainly there is very little in the earliest references to him at Kenfig to suggest that he was a person of any standing.

The first mention of Griffith locally comes in 1783 when separate entries in the Borough Minute Book (B/K 12) record that he claimed a foal found straying by the Hayward and was later admitted as a burgess. Later on he was also appointed and served for twelve months as an Aletaster which was an office that most of the better-off burgesses successfully avoided. Griffith, in fact, actually performed a second term in 1791.

It also seems from these early records that initially Griffith failed to acquire any great holding in the Borough. When listed for Land Tax in 1784 the sum assessed as his contribution was the modest one of two shillings (Q/D/LTA/NEW/8 1784) in respect of property owned by the Margam estate. Two years later, however, he appears as the sub-tenant of Hopkin Llewelyn at Llanmihangel Mill (PM 3453) where he seems to have lived out for the remainder of his time here.

In 1785 Griffith was quick to snap up the parcels of hay and fern belonging to **John Rosser**, himself a strange character who is one of those who served the Borough in the office of Petty Constable but was not a burgess at that time. This had been back in 1770, and in the same year he was declared a fit person to be a burgess, though he did not take up this office until 1785. The only reason he did so then, or so it seems, was that his wife Mary Yorwerth inherited parcels of hay and fern in the possession of Ann Yorwerth, though I am not sure how these two fit into the family tree. These he promptly sold to Griffith Thomas for two pounds (B/K 12) and thereafter had little to do with Borough affairs. He served as an Aletaster in 1786, and repaired the windows of the Town Hall the year after, but after that vanishes from the records.

Griffith, for his part, seems to have been happy to obtain these trappings of a Kenfig burgess, but does not seem to have made much use of his parcel of hay ground at Waun Cimla for he is one of those regularly reported for the state of his fences there. He was also one of those making illegal enclosures of waste land which in his case amounted to three perches of waste land alongside Heol-y-Marlas (B/K 12). When the Borough demanded in 1793 that he pay them 6d per year for it, he seems to have simply declined to pay.

That same year, however, Griffith placed before the burgesses a proposal that had implications far beyond its stated purpose of obtaining a permit to prospect for minerals beneath Waun Cimla and Cefn Cribwr Common.

It will be recalled [in *Part* 2 of *Kenfig Folk*] that in 1572 the Corporation had enclosed the land there to form Waun Cimla and its 29 parcels of hay ground. Ten years later, following an enquiry by Thomas Wiseman, this enclosure was declared to have been made without the permission of the Lord of the Manor, and therefore to be illegal. Through a combination of Wiseman's tact and the Earl of Pembroke's inertia nothing further was done, and the burgesses were suffered to remain in possession without paying rent.

Nevertheless, throughout the early part of the 17th century the Earl granted leases to various individuals to mine coal on the common in the area known as Tir Garw, thereby demonstrating that it was they, and not the burgesses, who owned the land there. Now, over a century later, Griffith Thomas approached the Corporation seeking permission to "search for, digg, raise and carry away all the coal and iron ore which shall, or may be found, on that part of the Burgesses' land called Tir Garw and Keven Kribbwr" – and they granted it!

By the articles of an agreement reached between them on 10th May, 1793 (B/K 12) the Corporation agreed that Griffith could operate any mine he made for 41 years at an annual rent of £12. They also added a rider that he must sell coal for domestic use to in-dwelling burgesses at the fixed rate of three pence per 'customary horse load'. In the event the place where he actually found coal was on his plot of hay ground, and it was there that he sank his pit!

Coal Pit in the Vale of Neath, 1788 Interesting as this event was in itself, it actually opened up a far larger can of worms. By granting him permission to prospect for and mine the mineral wealth that lay beneath the common at Cefn Cribwr, the Burgesses were acting as though the land there actually belonged to them. Historically we know that this was not the case as Thomas Wiseman had demonstrated two centuries earlier. Were they in fact 'testing the water' over the question of ownership, or did they in fact actually believe that common at The Rugge actually belonged to them?

These are questions that it is now virtually impossible to answer with certainty. They would have been in no doubt whatsoever that they had commoner's rights there and many of them may have mistakenly believed that this implied right of ownership as well which, indeed, is a commonly held but mistaken belief amongst the general public even today. Moreover, if somebody from their ranks did raise doubts over the issue, then it would be pointed out that the Margam estate had never acted as the owner of the common for as long as anyone could remember.

The one incident that perhaps indicates a degree of uncertainty on both sides concerning ownership was the occasion in 1779 when the Borough received payment from two individuals for permission to 'trespass' upon Cefn Cribwr Common. When the matter was laid before the Margam Steward at a Court Leet, he directed that the sum be devoted towards the purposes of the Borough and spent on 'redoing' the court of arms in the town hall. This seems to reflect that neither side was certain of its rights in this respect and fudged the issue with a compromise solution. If that was so, then by issuing the lease to Griffith Thomas the Burgesses were in effect throwing down the gauntlet to Margam to prove their right of ownership.

The Talbots did not respond, and their failure to do so meant that from this point onwards ownership of the Common at Cefn Cribwr passed to Kenfig Corporation. As I remarked at the time when Thomas Talbot took control of Kenfig Pool, 'you win some and you lose some!'

John Byng's visit to Pyle (1787) Although he did not visit Kenfig, John Byng's visit to Pyle (Andrews, 1934: 293) on a hot summer day in August 1787 is not without interest. He broke his journey at the White Hart Inn which we now know as *The Tap* (a.k.a. *Ye Olde Wine House*) where, he tells us, he was served 'sewin' that had presumably been caught locally and was quite plentiful. With it came "a variety of good cheese, Welsh and English – for they yet speak of England as a foreign country". Paying a visit to the local church he noted that the windows there were fitted with shutters "to prevent damage from the fives-balls, as the church wall is the general place for that sport".

It has to be remembered that churchyards then contained few, if any gravestones, and no doubt the one at Mawdlam was put to similar use at this period. Mrs Marianne Robertson Spencer (Spencer, 1935: 45) records that during the *Mabsant* revels held to celebrate the feast-day of the patron saint, Mary Magdalene, young men from the community used the church for a particular type of ball game. Of it she says only that it involved attempting "to throw a ball over the church tower or steeple, and was a game requiring great skill and dexterity". By the time she wrote her book in 1913 however, it was already something that "belongs to the past".

A New Solution for the Rabbits Also in 1787 the burgesses seem to have attempted a slightly different approach towards dealing with the continuing nuisance caused by the rabbits on the common. As mentioned earlier in this chapter the onus for eradicating the errant conies was placed upon John Loveluck as tenant of the Margam warren, and apparently met with a measure of success. This in turn may have prompted the Burgesses to try a new tack in attempting to control the nuisance, and four years on they and Loveluck concluded a novel agreement.

Under its terms he paid the Borough an annual rent of £4 10s 0d. and in return was allowed to take rabbits at two places on their common, one described as being on the east side of Wern Las (location not known), and the other to the east of the castle ruins. Presumably these were areas in which the problem with rabbits was most acute. At the same time an identical permit was concluded with Jenkin John in respect of the common land adjoining the Portland, for which he paid a rent of £1. 5s 0d. Both leases were to run for eleven years.

These agreements seemed to be to everyone's benefit. Loveluck and John, who were both operating commercial warrens on the fringes of the common, were now given the right to legally cull rabbits on part of the burgesses' land bordering their own. This in turn helped keep down the annoyance these were causing and eliminated the need for the Borough to pay people to go round stopping up rabbit holes. On the contrary, their annual income was now actually boosted by the rent due from the two lessees.

Financial Problems? The account submitted by Daniel Rees for his year of office 1792-3 is in fact the last to be included in the Minute books and taken together with those of his immediate predecessor Jenkin John (1791-92) seems to indicate that the Borough was experiencing financial problems. Both accounted for interest payments totalling £3. 5s 0d due on sums of £20, £40, and £5 loaned by a George Bartlett; Hopkin

Llewelyn (the current Constable of the Castle) and Rees Rees junior respectively.

No mention had been made of such payments previously, and Daniel also mentions that in addition he had received the sum of £10 "Received of the Club Society". This perhaps marks the start of one of the local Friendly Societies in the District – probably in this case Mawdlam - which had invested some of the income from members' subscriptions with the Borough at an agreed rate of interest. At a slightly later date a field on the site of what is now the Greenacres Motel was known as 'Erw Club' as it was in the tenancy of such a Society who were sub-letting it in the same manner as the Parish Charity land on Heol Broom to boost their income.

Unfortunately, and because the Portreeves' accounts for succeeding years seem not to have survived, we have no way of knowing how badly the Borough fell into debt. If, however, the interest due on the loan from the Friendly Society is included then it was costing them a total of £4.5s.0d. per annum just to service these loans at a time when their income from the general rate amounted to just £2.10s.0d.

The Return of Nonconformity In 1764 John Williams the Vicar of Margam had written that there was no Nonconformist organisation within the parish of Pyle & Kenfig but just a quarter of a century later, that was no longer true for in 1788 the first chapel appeared on the site of Capel-y-Pîl in North Cornelly.

At a talk given to the Kenfig Society by Eirian Edwards, formerly of Penybryn and now of Cardiff, told us that the moving light behind the resurgence of Nonconformity in the locality was William Thomas (1723–1811). Originally from the Port Talbot area he was converted to Methodism about 1740 after hearing a sermon by the noted Welsh preacher Hywel Harris. Later he farmed at Ty Draw, Pyle (just off the huge traffic roundabout on the A48 out of the village) and seems to have been a rather engaging sort of character. Contemporary accounts speak of him singing hymns and prayers at the top of his voice whilst going about his work, which could be clearly heard by travellers passing along the nearby main road.

Another story about him is that he would regularly visit the homes of local people, particularly the poorest members of society, and pay them a shilling to be allowed to give them what he called his 'witness' to Christ. By such means he built up quite a band of fellow worshippers in the district that became sufficiently numerous and organised to build itself a place to hold regular services.

Since Capel-y-Pîl lies outside the boundaries of the Borough it does not form part of our story, but has nevertheless provided a place of worship for Methodists from Kenfig up to the present day. [Since Barrie wrote this, the Chapel has been closed for worship, and sold awaiting development in 2012. Ed.] In 1852 a small chapel (Bethel) was built at Water Street to serve the congregation in Higher Kenfig. It stood on what became the access road to Newlands Colliery, but has long been abandoned and has since been converted into a private house.

Kenfig in 1790 The *Universal British Directory of Trade and Commerce* appeared in print in 1790 giving business people and others a detailed account of Britain at the time – town by town. Its description of the town of Bridgend contains the following brief account of Kenfig.

> Seven miles South-west [of Bridgend] is the borough of Kenfig, which though a straggling place, and inhabited by none but farmers, contains about 50 resident and 70 out-dwelling burgesses, each of whom has a vote for the member of the Glamorganshire boroughs. A great part of the land near the sea side at this place is overwhelmed with hills of sand, which are continually shifting from place to place, according to the direction of the wind.

In itself there is nothing particularly remarkable in this account but, for the first time we are given a picture of the Borough as it was viewed by the population beyond its borders, and it is not a particularly flattering one. Despite the fact that revolution in France had broken out the previous year, its excesses had not yet muted public expression of the need to reform the British Parliamentary system, with the abolition of 'rotten' and 'decayed' boroughs close to the top of their agenda. The writer clearly saw this 'straggling place' as one of the latter and his views were undoubtedly shared by many others outside its borders.

Chapter 12
War and Reform – 1790s

Throughout the latter part of the 18th century there had been a growing clamour in the country to reform the manner in which it was governed. Particularly obnoxious to those heading this movement was the manner in which the nobility were able to exercise direct control over the election of MPs to represent the Borough towns. This they were able to achieve because of the existence of boroughs like Kenfig, that were towns only in name which were, to paraphrase the author of the Universal Directory, simply straggling places inhabited by none but farmers.

The worst examples of this were the 'rotten boroughs' – places like Old Sarum near Salisbury which was nothing more than a grass-grown mound where a town had once stood. Here, on election days, small patches of grass were leased to individuals carefully chosen by the landlord as supporters of his candidate. For the duration of the election they became Burgesses of Sarum with a burgess's right to cast their vote. The result, of course, was a foregone conclusion.

Kenfig, it has to be said, was not quite in the same category. Its town may have been buried by the sand, but the Borough did contain a number of small communities, though none could claim to be any more than villages. Moreover, amongst the in-dwelling burgesses, there was a surprisingly large element of working class men who were entitled to vote; this, in certain quarters, was thought to be another good reason why such 'decayed boroughs' should be consigned to the scrap heap of history! There were at Kenfig many burgesses who were freeholders and free men, though the majority were now tenants of the Talbots of Margam and directly under their control. Nevertheless, the greatest criticism that Kenfig warranted as a decayed borough ripe for reform was the army of out-dwelling burgesses maintained by the landlord to 'promote the Margam interest'.

The excessive violence of the French Revolution that broke out in 1789, and our subsequent war with that country from 1794 to 1815 tended to curb the activities of the reform movement for a time. Following the victory at Waterloo and with the removal of the self-appointed Emperor Napoleon, the clamour for something to be done became increasingly strident and ultimately resulted in the Reform Act of 1832. Whilst the Borough as an element of local government survived this intact, its days were clearly numbered.

War with the French, incidentally, created a boom in the agricultural industry, benefiting both the local farmers and landowners. Whilst the farmers found a ready market and high prices for their produce as the government strove to feed and equip a huge standing army and navy, the landlords profited even more by creaming off most of the higher prices by raising the rents.

Until Nelson's victory over the combined French and Spanish fleets at Trafalgar in 1805, there was also the ever-present threat of invasion. Whilst the South Coast of England was considered the area most under threat, the burgesses at Kenfig were only too well aware of how, in the most recent conflict between the two nations, French privateers had been able to anchor in Swansea Bay with impunity (as earlier described by Sir Herbert Mackworth in 1782). But day-to-day life in Kenfig carried on. (D/D Ma 44 for subsequent quotes)

Admission Refused At the Spring Leet in 1791 the names of three men were put forward as candidates to become burgess and rather strangely two were 'disallowed' but subsequently admitted, whilst the one whose name went forward never seems to have taken up the offer!

Encroachments At an important meeting of the Burgesses held on 13th December 1793 several resolutions were passed that mark a further step in the increasing confidence of the Burgesses, and their determination to enforce their authority over that of the Portreeve. The occasion was a Court Baron presided over by the current Portreeve John Loveluck, but it is clear from the minutes of this meeting that it was the jurors who were making all the decisions. In the words of the entries it was they who "order that John Loveluck the present Portreeve" serve notice on Richard Robert to quit his tenancy of The Corporation House as described earlier in this history. Following their subsequent retraction it was again "the said jurors" who subsequently renewed Robert's agreement in September.

Other decisions taken at the December court were also made by the jury. They ordered "David Yorwerth, the present Hayward" to give personal notice to all persons keeping pigs on the common to set rings in their snouts to stop them grubbing up the vegetation, and ordered a fine of 6d for any who failed to do so. Most importantly they made an appointment to meet John Loveluck on Boxing Day at the Corporation House "and proceed from thence in order to survey the several encroachments made within the limits of this Corporation since the year 1773". It is the clearest indication yet that important decisions and key actions within the Borough were now being initiated by the burgesses themselves, and that the Portreeve had become merely a figurehead of their organisation.

Having carried out their perambulation of the Borough and viewed the various encroachments, Portreeve and jurors adjourned to the Town Hall and came to a decision. They had noted thirteen such enclosures (eight of which were on Heol Las) and measured them, but rather than order the persons responsible to restore the land to the waste, they determined instead to charge them rent. The sums varied from a penny per annum imposed on Rees Rees for a pig sty to 4s 9d due from Richard Yorwerth for two enclosures he had made on Heol Las. Morgan Howells of Sker, they noted, had made four such infringements, two on Heol Las and further ones at Greendown and Waun-y-Mer, but they were smaller and his annual rent was set at just two shillings.

Those "by whom the ground was taken in" were given the alternative of paying these rents or otherwise "to break down the ditches and walls, and make the same open with roads and common". It cannot be said, however, that the jury were unanimous in their decision, for Rees Rees and Rees Thomas (both of whom were responsible for some of the enclosures) together with Evan Jenkin stormed out of the meeting in protest and were fined 3s 4d.

Unfortunately the practice of entering the Portreeve's accounts in the Minute books ceases with those of Daniel Rees who had been replaced at the 1793 Autumn Leet, so we cannot say for certain that these rents were actually paid or not. It seems that initially the latter was probably the case for a year later – the first occasion upon which such rents fell due – all apparently failed or refused to do so. By the following Spring however only Rees Thomas and Griffith Thomas were still holding out. After that everything falls quiet, so presumably they too fell in line and paid up.

A New Tenant for The Corporation House. We have already noted how the wording of the minute books had gradually changed so as to leave no doubt that it was the burgesses and not the Portreeve who were now making the decisions in relation to the Borough of Kenfig. So it was that whilst it was the latter who on 13th October 'appointed' a Hall Day to be held "to take into consideration the method of choosing a tenant for the Corporation House" , the actual decision was made by the Eight Elected Burgess that he "appointed to interfere in the above affair".

The man they chose to replace the discredited Richard Roberts was William Leyson who had already volunteered to pay an annual rent of £8 per annum for the tenancy. In return he promised to keep "all the doors and glass windows of the said house in like manner as he shall receive them ... particularly such as shall be broken accidentally by rude and disorderly persons".

William was a relative newcomer to the area, and may have hailed from Tythegston where, in 1760, Leyson William and his wife Ann David had baptised a child of this name. A William Leyson is mentioned at the time of the *Caterina* wreck as one of those employed to assist with his horses in the salvage work, so he may have been resident within the Borough then. His admission as a Burgess did not however come until 1788, to be followed three years later by his marriage to a Mary William. Apparently illiterate, he was, like Howell Evan, an otherwise largely unremarkable individual.

Death of Daniel Rees November 1796 saw the passing of Daniel Rees of Pen Plas – the last Portreeve to have served for more than two consecutive years. After the change of rules forced him out of office in 1776 after his four-year term he had been appointed to the post on for one further year in 1793.

Daniel was tenant of Margam land at North Cornelly, and the owner of freehold properties in Kenfig Lower that included The Angel Inn, Ty'n-y-Towyn Farm, and Pen Plas where he lived. His son and successor was known as Rees Daniel after the Welsh fashion that had now all but died out in the borough. He seems to have been content to live a quiet sort of life, and although several times nominated for the post of Portreeve was only ever appointed to serve in that office once (1798). If he was married and had children I can find no record of either in the Parish Registers, and it would seem that he remained a life-long bachelor.

The French Invasion At a Hall Day in January 1797 it was reported that several Burgesses were in arrears with paying their rates, and the Eight Elected gave them a month to pay up or else face being disenfranchised. The stage was set for a confrontation, but was overtaken by events with the news that Wales had been invaded by a French army that landed near Fishguard on 22nd February.

Too few in number to pose a serious threat, and comprised largely of troops of dubious quality, the French surrendered just three days later. The vulnerability of the Welsh coastline had nevertheless been ruthlessly exposed, and the fears expressed by Sir Herbert Mackworth fifteen years earlier seemed now to have been fully justified. Two days after the French surrender the Burgesses met at the summons of their Portreeve Jenkin John "to take into consideration the method to furnish inhabitants of this Borough with arms for their defence in case an invasion should be made by an enemy on this [or] the neighbouring coast".

What decision, if any, was reached at the meeting we are not told, but at least the men of Kenfig had shown that they were as eager and willing as any to fight in defence of their homes and families. The rate defaulters apparently took advantage of the excitement as an excuse for not settling their arrears, and were again 'presented' on 3rd March, after which it seems that the invasion having proved a damp squib, they decided to finally pay what was owing.

The Reverend John Morgan At the Autumn Leet of 1797 the man appointed to be the Portreeve for the coming year was the Revd John Morgan of Margam who two years earlier had become tenant of Pwll-yr-Hwyadd Farm on Water Street. He was the first of several ministers of the Anglican Church to reside within the Borough, all of whom became burgesses and served as its Portreeve.

John Morgan had previously been a curate at Llangynwyd where his activities had brought him to the notice of the late Lynn Jones of Maesteg even though he only rates a brief mention in the latter's book on the vicars of that parish (Jones DLR, 1994). Like all good local historians Lynn and I exchanged the information we had collected about John Morgan to our mutual benefit, though it is to him that I am indebted for virtually all that I know about the Reverend Morgan's religious background.

It seems that John Morgan was born about the year 1750, and was admitted as a Deacon of St David's on 17th October 1779. Two years later he was ordained there as a priest, though unfortunately the details are not entered in the Bishop's Register which would indicate his place of origin. In all probability he was a West Walian, and shortly afterwards, as Lynn put it in his letter to me, became "one of the many young clerics from those parts who poured into the Diocese of Llandaff in search of a curacy".

In 1783 John became the curate of the combined parishes of Llangynwyd and Llangeinor (with Bettws), and since the Vicar of the day (William Thomas) was an absentee who rarely troubled himself with parochial affairs, John Morgan virtually ran the parishes himself and lived in the vicarage at Llangynwyd village. William Thomas paid him £30 per annum for his care of Llangynwyd and Llangeinor, and he received a further £10 from Henry Jones the incumbent at Newcastle in respect of Bettws. With a total income of £40 a year he would, as Lynn points out, have been considered 'passing rich'.

In 1789 William Thomas resigned the livings of Llangynwyd and Llangeinor and the Revd John Parry was appointed to succeed him at both, though he did not take up residence until early in 1794. When he did, of course, John Morgan lost not only his living, but also his home in the vicarage as well.

Fortunately later that year, or early in the next, Dr John Hunt became the Perpetual Curate at Margam (in effect its Vicar). He was an Englishman and needed a curate able to conduct services in the Welsh language at the Abbey Church, where they were held on alternate weeks. The Margam registers show that John Morgan conducted many of the baptisms, burials and marriages at this church (for which he would have received the fees) throughout Hunt's term of office (he died in 1816) and afterwards. Whether he acquired the tenancy of Pwll-yr-Hwyadd himself, or whether this was made available to him as part of the deal that brought him to Margam, is uncertain. What is obvious however is that having been admitted as a burgess in 1795 he entered wholeheartedly into the affairs of the Borough and within two years was admitted as the Portreeve, the first of three such terms he served in the office.

In 1799 he was inducted as the Vicar for the parish of Pyle & Kenfig, which was then held with the parish of Margam, and is indeed the first incumbent with sole responsibility for its affairs that I have identified since the town of Kenfig was abandoned. He still continued nevertheless to carry out the duties of his curacy at Margam for, to again quote from Lynn Jones's letter, Dr Hunt and the Reverend W B Knight who succeeded him "were gentlemen and had responsibilities elsewhere, they were not inclined to exert themselves on the mundane duties at Margam!"

Defence of the Realm During the course of his year in office, on 9th March 1798, the Rev Morgan called a Hall Day meeting "to take into consideration the method of contributing a reasonable sum of money to enable [the] Government to carry on the war against our enemies; to defend our country and properties".

The failed French invasion at Fishguard twelve months earlier was evidently still very much on the burgesses' mind, and if their gift of ten guineas (£10.50p) seems rather paltry, let me remind you that it is more than four years' income from their General Rate (£2.50p per annum). It would have done little if anything to help equip and man even the smallest of the ships in Britain's Royal Navy, but given the Borough's circumstances it was, like the widow's mite, a generous gift out of all proportion to its actual value.

The Reverend Richard Warner As the 18th century drew to a close Kenfig was paid a visit by another of those tourists whose accounts have survived to the present time. Unfortunately the Reverend Richard Warner who visited in 1799 tells us nothing of the community that existed here or of the state the Borough itself. Instead it was the castle, and in particular Kenfig Pool that captured his attention. Amusingly, having emphatically rejected the story of a city beneath the lake, the Reverend gentleman goes on to give a detailed account of just how such an event might have occurred through the collapse of an underground cavern! (Warner, 1800: 80-1)

Our journey of today commenced with a visit to Kynfig Lake, a pool of fresh water surrounded by the sands, about a mile and a half in circumference. At one end are the ruins of a small castle said to have been the residence of [Robert} Fitz-Hamon, but probably without foundation as the conqueror of Glamorganshire would have chosen a better situation, and a larger mansion. Equally void of credit is the popular tradition of a city having formerly stood on the spot which the lake now occupies The formation of a lake in the situation of Kynfig Pool is difficult to account for, unless we have recourse to some secondary cause such as an earthquake, or the falling in or giving way of the superficial crust of earth, by the absorption of its foundations into some immense cavity or inferior gulph, after being sapped and undermined by subterraneous waters – an opinion which the least knowledge of geology will render very probable.

KENFIG POOL

It has to be said that there is no evidence whatsoever to support Warner's hypothesis about the formation of this lake – unless of course one includes the legend that a city once stood at this spot!

As the year 1799 drew to a close the war in Europe and on the high seas still raged, whilst at home agitation for reform of the Parliamentary system was becoming more strident and attracting increasing support amongst the ranks of the 'movers and shakers' of society themselves. Change was on the horizon, and for the ancient Borough of Kenfig, which had now existed for over 650 years, the future that lay ahead was an uncertain one.

Chapter 13
The Borough 1800-1814

In this, the last part of my history, we follow the story of the people of Kenfig as they enter the dawn of the modern era. It is a time marked by the arrival of the first railways, of industrial development and urban expansion in the hinterland, but in which the life of the Borough itself remained but little changed. As the industrial 19th century surged onward the straggling, tattered and sleepy communities that comprised the Borough still followed the age-old round of the agricultural year whilst all about them quarries and mines opened and new towns and villages sprang into being. More than ever now the 'Ancient Town and Borough' appeared an anachronism which had little or no relevance in the modern era. Increasingly the Burgesses and their organisation became objects of amused curiosity and even ridicule.

Not surprisingly therefore as the 19th century progressed the Borough organisation increasingly turned in upon itself. The Burgesses, or so it seems to me, were now seeking to secure for themselves whatever benefits they could from their dying organisation – making hay whilst the sun still shone and their organisation still survived. This is a process that now too becomes more apparent in the Minute Book as the Borough Recorders became less reticent about entering details of Corporation business in its pages.

Previously we noted how, after the fall of Portreeve Richard Jenkins, a hereditary element was introduced into the qualification for admission as a Burgess. Initially it appears to have been intended to combat falling numbers due to the loss of dwelling houses traditionally regarded as 'burgages', and for a time both qualifications existed side by side. Then, at a Court Baron held on 28th February 1800 the Portreeve and Council took a decisive step that effectively weighted preference in favour of the hereditary principle. Whilst not actually banning the older residential qualification the Recorder's Minute declares that "no person shall be admitted and elected Burgess …at a less premium than five pounds and five shillings to be paid to the Corporation Treasury". For sons of Burgesses however the fee was set at just two shillings. Whatever the true intent of this decision (and none is given) the effect was to deter any new arrivals taking up the residential qualification through occupation of one of the Borough's traditional 'burgage' dwellings.

Was this measure perhaps aimed in particular at the tenants of the Margam farms and cottages – especially those in Higher Kenfig; an attempt, perhaps, to distance the Borough from the political aspirations of such local landowners? Or was it simply a means of extracting a greater return from this source of revenue? Political reform was indeed in the offing, but locally landowners such as the Talbots of Margam still invested large sums to secure their political 'interest' by creating Burgesses in those boroughs under their control. Whether the Talbots would be prepared to pay such an enhanced fee merely for this purpose was nevertheless a moot point!

Whatever the true intent the result remained the same. When electoral reform removed the landowner's ability to influence voters they ceased to finance the admission of Kenfig Burgesses, and of those who moved into the Borough as new tenants of 'burgages' some certainly chose not to apply for admission. Well before the abolition of Kenfig Borough in 1886 therefore, the residential Burgess qualification ceased to exist.

Such reluctance on the part of new arrivals to pay the enhanced fee is apparent right at the outset following the introduction of this new rule, and despite the unequivocal nature of the order as set out in the minutes, it seems that a lower rate could be negotiated by those of sufficient status or influence with the Corporation. Thomas Porter, who took on the tenancy of Caeau Gollen (Glasfryn) in 1802, is a case in point. He was a newcomer to the area who occupied a traditional 'burgage', and the Burgesses charged him just one guinea (£1.05p) as his admission fee, even allowing him to pay this sum in two instalments. The following year Jehosaphat Powell was charged the same amount when he took up residence at Llanmihangel Mill even though his wife was the daughter of a former Burgess. In 1804 newcomers John Jones of The Angel Inn and William Owen paid fees of three guineas each which, although a considerable sum, was nevertheless a 40% reduction on the 'official' rate.

Nor were these reductions applied exclusively to in-dwelling Burgesses. That same year Robert Savours, a mere out-dweller, was also charged just one guinea. This, claimed the Burgesses was, "out of good will towards the said Robert Savour", adding self-righteously that, "it is not to be a general Rule to admit any for that value". Despite this the following year saw two more out-dwellers admitted at 'special rates'. Thomas Major junior was only charged two shillings (the fee for a Burgess's son) "It being our good will towards the said Thomas, he being a servant of Mr Talbot's". A few weeks later, and without any further comment, they also admitted a Hopkin Rees for the fee of one guinea.

In practice therefore it seems that the Burgesses were simply content to extract from new entrants whatever they could get, and even went so far as to bend the facts if they really wanted the prospective candidate to join their number. In 1812, following the death of the surveyor John Williams, the tenancy of Newlands Farm in Higher Kenfig passed to a John Roderick (often spelled Rhoderick in contemporary records). His is an unusual surname which I have not noted previously in connection with the Borough, yet his admission as a Burgess was approved on the grounds that he was a Burgess's son! This, of course, meant he was only charged a two shilling entrance fee, and similar manipulation of the facts is apparent in the admission of David Hopkin of Newton Nottage at the Spring Leet the same year. He was declared a fit person on the grounds that he was "married to a Burgess's daughter" even though he was an out-dweller. This meant that he too paid the lower two-shilling rate, and it is perhaps not co-incidental that the Burgess's daughter in question was the sister-in-law of the influential Joseph Rees of Kenfig House Farm!

David, it seems, was paying to become an out-dwelling Burgess off his own bat, and the same seems to be true of John Beynon – son of the old mischief-maker of that name whom Alice Yorwerth had taken to court for slandering her in 1768. John junior kept a shop in North Cornelly and in 1814 acquired some freehold land in Kenfig Lower. When he attended a sitting of the manorial court to have the transfer of the latter formally ratified the Burgesses admitted him as an out-Burgess at the same time!

The only practical advantage Beynon and Hopkin would have reaped from their admission was the right to vote in elections for an MP to represent the Glamorgan Boroughs, so perhaps both were just politically active individuals keen to secure the vote. On the other hand, were they merely acquiring the title because it still had a certain 'snob value' – rather like those who pay large sums of money today for the title deeds of lordships and manors that have long become defunct?

Part of the reason behind the Corporation's decision to raise the admission fees to such a high level may have been that towards the end of the 18th century the Borough was in some sort of financial difficulty. Because of this it had raised loans from individuals and local organisations though the details are rather sketchy because about that time the practice of entering the details of the Portreeve's annual account in the Minute Books was discontinued. It becomes apparent, however, that in order to pay off these debts every Portreeve subsequently paid £2 per annum out of the rates and other sources of income into a special fund established to repay these loans. Not until October 1807 however were the Corporation able to note with satisfaction that this object had been achieved and the special fund could be discontinued.

Another interesting development in this first decade of the new century is that decisions of the council are once again recorded in the Minutes as having been taken by "The Portreeve and the Eight Elected Burgesses". This seems to imply that some of the former status of their Chief Officer had been restored following the brief period during which his actions had apparently been dictated by the council. The limitation on his term of office to a single year nevertheless remained and undoubtedly his capacity to act independently of his council continued to be fairly limited.

This partial restoration of some of the traditional dignity and authority of the Portreeve's office was probably due in part to the presence of the local vicar, John Morgan, amongst the ranks of the Kenfig Burgesses. Admitted in 1795 he held the office of Portreeve on three occasions between 1797 and his death in 1820. Morgan was hugely proud to be a member of such a venerable organisation, and so far as he was able sought to learn what he could about its past history. As their Vicar he would have been accorded enormous respect by his council on those occasions he served as their Portreeve, and would most likely have insisted upon a similar attitude towards the current holder of that office when he himself sat as a council member.

New Rules for Waun Cimla In 1807 the Corporation also laid down new rules relating to the sub-letting of plots of hay at Waun Cimla. For those wishing to rent or let their plots to others, the existing rules limited the amount that could be charged to no more that 3s 4d per acre and 4d per piece in respect of 'the lattermath' (later or second mowing). Now, however, "In consideration of the advanced rate of the rental of lands, and the present grievous burden of taxes on Land Holders" these rates were raised to five shillings and one shilling respectively.

Meanwhile the Corporation were still struggling to get the Burgesses to pay their rates, and its officers to perform their duties. In 1802 the Aletasters were reported for 'not performing their office' and two years later the Hayward was fined and dismissed from office for not being present at Court, whilst former Portreeve Thomas Thomas was reported for failure to pay the balance of his account into the Borough Treasury. In 1802 and again in 1805 they had to badger some Burgesses on several occasions before they paid their rates, and there seems to have been some form of altercation over the non-appearance of eight Burgesses at a manor court held in August 1804 when each was fined two shillings.

Such non-appearances were not unusual, and several of the better-off frequently chose to pay a fine rather than sit through the tedious business normally conducted at such sittings. On this occasion, however, the eight people concerned went a step further and deliberately refused payment. It seems also that they had some grounds for their intransigence, for when the matter was again debated at the Autumn Leet court their fines were reduced to sixpence (2½ p) each. With this they declared themselves satisfied and paid up on the spot. To the delight of the Recorder and those present, the newly appointed Portreeve, Richard Jenkins then "ordered the same to be drank in Ale immediately"!

The Rabbits – A Progress Report On the rabbit front all appeared to be going swimmingly. The permits granted to John Loveluck and Jenkin John were having the desired effect of keeping the number of conies on the common in check, and indeed on 3rd December 1802 the Corporation actually introduced a measure that seems to have been designed to prevent them being exterminated altogether! This introduced a 'closed season' between 3rd December and 25th March during which neither the Burgesses nor anyone else would be allowed to dig for rabbits on the common, with a hefty fine of forty shillings (£2) for anyone caught breaking this embargo.

The leases to the 'rabbitries' bordering the commercial warrens came up for renewal on 25th March 1803 and, satisfied with the manner in which the system was operating, both the lessees and the Corporation were happy for it to continue. A delay was however caused by the death of John Loveluck on 14th March whilst negotiations were still in progress, and new leases were not signed until 17th June with Ann Loveluck taking up her late husband's option. She was now also recognised as the tenant of the lands rented from the Margam estate, though in practice the day-to-day operation of Mawdlam Farm and the Warren was undertaken by her eldest son William.

The new rabbit leases were back-dated to 25th March, and were to run for five years with the Lovelucks paying a rent of £8 per year, and Jenkin John forty shillings (£2). Both were again renewed in 1808 and in September of that year the area covered by William Loveluck's permit was extended to include land in the vicinity of Twmpath Mawr* on the boundary with Sker Manor and adjacent to a commercial warren being operated there by the current tenant, Micah Williams. Loveluck was also given leave to cull rabbits in a "small circular spot of one hundred yards on the north, east and south sides of the remains of our old castle".

The scheme therefore seemed to be working well, and no doubt several Burgesses were congratulating themselves on turning what had been a persistent annoyance into an asset that now earned a steady income for the Borough coffers. Unfortunately none of them possessed a crystal ball enabling them to see into the future!

Financial Problems In the Borough Minutes for January 1817 (B/K ALE) comes the hint that recent improvements to The Corporation House had somewhat depleted the Borough Treasury with a decision taken by Portreeve and Council that they should borrow the sum of £25 at a 5% rate of interest. The reason was that they wished to use this sum to

---

* The exact location unknown, but was almost certainly the hillock known as Thorborough which had been a key boundary mark in the dispute with Jenkin Turberville of Sker in 1592.

repay an existing loan obtained from a Friendly Society at Mawdlam, and clearly did not have sufficient funds in their Treasury.

Friendly Societies were to become a common feature of life in the district during the years that followed, though this is the only mention I have come across of one existing at Mawdlam. Presumably it subsequently amalgamated with one of the larger Societies in neighbouring North Cornelly whose activities are regularly reported in *The Glamorgan Gazette* from 1866 onwards (Jones D, 1997).

These Societies were also known as Benefit Clubs, the members making regular contributions to its funds which were used to assist any member and their dependants who fell on hard times through injury, loss of employment or death. Perhaps this transaction actually marks the end of this particular Society at Mawdlam and the transfer of its members and assets to another branch.

A Salary for the Portreeve The financial difficulties in which the Borough now found itself seem to have been quite severe. At a Hall Day held on 1st October 1819 it was pointed out that the roof of the Town Hall (which was tiled) was in a bad state of repair, but the recommendation was that it be temporarily repaired with a reed thatch "until sufficient materials can be provided to make the same effectual". The implication is that funds to purchase new tiles were apparently wanting. A virtually identical entry appears in 1823 without any indication that the roof was subsequently repaired with tiles in either case. By September 1827 the Council was reporting that "the roof of the Corporation House, and more particularly the roofs of the cross houses, to be very ruinous and out of repair" declaring that "the same ought to be tiled as soon as possible".

It was perhaps in view of the current financial crisis that at the same Court a landmark decision was taken to henceforth pay their Portreeves a fixed salary of three guineas (£3.15p) at the end of their twelve-month term of office. Hitherto the Portreeve had paid into the Treasury the sum of £2 10s. 0d. (£2.50p) collected as the General Rate and kept the remainder.

Inflation had steadily eroded the real value of this fixed sum and the powers and responsibilities of the Borough's chief officer had likewise been reduced, so this practice was long overdue for an overhaul. As we have already noted the appointment of a Treasurer had already usurped the Portreeve's duty to present an annual account of the Borough finances, so the Corporation now formally recognised this fact. In future they decreed, income from the rates and other sources was to be paid direct to their Treasurer/Recorder, and it was he who would now pay the Borough Officers for their services and settle all lawful debts incurred by the Corporation.

Chapter 14

The Corporation House

The early 1800s were important ones in the history of 'The Corporation House' (the present-day inn, *The Prince of Wales*) which, being some two centuries old, was starting to show its age. I suspect indeed that the debts accrued by the Borough in the closing years of the previous century were largely due to urgent and extensive repair work required to the building and certainly the early decades of the new century saw a major refurbishment of both the town hall and the associated alehouse. With these changes there also came a change of name. Up to, and including, the year 1822 the licensed premises are usually referred to as 'The Corporation House' or sometimes as 'Ty Newydd'. Why the premises was known by both names I cannot say for certain but my guess would be that originally 'Ty Newydd' applied only to the alehouse and living accommodation whilst 'Corporation House' referred to the whole, or perhaps just the Town Hall. As is the way of such things however, with passage of time this fine distinction became blurred and by the 1800s both names were being applied indiscriminately. When the alehouse licence was renewed in the autumn of that year it was for premises "at the sign of *The Prince of Wales*". For the first time too, its rival at Mawdlam appears under the name by which we know it today - *The Angel Inn*; previously it had simply been known as *Ty yn Mawdlam* (The House in Mawdlam)

It is nevertheless likely that the new name 'Corporation House' had been bestowed upon it some years earlier. In 1822 the title 'Prince of Wales' was actually vacant, ever since the Prince Regent had ascended the throne as King George IV in 1820.

There was a rapid turnover of tenants acting as landlord of *The Prince of Wales* during the early years of the 1800s. (details are given in Part 4 of this series about *The People & Places of Kenfig*). While this was taking place, the premises themselves underwent extensive renovations. It will be recalled that at this time the building was 'U'- shaped, surrounding three sides of a courtyard facing northwards. Immediately in front of this was the junction of Heol y Lane with Heol Kenfig - the former still passing along the east side of the premises as it had done since it was first erected in the early 17th century. The major refurbishment that followed in the first decade of the new century was spread over a period of several years, and the actual details of what was taking place during that time are rather confusing. Not only are the details in the minute books rather sketchy, they are often contradictory and generally confusing for it seems the Burgesses chopped and changed their plans even whilst work was in progress.

In part the lack of information is because of a further alteration in the Borough administration made by the Corporation in October 1807. As we have previously noted, in 1794 the responsibility for accounting for the organisation's annual income and expenditure had been transferred from the Portreeve to the Recorder. This was now taken a stage further by the creation of a new office of Borough Treasurer, "to receive the rent and all other sums of money due to the Corporation, and also to pay Taxes and all other lawful demands on the same". To keep these accounts he was provided with a proper ledger, and for his services received an annual fee of ten shillings and sixpence (52½ p).

The council appointed Joseph Rees, the current Recorder, to fill this office, and in the main it seems that the two offices were normally held by the same person. The general idea seems to have been that, as occasionally happened whilst work was in progress on the Corporation House, their Recorder could opt out of this role and as Treasurer concentrate upon overseeing and financing some other activity. At the Autumn Leet of 1812 for example, when the renovations were drawing to a close, Thomas Porter of Caeau Gollen was appointed Recorder for the year ahead but Joseph is still referred to as the Treasurer during this period. In general, however, both offices were normally held by the same person.

Unfortunately the Treasurer's account book containing information regarding the improvements made to the Corporation House has not survived, so in charting the work we have to rely solely upon the sparse and rather confusing entries in the Borough minutes. Thankfully a rough sketch plan of the ground floor of the building was drawn in the minute book in 1810 to illustrate the set of current proposals, which seem in fact to be the ones that were ultimately adopted.

Prior to the alterations it seems that the ground floor beneath the Town Hall was divided into two large rooms that comprised the living quarters for the licensee, his family, and their live-in servants. The one at the western end would have been a living-room cum kitchen that probably incorporated sleeping accommodation for the servants. From this room a doorway gave access directly into the kitchen garden which occupied the area of the present car park. The other ground floor room was the sleeping accommodation for the licensee's family, the interior probably being divided up by curtains or partitions to provide a modicum of privacy.

To our eyes this appears a rather archaic and inconvenient arrangement, and indeed this was also the case in 1800, but when the Town Hall had been built two centuries earlier it was the normal practice as I discovered (Griffiths, 1990: 87) during my earlier project into the manors of Stormy and Horgrove. Here William Lewis who died in 1674 was tenant of one of the largest farms in Tythegston Higher, but details relating to his house contained in his will showed that it too consisted basically of two rooms – a ground-floor hall with a chamber above. Similar arrangements are likewise apparent in the surviving remains of other such 'long-houses' in Horgrove Manor at Ty Mawr (Haregrove Farm), Parcau Issa and Ty Isha (Griffiths, 1990: 112-3).

Whilst the need to modernise the living accommodation may have been an element in carrying out these improvements, what perhaps prompted them in the first place was an alteration made to the course of Heol y Lane at about this time. Instead of continuing along the eastern side of the building it was diverted to its present course through the licensee's kitchen garden and along the southern front of the building. Neither the date of this diversion, nor the reason it was considered necessary, is even hinted at in the Borough Minute Books. Maybe there had been problems with land-slips on the slope of the field bordering the lane alongside the Corporation House, or perhaps the Burgesses simply wanted to extend the east wing of the building in that direction as seems to be hinted at in alterations proposed in October 1808.

At this meeting Joseph Rees was authorised, as a matter of urgency, to make temporary repairs to the building. This involved work to the roof of the brew-house in the west wing and to a serious leak that had developed above the entrance to the Town Hall which in turn had apparently caused damage to "the joists and ceilings of the little parlour"(B/K 12) or bar in the east wing. Having taken steps to remedy these defects, Portreeve and Council then went on to consider improvements to the living accommodation provided for the licensee. To implement these they proposed moving the brew-house from its location in the west wing to "the present stable" – which was situated at the northern end of the east wing. The original brewhouse they then proposed to convert into "lodging rooms etc". In addition they decided to turn a loft over the 'little parlour' into another bedroom and to create an 'entry' which would provide convenient access. This last, presumably, would have involved the building of a stairway. As the old brew-house had apparently served as the cellar for the inn, it was additionally proposed "to make a slope house (a lean-to) in the back part of the house" to serve this purpose. Together with the need to provide a stairway in the eastern wing, this may have involved extending the building onto the adjoining Heol y Lane.

These proposals mark the start of a piecemeal development of the north side of the building apparent today where the eastern wing is noticeably wider than its western counterpart - possibly because it now incorporates the 'slope house' and the stair-well authorised in 1808. The reference to the "back part of the house" therefore perhaps relates at this time to the eastern wing adjoining Heol y Lane.

Certainly the Borough was faced with some problems at this time which seem to have stemmed from a re-orientation or proposed re-orientation of the building consequent upon the diversion of Heol y Lane. What had been the back-door from the hall of the licensee's living quarters into his kitchen garden now became the main entrance for patrons requiring access to the bar, and was perhaps the reason for the proposed removal of the original 'living room' to the former brew-house.

Upon consideration, however, this aspect of the alterations was not considered entirely satisfactory by the Corporation, and a fresh proposal was put before the council at a Hall Day held on 2nd June 1809. It envisaged the demolition of "the two cross-houses (the two projecting wings) in the back part of the Corporation House", and replacing them with "a double house parallel with the Town Hall (with a leaden gutter between them both, viz. on the middle wall)". This extension would then be fitted out with "bedrooms above stairs and cellar, etc below". A harassed Joseph Rees was instructed to obtain the necessary materials and employ workmen for the task, whilst the Corporation boldly committed itself to "find money to forward the work until it shall effectually [be] completed".

It did not take them long to realise however that such an ambitious scheme was well beyond their limited resources, and the following February they settled on the more modest adaptation of the existing premises outlined by the sketch plan drawn in the minute book. The two large rooms beneath the Town Hall were now divided into three, the one at the western end being the kitchen; the eastern one a second bar/parlour; and the middle room a bedroom. These rooms and the ones in the two 'cross-houses' were to be linked by a corridor running along the north side of the main building. A short corridor leading off this between bedroom and kitchen gave access to the new main entrance on the south side. Today this entire area is taken up by the public area of *The Prince* but the layout displayed in the 1810 sketch-plan is nevertheless still evident.

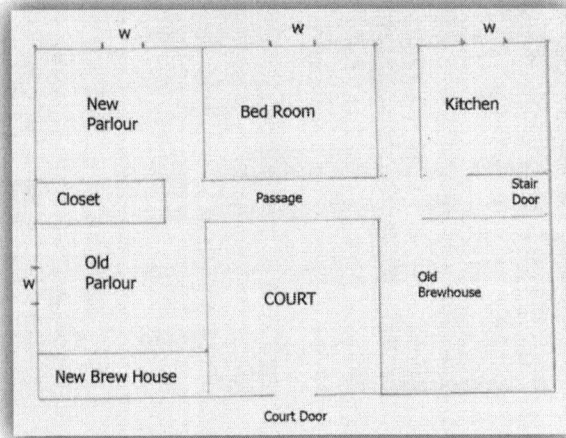

A PLAN OF THE GROUND FLOOR OF THE PRINCE OF WALES ILLUSTRATING PROPOSED ALTERATIONS IN 1810.

Mention is also made of the fact that work intended to create an additional bedroom in the loft above the 'old parlour' had been held up due to a delay in repairing the ceiling there, but would be completed as soon as this was done. The sketch-plan also indicates that at the western end of the main passageway there was a 'stair door'. This one assumes indicates that the earlier alterations to the former brew-house in the west wing had been completed creating a bedroom upstairs and a living room on the ground floor. Another point of interest is that the former 'lock-up' beneath the external stairs at the opposite end of the corridor had been converted into a closet or cupboard. Outside the building the former courtyard had been converted into an enclosed yard by building a wall and gate across the open side.

The Eight Elected Burgesses assigned responsibility for getting this work done to Joseph Rees and the Portreeve who, at this time, was the Rev John Morgan. The latter contributed virtually all the material relating to Kenfig included in the Carlisle 1811 *Directory of Wales*. In it he says that the Town Hall had been "lately erected" at a cost of about £400, and whilst the claim that it was entirely rebuilt is clearly erroneous, the cost involved was massive and caused the Borough to once more plunge into debt. Nor, would it appear, had the work here been completed by the time the book went into print.

TOWN HALL INTERIOR TODAY (LOOKING SEAWARD)

In November 1812 the Corporation authorised Joseph Rees to purchase sufficient pantiles to roof the new stable 'without delay' and agreed to pay Evan Jenkin (the current licensee) the sum of one pound compensation "on account of the stable not being finished according to agreement". Where this building actually stood I cannot ascertain, but most likely it was erected in the garden which was already in part occupied by the common pound for stray animals. At the same court the Corporation raised Joseph Rees's fee as Treasurer to one guinea (£1.05) presumably in recognition of his efforts in implementing these alterations over the previous four years. I get the feeling he had earned every penny of it!

As with previous tenants, Thomas's agreement stipulated that he was to keep all the windows of the property in good repair with the exception of those in the Town Hall itself. For damage to these he was only liable if they were broken "by the said Thomas Thomas or any of his family or servants, or occasioned through neglect or by means of amusement, dancing, or the like effect". The tenancy agreement signed

TOWN HALL INTERIOR TODAY (LOOKING INLAND)

by his predecessor Evan Jenkin (B/K ALE) in 1811, had also contained such a clause making him liable for damage caused "by dancing or any other unnecessary meetings of the like".

Mabsant Revels This is a timely reminder that whilst the primary function of the Town Hall was to house the manorial and Borough courts, it also served the people of Kenfig as a kind of community centre where they met socially for dances and other celebrations. Such events rarely if at all rate a mention in contemporary documents, but festivities at the Hall are known to have been an important element in the local Mabsant festival.

Marianne Spencer (1913) gives us a description of the local Mabsant revels which took place in November. They dated back to medieval times and were held to mark the festival of the patron saint of the local church – although when she wrote about the practice, it had sadly come to an end. This was probably the result of the upsurge of religious enthusiasm during the religious revival of 1904 when the playing of games, dancing and consumption of alcohol was condemned as sinful and depraved. The revels were, nevertheless, one suspects, quite mild compared with what passes for 'normal' weekend behaviour at nightclubs across the country today!

It is unlikely that Mrs Spencer ever participated in these revels herself, but she certainly visited Kenfig and spoke with people who had, and who remembered the old revels with considerable affection. Part of the celebration, she tells us, was a ball game played in the churchyard at Mawdlam where the "young men" of the community endeavoured to "throw a ball over the church tower or steeple". There was evidently rather more to it than this for Mrs Spencer adds that it was a game requiring "great skill and dexterity".

The highlight, however, was undoubtedly the Town Hall dance where she describes how the room was specially decorated for the occasion with flowers and greenery and then lit by candles "stuck with a dab of clay against the walls". Music was provided by a harper who arrived early in the afternoon and took his seat on the long table that still occupies the western end of the hall today. Although the serious dancing did not start until nightfall, amongst the young ladies of the locality it was accounted a great honour to be the one who actually opened the event by tripping the first set of the day with her partner. Mrs Spencer tells the tale of one ingenious young milkmaid – perhaps one of those from whom she obtained her information – who successfully achieved this distinction despite supposedly being at work at the time the harper struck the opening chords to begin the proceedings.

In those days cattle were actually milked in the fields, so at the time the dancing was due to start the young lady in question was actually trudging her way from the farm with milking stool and pail to carry out her duties. Once out of sight of her employer however, she ditched her equipment and ran to the Town Hall where, forewarned, her boyfriend was already waiting. Kicking off her heavy working shoes she danced the opening dance with him in her stockinged feet, then raced back to resume her work as though nothing had happened. Later that evening, dressed in her 'Sunday-best' she was back again at the hall enjoying the congratulations and plaudits of her friends for her piece of ingenuity.

The centre of the floor was kept clear for the dancers, but the walls were lined with benches where they could relax between dances - the girls in their voluminous frocks and dresses balancing precariously on their partners' knees. Children gawked through the open door at the top of the stairs as the dancers whirled and twirled across the floor in the flickering candle light, whilst ladies of an older generation sat knitting and nodding in time to the music, recalling the time when they too had vied for the honour of being first dancer at the festival. Then, as the dawn of a new day was breaking, and with the strains of the harper's final set still tinkling in the memory, everyone made their way home to snatch a few precious hours of sleep, and the Mabsant revels were over for another year.

The Hall Chest A wooden chest was kept by the Borough within the Town Hall to hold the Charters, documents and its Treasury. It was wooden, and as was the general pattern of such items it was probably very large and heavy to prevent removal. The lid was secured by three locks, each of which had a separate key. A brief mention in the minutes for the year 1816 shows that at this time these keys were held by three different Burgess who all had to be present for access to the coffer to be gained.

Mention was made of this fact at the time, because a Burgess named Howell Evan who lived on Heol y Lane, refused to surrender his key to the Portreeve when required. At the Hall Day on 30th January his fellow Burgesses gave him eight hours to comply or else be disenfranchised, and after this we hear no more of the matter. Of particular interest, however, is the statement that this key "Belongs to Heol Kenfig" confirming the existence of a custom. This was noted in Glamorgan Gazette, 20th August, 1869, when the Cambrian Archaeological Society visited Kenfig. The report of their visit describes how the Borough archives were "jealously kept by three aldermen of the borough" and housed in "a safe built into the wall" at the Town Hall which by then had replaced the ancient chest.

The writer then continues, "This safe has three locks, and the key to each of these locks is kept by three members of the corporation. To this day there are 3 streets in the borough of Kenfig called respectively Blue-Street [Heol Las], Water-street, and Kenfig-street [Heol Kenfig], and the rules of the corporation provides that each key must be kept by a resident in each of the above streets. These men are called the Aldermen of these streets. Mr Freeman said the like custom prevailed at Taunton in Somersetshire".

During the intervening years between the Censuses William was involved in an incident which saw him (not for the first time!) at odds with his neighbours – in this instance at a vestry held in the Angel Inn in 1843 to appoint Trustees for the charity lands in Kenfig. He was the Clerk for this body, and during the course of the meeting deeds and papers relating to the organisation were stolen from him. The entry in the Borough Minute Book is somewhat damaged by damp, but the 'thieves' were none other than two respectable farmers from the parish - David Jones of Tytanglwys and Evan Jones (alias John) of Pwllygath. They had taken this unusual step in order to demonstrate the scant security afforded these documents which included deeds and leases relating to the lands at Kenfig which the Charity owned. They declared that they had no intention of retaining the items, but would only restore them if the question of their security was properly addressed.

It seems that others too felt the same way, and accordingly it was settled "that a box should be made for the purpose of keeping the said wills, deeds, etc with [two separate?] locks & keys, and that one key is to be kept by the Churchwarden of Kenfig, & the other key is to be kept by the Churchwarden of Pyle; & that the box is to be kept within the iron chest which is fixed within the Town Hall, Kenfig, for ever"

Chapter 15

Alarms & Excursions

Alongside the refurbishment of their Town Hall, the visits of tourists and the excitement of the Bando matches on Kenfig sands, many other incidents punctuated the everyday lives of the Kenfig Burgesses during the early decades of the 19th century. Some were fairly mundane, others rather more notable, but all formed part of the fabric of the society in which they lived.

Who Shot at Rees Hopkin in 1803? In August of 1801 there occurs one of those annoyingly brief references to an incident in our area from the records of the Glamorgan Quarter Sessions. It arose from a serious incident involving Rees Hopkin who, whilst not a Kenfig Burgess, was someone we have met previously as the tenant of Ty Draw farm in South Cornelly who engaged in a long-running boundary dispute with Morgan and Owen Howell of Penymynydd.

Morgan Howell acquired the tenancy of Penymynydd from the Tythegston estate sometime prior to 1790 at which time he was still the tenant of Sker Farm. In this year he was reported at the manor court for failing to maintain a gate leading from his field known as Broomslon into another of the same name belonging to Rees. That was in April, and Morgan was given two weeks to do the work or else pay a fine of ten shillings (50p) (B/K 12). He apparently chose to ignore this for, at the October Leet he was again ordered to carry out the work by December or pay fifteen shillings.

This gate was apparently an element of "a passage or thorough-fare way thro' the lands of Rees Hopkin within the land of Morgan Howell" – an access route, the maintenance of which was clearly a bone of contention between the two, for in October 1791 Morgan was ordered by the manor court to fence it. By 1793 Owen had apparently taken up residence at the farm, and (the necessary fencing still not having been put in place) was ordered to carry out this work himself. This he apparently did, but clearly there was by now bad blood between the two farms and this culminated in Gwenllian the wife of Rees Hopkin suing Owen for defamation of character in 1797. The details are not recorded, but Owen totally ignored the first summons to appear before the Consistory Court at Llandaff, and then two subsequent ones with the result that he was served with a notice excommunicating him from the Anglican church (LL/CC/G 1510).

This did capture his attention! He may have had aspirations of one day becoming the Portreeve of Kenfig (though he never held the post despite frequent nominations) which would have been impossible whilst this sentence was in force. Within a few days he had capitulated and the notice had been withdrawn. Owen and his family, let it be said, were not the easiest of neighbours to live with, but the same is evidently true of Rees Hopkin and his family. In 1787 he had prosecuted Mary and Gwenllian John for stealing his barley, a case that was subsequently thrown out by the jury at the Court of Quarter Sessions (GQS MSS). He was frequently at odds with other neighbours over the maintenance of their joint boundaries, and in 1804 the Kenfig Corporation had to replace a mere stone in one of his fields that mysteriously vanished (B/K 12). The same thing happened again in 1823 (B/K ALE).

So who was it that shot at him in 1803? Surprisingly perhaps it was not Owen Howell or one of his family! The only details that can be gleaned from the Glamorgan Court files (GQS Gaol Dockets & GS/Wales 4 630/8) are that it was a yeoman named Rees Thomas "of ye Par[ish] of Pyle & Kenfig". This at least is sufficient to eliminate Rees Thomas of Kenfig, current head of the Rees/Thomas family, for had he been the culprit his place of residence would have been shown as the Borough of Kenfig. The Rees who stood trial for the alleged offence evidently lived outside the Borough, but other than this I have discovered nothing further about him. The wording of the charge describes him as "an ill-designing and disorderly person of a wicked and malicious disposition", and accuses him of using "a certain gun loaden with gunpowder and a leaden bullet" to shoot at Rees Hopkin.

He apparently missed, for there is no mention that Rees sustained any injury, but nevertheless this was a serious offence amounting to attempted murder, and Rees Thomas was on trial for his life. There were five witnesses for the prosecution besides Rees Hopkin, though with only their names to go on it is difficult to be certain of their identity. Although not Kenfig folk, Evan William and his wife Catherine were probably the parents of John William (1814-1853) a collier who lived on Heol Las in the 1840s. John William and his wife Mary could be the surveyor of that name living at Newlands Farm, but the names are common in the area at this time and Margaret Harry, the final witness, could be one of two people of this name with Kenfig connections, but again there is no certainty. Having heard their testimony the jury brought in a verdict of 'Guilty', and Thomas Rees was sentenced to be hung, though again there is no certainty that this was carried out as it may well have been commuted to one of transportation to the colonies.

This incident, and Owen's brief excommunication, seems to have had the effect of calming the feud between the two, though it was still liable to flare up from time to time. As already indicated Owen and his family were not the easiest of neighbours to have at the best of times! In 1804, for example, the manor court had found him guilty of 'adjusting' the boundary of one of his fields so as to encroach upon the land of an adjoining holding, then the following year he again found himself the target of complaints regarding the state of his boundaries emanating from Rees Hopkin. A ditch for which Owen was responsible adjoining "a certain garden belonging to Ty pen Heol Draw" was alleged to be out of repair and also a fence separating his field called *Caer Gikell* (Probably Cae'r Stickel–The Style Field), from one of Rees's called *Shislon*. The complaints were upheld and Owen given until 1st December to make the necessary repairs or else pay a fine of five shillings in respect of the first and ten shillings the second.

These complaints may have been in the nature of a 'pre-emptive strike' on the part of Rees, for it then emerged that he had made a gateway creating access between one of his fields and Heol y Broom through a fence and ditch that formed the boundary to part of Owen's property. This sounds as if it was part of the disputed access-way through Penymynydd Land that had caused friction between them previously. Rees in turn was given until Christmas to "remove his aid gate and shut up the gate way" or else be fined five shillings himself. With that, and with honours roughly even, the two had to be content though Owen failed to carry out his part of the work on time and had to be allowed a week's extension. With this evidence that the manorial court was not going to pull any punches, the feud once more died down.

At the next Autumn Leet (1806) Owen was once again in trouble over his boundaries, though on this occasion it was largely through the neglect by his tenant, Yorwerth Yorwerth of a boundary with the lands of Elizabeth the widow of William Thomas of Pool Farm. Both parties contended that responsibility for maintaining this boundary was not their responsibility, and the court took evidence concerning its history stretching back over more than forty years. In the end it found in favour of Owen and Yorwerth, ordering Elizabeth to carry out the necessary work herself.

Four years later his fellow Burgesses were bitterly complaining that Owen was "worrying the Burgesses' sheep on the common with dogs", a curious act on his part unless perhaps he was attempting to drive them away from the area of Kenfig Down nearest to his house and keep the grazing there for his own stock. Whatever the reason the Burgesses were not impressed. They sent their Sergeant to warn him that any repetition would incur a fine of 13s 4d on each occasion; being disenfranchised, and possibly civil court action for damages by the injured parties. We thereafter hear no more about the problem!

The Wreck of *The Perseverance*. Ships still regularly came to grief on the navigational hazards off Kenfig's shore though most remain unrecorded. A mast from one such vessel was recovered from Kenfig Sands in February 1808 (D/D Ma 51), though the only wreck known to have occurred during that year happened two months later at 3 am on the morning of Tuesday 5th April.

In a report in the *Cambrian* newspaper dated 9th April, 1808 this vessel was *The Perseverance* on passage from Cork to Bristol with over sixty passengers aboard and a mixed cargo which included butter, soap, provisions, wine and whiskey. Whether due to bad weather or faulty navigation the vessel hit a sand bar off the beach at Kenfig and became a total wreck. Happily all passengers and crew were saved, but as usual a large crowd gathered to view the spectacle, and no doubt help themselves to whatever they could. On this occasion however a detachment of cavalry from Swansea and a party of Sea Fencibles [naval militia] were quickly on the scene and very little looting actually took place.

Certain individuals nevertheless managed to get their hands on some of the whiskey, and drank to such excess that several were taken seriously ill and two subsequently died. Again it is worth noting that no burials are recorded in the registers of the parish during this month, so whoever these people were they were probably not local.

The newspaper report mentions that local 'gentlemen' subsequently provided carts to help remove the contents of the ship to safety in what seems to have been something of a race against time as by the 8th April the vessel had broken up. An entry in the Margam Accounts dated 10th June of that year (D/D Ma 52) records that one of the estate wagons had been used for three days assisting at a wreck on "Margam Sands" and that the sum of three guineas had been received by way of payment.

An Unwelcome Yuletide Gift! At the Autumn Leet of 1813 the Burgesses noted that Lord Vernon of Briton Ferry had passed away, though they were at this time ignorant about who would inherit his Paschal Hill and Freehold lands within the lower Borough. As Lord of the manor of Briton Ferry it will be recalled that he was also the owner of Llanmihangel and Marlas Farms, the latter being the home of the spinster Mary Jenkins who was now about 63 years of age.

The news of the passing of her landlord probably did not concern her overmuch for her tenancy of the house and its land was assured for the remainder of her natural life by the lease taken out upon it by her late father. All this changed dramatically however when, shortly after Christmas she received a printed letter(PM6418), actually despatched from London on Christmas Eve, by Alex Mourray, one of the Trustees of Lord Vernon's estate. This informed her that following a recent ruling at the King's Bench Divisional Court in the case of *Cox vs. Day*, her lease, along with many others in the estate, had been declared null and void. The letter asked her to forward them certain particulars concerning the agreement she currently held and without prejudice to any legal action she herself might decide to take to challenge the decision.

As regards her chances of success by taking such legal action through the courts the letter was, however very downbeat and concluded rather menacingly, "if you, or any of the other Lessees under similar Leases, be advised to submit the Question to legal adjudication, Proceedings for that purpose will be instituted against such Lesees, so that the same may be decided at the next Assize". What effect such a letter had upon an elderly spinster like Miss Jenkins can well be imagined, and the fact that it survives in the Margam Archive collection shows that she evidently turned to her kinsman Griffith Llewelyn and his employer Thomas Mansel Talbot for help and advice. Without knowing anything about the legal niceties of this case other than what is stated in the letter, it nevertheless seems to me that she actually had good grounds for opposing it.

The Vernon leases had been declared defective on the grounds that they were "incompatible with the powers vested in his lordship by the Marriage Settlement" when he wed Lady Louisa Barbara Mansel of Briton Ferry the only child of Bussy Mansel. This appears to imply therefore, that the court ruling related only to leases issued by Lord Vernon following this marriage, and this is indeed confirmed elsewhere in the letter. Mary's lease had been taken out by her father Richard from Lady Louisa personally in 1754 and prior to her marriage. On the face of it therefore it was not one to which the ruling of the King's Bench applied.

This case concerning the Vernon leases had in fact been prompted by political considerations. Holders of such leases were entitled to vote at General Elections, and would obviously have voted in accordance with the wishes of their current landlord. At a stroke therefore the court ruling had wiped them from the electoral register. In the event some did indeed fight to overturn the verdict through the courts, though it proved to be a long and arduous battle.

Initially it seems that in a fresh action before the King's Bench they overturned the original ruling, but this in turn was then overruled by the Court of Exchequer as Lewis Weston Dillwyn (1963: 32) noted in his diary on 24th May, 1819.

> This morning the distressing news arrived that the Court of Exchequer by a majority of 4 Judges against 3 have reversed the Judgement of the King's Bench and decided that the leases on Lord Jersey's Estate are bad. It is an infamous proceeding, and I would not have his Lordship's conscience for all his riches. The Black lettered Noodles of the Exchequer will however be appealed against to the House of Lords.

The appeal was heard by the Law Lords in May, 1821, and to everyone's relief the validity of the Vernon leases were finally confirmed.

Assault upon Joseph & Elizabeth Rees Perhaps when I eventually delve more fully into the records of the Glamorgan Court of Quarter Session I will discover the story behind a brief item in the Cambrian Newspaper of 21st February, 1818, though given that these records are often fragmentary and incomplete, maybe it will still remain a mystery. The newspaper report is very brief and merely records that the Rev Knight (of Tythegston Estate) in his capacity as a Justice of the Peace for the County, had directed that the sum of two guineas imposed upon "Evan Jones of Kenfig, blacksmith" for an assault upon Joseph Rees and his wife Elizabeth, be paid to the Treasurer of Swansea Infirmary.

Joseph, through his activities with the Kenfig Corporation, has frequently figured in this history, but Evan is something of an enigma. I assume him to be a man named **Evan John** who nevertheless frequently used the surname 'Jones' in contemporary records, and who first appears in local records in 1807 when he is shown for the rent of £1 for a cottage and garden belonging to the Margam Estate in Higher Kenfig. This was one of the cottages on Water Street adjoining Pont Felin Newydd, and on the face of it there appears to have been no good reason why he and Joseph should have had such a violent altercation. Evan John was not even a Burgess at this time, but is probably the person of this name from Higher Kenfig recorded as being admitted in 1824.

A General Election. In 1818 the Burgesses received formal notice that an election was to be held at Cardiff on 22nd June for an MP to represent the Glamorgan Boroughs. Since 1790 the seat had been held by members of the Stuart family of Cardiff Castle – the Marquises of Bute – and previously by the Mackworths of The Gnoll, Neath. All represented the Tory Party, and had been appointed without the need of a formal election. In fact, there had not been a contest for this office since 1734 (Grant, 1988: 234), so the announcement caused no small stir amongst the Kenfig Burgesses, and they took the unusual step of recording the result in their minute book.

During the initial stages of the contest Lewis Weston Dillwyn of Penllergaer had thrown his hat into the ring as a possible contender for the Whigs, and on 10th June apparently met with the Burgesses at Pyle Inn in an attempt to secure their support (Dillwyn, 1998: 24). Unfortunately, as he noted in his diary, "Kenfig owing to the unlucky pre-engagement of the Margam interest was obliged to be against me, but the hearts of all the Burgesses appeared strongly in my favour and they will none vote against me unless absolutely driven which is not likely."

In the event a Frederick Wood secured the Whig nomination, but was unable to prevent the election of Lord Patrick James Herbert Crichton-Stuart of Cardiff Castle. The contest also seems to have prompted the Margam estate to bolster its own political clout by financing the admission of a considerable number of Kenfig out-Burgesses in the months that followed. On 18th October twenty individuals (only four of whom lived within the Borough) were nominated and subsequently admitted, to be followed by the nomination and approval of no less than forty (all out-dwellers) at a Court Leet just five days later.

Suicide at Upper Kenfig Farm. Since the inquest on the still-born child found at Marlas House in 1775 no record of the Portreeve's role as Coroner for the Borough subsequently appears in the Borough Minute Books until 1818. From this time onward some note, usually very brief, was made of all such courts in these records. The first relates to the death of a man named William Thomas which had occurred "at the dwelling house of William Williams" that can only be the farm on Water Street known as Kenfig House Farm or sometimes as Upper Kenfig Farm (In order to avoid confusion with Kenfig House Farm in Kenfig Lower I have generally adopted the practice of referring to this farm by the latter name.).

By a strange coincidence William Williams was also the current Portreeve but nevertheless presided over the court in his capacity as the Coroner, and if there was any connection between him and Thomas, none is mentioned in the record. The Inquest was held at the farm where the Jury viewed the body of the deceased and heard the testimony of the witnesses.

This evidence showed that on the night of 22nd /23rd August Thomas, "not being of sound mind, memory and understanding, but insane" went to an outhouse at the farm and hanged himself with a rope he had fastened to one of the beams. The Jury returned a verdict of suicide with a rider (normally added in such circumstances) that he had done so whilst of unsound mind. Such a proviso enabled the next-of-kin to have the body interred in consecrated ground from which suicides were traditionally excluded.

Who, or what William Thomas was I have no knowledge but the fact that William Williams sat as the Coroner suggests that he was not one of his employees. The record is also of interest in showing that the Higher Kenfig element of the Borough was included within the Portreeve / Coroner's area of authority. Being located in different Parishes the two elements of the Borough were otherwise usually considered as separate entities for local government and administrative purposes.

Chapter 16

Surveys and Inspections

Kenfig in 1814 In 1814 the Margam estate undertook a massive and comprehensive survey of the lands over which it held sway. Maps were drawn to indicate their location and size, each accompanied by a written key listing every house and field depicted; the area it covered; and its value. It is the earliest detailed depiction of Kenfig Borough of which I am aware, and as such has often been a key element in my research. At the same time (at least where Kenfig Lower is concerned) the maps are in one respect as interesting for what they omit as for what they actually show.

In Higher Kenfig, with the exception of Llanmihangel farm (still part of the Briton Ferry estate), every square inch of land was owned by the Talbots, so this survey is of huge assistance to the local historian as this manor is not covered by the Tithe survey of 1846. The monks of Margam Abbey, to whom the land originally belonged, had been exempted from paying church tithes by Papal decree, a privilege that was inherited by the Mansels and Talbots as their successors. In Kenfig Lower, however, Margam was merely the largest landowner, and here the survey is rather more patchy. Marlas belonged to Briton Ferry; Penymynydd to Tythegston; and the former land of Ty'n y Towyn Farm to Rees Daniel, so none of these are shown. There were also other smaller freeholders like the Price family, the Bennets, Lewis Leyson whose land and houses are likewise not depicted.

The net result is that most of the houses and cottages in the Manor of Kenfig Borough are not shown on this survey map even though many of the occupants owed a (purely nominal) freehold rent to the Talbot family. Nevertheless, there is still much that can be learned from the document. It shows, for example, that at this time the area covered by the Margam rabbit warren in the dunes extended well inland from the coast to a point beyond the eastern shore of Kenfig Pool and was physically marked with boundary posts set at regular intervals. In all it was estimated to contain 1,042 acres let to William

Loveluck who, rather more surprisingly, is also listed as the tenant of Kenfig Pool. What, exactly, were his rights and responsibilities in connection with the lake I have yet to discover, but certainly the Talbots continued to use it for their own pleasure purposes and the cost of repairs to the boat and the boathouse continue as a regular feature in the estate accounts.

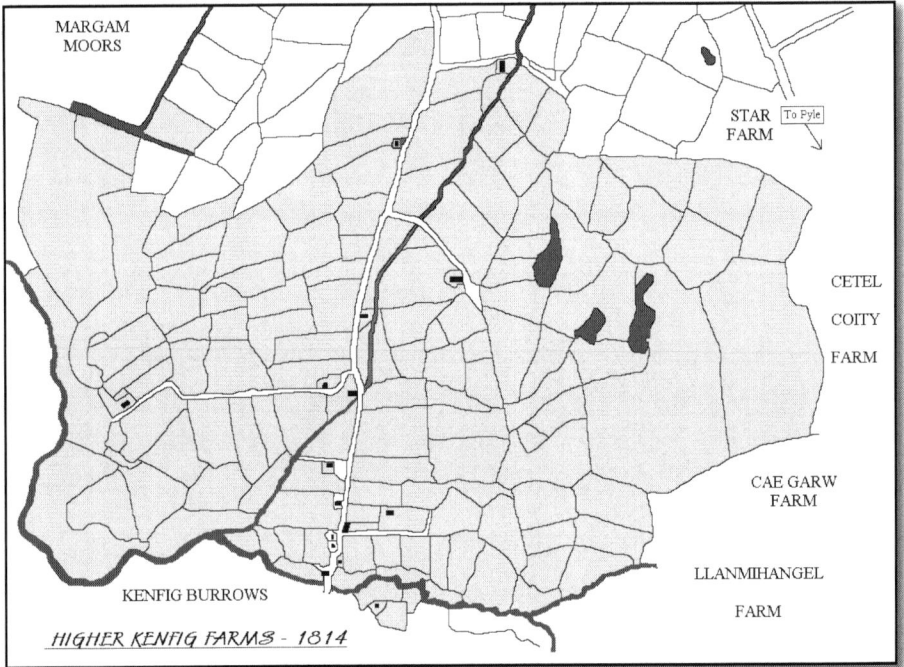

MARGAM MOORS

STAR FARM — To Pyle

CETEL

COITY

FARM

CAE GARW FARM

LLANMIHANGEL FARM

KENFIG BURROWS

HIGHER KENFIG FARMS - 1814

In his account of Kenfig that he provided for Nicholas Carlyle, the Reverend John Morgan mentions that he had seen a document kept at Margam House that is evidently Thomas Wyseman's report of 1592 on the boundary dispute with Sker. The archives of the Margam estate contain many thousands of documents, and it is probably significant that this particular one was so readily to hand. Others often vanished in this mountain of paperwork without trace – like Thomas Wyseman's other report relating to the Burgesses' enclosure of the common at Waun Cimla in 1572. It is interesting to speculate therefore that maybe it was the discovery of this document that had led to Thomas Talbot's assertion of his exclusive rights to the fishing at Kenfig Pool. Perhaps too it had enabled him to push the recognised boundary of the warren so far inland for, as Wyseman's research indicated, the western limit of the common called Kenfig Down was defined as the area known as 'the burrows' adjoining the coast. In 1814 the dunes reached as far as the Kenfig – Nottage road and beyond.

Margam Land in Kenfig Lower 1814 The bulk of Margam's enclosed land in Kenfig Lower was in the hands of just three tenants – Elizabeth, widow of William Thomas of Pool Farm with just under 97 acres; Joseph Rees of Kenfig House, 64 acres; and John Rees of Kenfig Farm 48acres. The next largest tenant after him was William Loveluck of Mawdlam Farm with just 21.

Because the farms of Kenfig Lower were comprised, to a lesser or greater extent, of freehold land and holdings belonging to other estates as well as that belonging to Margam, the 1814 survey is of little assistance in determining the actual size of farms here, but the figures for the farms of Higher Kenfig are as follows.

HIGHER KENFIG FARMS – ACREAGE IN 1814

Name of Farm	Size in Acres
Llanmihangel	268
Upper Kenfig (Kenfig House) Farm	200
Ty'n Cellar Farm	148
Newlands Farm	112
Farm Fach	51
Pwll y Hwyadd	36
Morva Bach Isha	45
Ty Du	33
Caeau Gollen	17
New Mill	12

What the survey does show is that in general the Margam land in Kenfig Lower is not of such good quality as that of its neighbour. In Higher Kenfig land valued at thirty shillings an acre and above is not uncommon, but in Kenfig Lower there are no fields that exceed this figure.

Thomas Talbot's Promise Thomas Mansel Talbot, who has figured frequently in our story of Kenfig over the past half-century passed away in 1813, an event that must have caused more than normal consternation in the Loveluck household at Mawdlam Farm. It will be recalled that the farmhouse and outbuildings had been created by John Loveluck out of two derelict cottages belonging to Margam and held on lease by Mary Evan of The Angel Inn. This work had been at his own expense on a verbal promise from Talbot that when Mary died the tenancy would pass to him and that this would be consolidated with his other Margam holdings into a single lease. Unfortunately John died in 1803 and Mary complicated the situation by living for four years longer.

John's widow Ann, and his eldest son William, continued to improve the new farmhouse and outbuildings after his death, but in the years following Mary's death in 1807, when the verbal agreement was due to have taken effect, there was no word from Thomas Lord Mansel. One might reasonably ask why William or his mother did not approach his Lordship over the matter themselves, but this is just another example of the enormous social gulf that lay between them two centuries ago. His Lordship might take exception at being approached regarding his failure to keep his promise, construing it to be a slur upon his honour – and the nobility tended to be extremely touchy about what they construed to be their honour in those days!

William may indeed have attempted to enlist the support of Griffith Llewelyn the Margam Agent, with whom he would have had some contact through the Borough organisation. but if so then he apparently achieved little success. Towards the end of his life Thomas Talbot, although he remained mentally alert, suffered from fits and was inclined to be hot tempered (Martin, 1993: 43), so it must have seemed to William that the family's chances of getting the ailing Thomas Talbot to honour his promise had gone.

It was nevertheless probably Griffith Llewelyn who suggested to Loveluck that with Thomas Mansel Talbot dead and buried it might be worth his while making a formal petition to the Trustees administering the Margam estate on behalf of Thomas's son and successor Christopher Rice Mansel Talbot. This William duly did in the form of a letter dated 30th May, 1815 (PM 8668). Attached to this document in the Margam archives are several others that Llewelyn had apparently rooted out from the archives and appended to it for the information of the Trustees. Amongst them is a note penned by Thomas Talbot himself about the time of John Loveluck's death in 1803.

Llewelyn, it seems had indeed approached Talbot on Ann and William's behalf at that time, and reminded Talbot of his promise to his former gamekeeper. Although Thomas's handwriting is pretty awful, it is clear from the note that he recalled his agreement with John, though was a little vague about the details. He had perhaps forgotten that the implementation of his promise depended on the death, not of John himself, but of Mary Evan, and was confused as to the course of action proposed by Llewelyn and why a lease to the Lovelucks had not already been drafted. "Be it as it may, I think my offer of letting the widow have the [tenancy?] on the same terms poor John had, should have been drafted", he wrote, directing his agent to "make everything known to the family."

Armed with this note and details of the current Loveluck tenancies, it seems Llewelyn was able to secure a lease for William from the Trustees currently administering the Margam estate on behalf of young C.R.M. Talbot. Even though John Loveluck and Thomas Talbot were now in their graves, the promise made between them some sixteen years earlier was duly honoured.

A Natural History Note. The dunes at Kenfig must at this time have abounded in wildlife, particularly in and around the Pool, but a bird that got caught in a gin-trap set by William Loveluck in January 1816 was a sufficiently exotic arrival to rate a brief mention in the Cambrian Newspaper. This was a golden eagle with a wingspan of just over seven feet. The breed is now extinct in Wales.

Government Inspections In 1830 the clamour for electoral reform reached a climax with the introduction of the First Reform Bill which was approved by the House of Commons but rejected by the House of Lords. During the next two years agitation in the country reached such a crescendo that many feared it would erupt into civil war but, through various shifts and manoeuvres, sanity and common sense finally prevailed and the Reform Act of 1832 became law. The worst of the old 'rotten' Boroughs were eradicated, and the right to vote determined by virtue of a person's annual income. Ironically this meant that in future those Kenfig Burgesses admitted from the lower end of society such as the labourers and craftsmen would be denied the franchise since their income fell well below the stipulated amount.

Kenfig nevertheless survived the cull of rotten and decayed boroughs, and featured in the reports of two Parliamentary commissions held about this time. The first Report from Commissioners (1832: 121-2) published in the year the Bill became law reported on the *Proposed Division of Counties and Boundaries of Boroughs* whilst the second Report (1834: 269-70) followed a year later and was concerned specifically with the organisation of existing municipal corporations. A Commissioner for each enquiry visited the Borough in person and their reports paint an interesting picture of the Kenfig they saw.

The commissioner who visited in 1832 was a Mr W Wylde with whom the Burgesses seem to have established a good rapport. Kenfig he describes in terms that have become familiar to us from those who had visited here during the previous half century - "a straggling village lying on the edge of the sand hills bordering the eastern shore of the Bay of Swansea". He noted that for the purpose of Parliamentary elections it was combined with the other six Glamorgan Boroughs to return an MP to Parliament and that under the aborted Reform Bill of 1830 would have been combined with Swansea, Aberavon, Lougher and Neath to vote in an MP for these Boroughs only.

Already we have seen how, with Parliamentary Reform in the offing, the Margam estate had made an all-out effort in 1824 to boost the number of out-Burgesses it controlled within Kenfig by sponsoring the admission of 72 new Burgesses. At the time of Mr Wylde's visit there were in all 270 Burgesses which was probably the highest total in its history, though of these only 57 were in-dwellers. The Commissioner nevertheless noted that only 158 Burgesses had actually turned out to vote at the 1831 election.

Quoting from the 1831 Census Wylde states that the total population of the Borough amounted to 485 of who 276 lived in Kenfig Lower. In the latter there were 58 inhabited houses (a rise of nine since the Census of 1821), but he was unable to give comparable figures for Higher Kenfig as for the purposes of these returns it was included in the totals for the parish of Margam.

The principal purpose of the commissioner's visit was to report on the Borough's boundaries, and in this connection a proposal had apparently been put forward that it might be beneficial to enlarge the Borough by including the neighbouring village of Pyle. Given that the long-standing antipathy between the two communities was still very much alive we can well imagine that this was an idea that did not sit too well with the Burgesses and no doubt they took the opportunity to press their objections at the meeting with the Commissioner. What the inhabitants of Pyle felt about this proposed merger we cannot say, for Mr Wylde appears to have chosen not to consult with them, and any arguments they may have offered for or against such a merger were therefore lost by default.

Nearly a century and a half after the visit of Thomas Wyseman the question of the Borough's ancient boundaries was one with which the Burgesses were evidently still very uncomfortable! They told Wilde that they possessed three ancient charters, but apparently only produced the one from Isabel Countess of Worcester, for his inspection. This, as he noted, did not give any details of the boundary whatsoever, and the Burgesses seem to have held back the one by Thomas le Despenser dating from 1397 (which did)! In default they trotted out the manorial survey from 1661 which set out the limits of the enlarged boundaries current in their day.

Perambulating the boundaries – also known as 'beating the bounds' - was a task undertaken at fairly regular intervals to ensure that all boundary marks were in place and also to familiarise them in the minds of the younger generation – traditionally by giving them a caning to ensure that the name and location remained imprinted on the memory! The last perambulation of these, they told him, had taken place about six years earlier, and confirmed that "No part of the boundary is doubtful or disputed".

With this Wylde seems to have been content and in connection with any proposed amalgamation with Pyle noted that the two communities were currently in effect "two hamlets of one Parish .. though they have separate churches". With Pyle's population totalling 475 in the recent Census, he continued, "the two, taken together, would form but a small Parish" - both being entirely agricultural with "no manufactory or even coal working existing in either". In terms of population he conceded this might give Kenfig "rather more weight amongst the Boroughs with which it is associated" but, he added, "nothing can give it any community of interest with them, Kenfig being purely agricultural, whilst all the others are more or less commercial or manufacturing". The boundary of the Borough of Kenfig, Wylde concluded, should therefore remain as it was.

From the Burgesses' point of view his visit had therefore been a success. The thorny question of their 'ancient boundaries' had been avoided, and the dreaded prospect of amalgamation with their arch-rivals at Pyle successfully scuppered.

Wylde for his part seems to have experienced no difficulties in his dealings with the Burgesses, and to have been favourably impressed by the current Portreeve, Joseph Rees, whom he describes as "an intelligent farmer". This is in marked contrast to the report submitted by James Booth for the Commissioners on Municipal Corporations compiled on 30th December 1833. He describes the Burgesses he met with as "being of the class of farmers, little conversant with business, and imperfectly acquainted with the English language". His comment on their business acumen is probably an accurate assessment, but his claim regarding their command of English seems to have rather a hollow ring. Welsh was undoubtedly the first language of the community at this time, but Joseph Rees, his brother Rees, William Loveluck, and Thomas Thomas were all Burgesses who had held the office of Recorder, and kept the minute book record in quite good English. To these we may also add Jehosaphat Powell of Llanmihangel Mill who was the Portreeve at this time and who subsequently drew up a petition – in good English – protesting against the operation of the Turnpike system in the locality.

Significantly the enquiry made by James Booth in December 1833 seems to have been far more detailed than that of his predecessor, and his comment about the Burgesses' imperfect English is made in connection with their answers to questions he put to them about the Borough organisation. Obtaining such details was the main purpose of his visit, but the Kenfig Burgesses were, as we know invariably highly suspicious of strangers asking questions of this sort! Wylde had merely been looking at the question of extending their boundaries, and not even bothered to properly inspect their ancient charters. Booth probed far deeper, and required the production of all the charters in their possession including the one by Thomas le Despenser, "the date of which I could not decipher". Having done so, however, he then dismissed them all as mere curiosities since "none of these charters are ever referred to, or regarded in practice".

James Booth and the Burgesses, it seems, took an instant dislike to each other with the latter adopting a 'no speeka da Eenglish' routine to avoid questions they did not wish to answer. Certainly some of the information the Commissioner subsequently included in his report appears to be incorrect when set against information contained in the Borough Minute Books. Nevertheless his remarks do shed some additional light on the duties of the Officers of the Borough not mentioned in other sources.

Starting with the **Constable of the Castle** he noted that this official was appointed by the Lord of the Manor; was responsible for the appointment of the Portreeve and other officers but otherwise played no part in the affairs of the Borough. The candidates for the office of **Portreeve** he tells us were selected by the **Aldermen** who were all Burgesses that had previously held the office but that the latter otherwise fulfilled no useful function. Of the Portreeve's duties he says that he appointed the "overseers of the poor and surveyors of the highways, and grants certificates of eligibility to keep public-houses, for which duties he received an annual salary of three guineas. No mention whatsoever is made of his role as the Coroner and a local magistrate, but there is the interesting statement that he conducted "monthly courts for the transaction of the ordinary business of the borough".

This is clearly a reference to the monthly Courts Baron which were still being religiously entered by the Recorder in the minute books. Nominally these, and the two Courts Leet, were of course held to transact business specifically relating to the Manor of Kenfig Borough, but for some time now the records show that virtually no manorial business was actually being transacted.

During the 18th century we noted how, because these Courts Baron were presided over by the Portreeve, it became increasingly common for routine Borough matters such as the transfer of parcels of hay and fern to be dealt with during the course of the sittings. Booth's report therefore confirms what had long been apparent in the Borough minute book - that by this time the purely manorial element of Courts Baron had ceased to exist and that the sessions had become 'Hall Days' in all but name. The jury that presided now invariably consisted of the 'Eight Elected Burgesses' who were the Town Council, and where specific Hall Days are held, they seem to have dealt only with urgent business that could not wait until the next Court Baron. Similarly the only business routinely conducted at the two annual Courts Leet presided over by the Constable of the Castle was the appointment of Borough Officers at the Autumn sitting. In practice therefore the ancient manorial courts now existed in name only.

Turning to the office of **Recorder**, Booth tells us that he was appointed by the Portreeve, and confirms that it was effectively combined with the office of Borough Treasurer. The holder therefore received two salaries of one guinea per annum for each, and in addition a fee of 7 shillings on the admission of each new Burgess. Booth also noted that Joseph Rees (the current holder of the office) had occupied the post for roughly four years out of every five since the death of his father in 1799, and that the latter had held it in similar fashion prior to this.

Of the **Sergeant at Mace** the report claims that his only duty was "to attend upon the Portreeve", implying that his role was largely a ceremonial one. No mention is made of his organising the collection of rates and taxes as had been the case in the previous century but it is difficult to believe that such duties had ceased entirely. The collection of national revenues may by now have been achieved by other means, but the Sergeant may well have still been responsible for purely local collections such as the Poor Rate and the Borough Rate. Booth reports that he received no salary, but was paid sixpence on the admission of every new Burgess.

His 'job description' for the **Hayward** and the **Aletasters** also seems to imply that their responsibilities had been considerably reduced in recent years. There is no mention of the latter being used to collect the Borough rates, the report describing their office as "little more than nominal". In the case of the Hayward Booth certainly seems to have sold his duties short, stating that he was only responsible for the seizure of stray livestock. This completely ignores his role in enforcing the rules and customs relating to the common land with which, as the minute books show, he was still actively engaged at this time. The continuing importance of this role was recognised by the fact that he was in receipt of an annual salary of £1. 5s. 0d whilst the Aletasters received nothing.

I suspect that in fact Booth, struggling to obtain any coherent response to his questions from the Burgesses, simply assumed that the seizure of strays was the Hayward's only responsibility because this was normally the sole duty of other such officers appointed at manors elsewhere throughout the country. This seems to be borne out by the fact that he makes no mention whatsoever of the office of Petty

Constable, and in fact states elsewhere in his report that "there is no local police and no gaol".

Although the former lock-up in the Corporation House had indeed ceased to exist, Kenfig's Petty Constable was certainly still active. Normally, however, these officers were appointed at Parish level but as was noted in the very first part of this history it is a curiosity of the district that had formerly been the Lordship of Margam that its constables were appointed at manorial (or in Kenfig's case – borough) level. It seems therefore that because of the truculent attitude of Burgesses, and the alleged difficulty in communicating with them, Booth simply assumed that the roles of Hayward and Petty Constable were the same as he had encountered elsewhere.

His report's description of the Borough commons is nevertheless accurate as is that of the system employed for allocating the 29 plots of hay at Waun Cimla which he says was valued as being worth about £15 per annum. The area of common land suitable for pasturing livestock was, he was told, about two to three hundred acres, though "the remaining waste lands were stated to be of still greater extent, [but] are covered with sand, and of no value".

Since Wylde's report the 1832 Reform Act had come into force and as originally intended Kenfig was now combined with Swansea and the three other West Glamorgan Boroughs to return an MP of their own. The practice of admitting out-Burgesses purely for the purpose of voting at elections had been terminated, and already the number that remained of those that still survived (having been admitted prior to the Act) had fallen dramatically to 123. The number of current in-dwellers is given as 51. The apparent reduction of this figure from the 57 Burgesses quoted by Wylde just 12 months previously may well be due to the fact that he included 'female Burgesses' whilst Booth eliminated these from his total.

Another curious anomaly about this report is that despite stating at the outset that the boundaries of the borough were "correctly described in the map which accompanies the Boundary Report for Kenfig", Booth seems to have been unaware that Higher Kenfig formed a part of it and lay within the Parish of Margam! Consequently the statistics he quotes regarding population etc. relate only to Kenfig Lower giving the impression that the Borough was actually more sparsely populated than was actually the case.

Cash received for pasturing cattle on one of their commons, producing about	£10. 0. 0
The rent of a public-house and gardens, let at rack-rent	£6. 0. 0
Rent of four small tenements engaged to be let on long building leases, producing togeth.......	£4.16. 0
Rent for a piece of hay ground on Kimla	£0. 6. 8
A payment, called a rent, of 1s 6d by each of the Burgesses holding a plot in Wayn Kimla, producing annually about	£2. 2. 0
A similar payment of 1s 5d from each of the other resident Burgesses, producing about ...	£1.15. 0
Total Revenue about	**£24.19. 8**

Perhaps the most interesting item in the entire report however is a summary of the sources from which the Borough derived its income: Presumably the sum of £10 paid for pasturing cattle relates to the common at Cefn Cribwr, though I have not noticed any references to such in the Minute Books. The four building plots mentioned were also situated on land here, and payments under this heading were set to increase over the coming years as the development of the community that was to become Kenfig Hill progressed further. The payment of 6s 8d for the plot of hay at Waun Cimla was of course merely an annual instalment on the sum of £2 due from a Burgess who had recently been admitted as the holder, and would have ceased once the whole amount had been paid. It is also interesting that those Burgesses holding plots at Waun Cimla also apparently paid enhanced annual rates (here called 'a rent') which is again something not alluded to elsewhere in any of the Borough records I have examined to date.

Summarising the Corporation's annual expenditure Booth lists the payment of the salaries of the officers; rates, taxes and "small incidental expenses"; the repair and upkeep of the Town Hall; and "the purchase of ale at their meetings for business".

This last remark and the general tenor of his report suggests that James Booth was not very impressed by Kenfig, but even allowing for such prejudice it is clear that the organisation was in decay and fast becoming irrelevant in the new age that was dawning. The Reform Act and the reports submitted by Wylde and Booth may have allowed it to continue unchanged as an organisation, but its days were now clearly numbered.

Chapter 17

Kenfig's Hill

The story of Kenfig Hill has yet to be written, and since it lies beyond the boundaries of Kenfig Borough it is a subject that is also outside my own terms of reference for this history. Nevertheless the origins of the village are closely bound up with the fortunes of the Borough and cannot therefore be entirely ignored. So, and without delving too deeply into the subject, this chapter is devoted to the birth of this new community as chronicled in the Borough's records. Hopefully it will one day prove a useful starting point for some future local historian seeking to tell its story.

The land known to the Burgesses as 'The Rugge' has been mentioned on numerous occasions since it first appears in Thomas le Despenser's charter of 1397. By that document he gave them certain limited rights to use it as a common upon which to graze livestock. Except for a small portion in the south-western corner bordering the land of Pwllygath Farm it lay within the parish of Tythegston Higher, bounded by Nant Craig yr Aber stream on the north and the road from Cefn Cribwr to Pyle on the south. To the east the boundary was marked by a bank and ditch which Neville Granville (1980:39) believes extended northwards from Bwlch Cottages opposite the Wesley Chapel.

Some purely random observations I made whilst walking my dog along the footpath on the track bed of the former DLPR tram road seem to confirm Neville's assumption. To the east of this boundary, pockets of woodland and forest plants still survive in hedgerows and scrubland, whilst to the west they are entirely absent. Originally, when all the land here was unimproved waste, woodland and scrub provided the natural habitat for such plants, but when 1572 the Burgesses cleared their land to create the large open enclosure called Waun Cimla, this cover was removed. The internal division of this enclosure into 29 plots was by means of wooden fences which, unlike the hedgerows of the fields further east, did not create a suitable refuge to allow woodland species to survive. Thus it was that the marked difference between the two areas apparent today was created.

Although the Burgesses' enclosure of Waun Cimla was done without the sanction of the Lord of the Manor, and subsequently investigated by Thomas Wyseman on his behalf, no action was ever taken against them. In the 17th century a coal mine operated here under a lease from the Earl of Pembroke and following its closure the Burgesses increasingly acted as though they were the real owners of the land. This ultimately culminated in their actually assuming that right and issuing a lease to Griffith Thomas to prospect for coal here in 1793.

Whilst the relevant documents proving that ownership properly rested with Kenfig's lord existed somewhere amongst the massive archive of monastic and estate documents mouldering away at Margam House, the Mansels and their successors the Talbots were totally unaware of their existence. The Kenfig Corporation's action went unchallenged and emboldened by their success, the Burgesses went on to exploit the opportunities this now offered in the light of the burgeoning industrial developments at Cefn Cribwr and elsewhere.

Their land at the Rugge lay on the north-facing slope at the western end of Cefn Cribwr ridge and was divided into three elements. The enclosed land of Waun Cimla occupied most of the central portion from the eastern boundary to a point just west of School Road and the lower end of Prince Road. Between this and the stream at the foot of the ridge was an area called Tir Garw (Rough Land) which was technically common land but was never used as such because this was where early coal mining operations had been carried on and the ground was consequently unstable. It had therefore become overgrown and was largely covered by scrub and woodland.

The remaining land on either side of Prince Road and continuing up onto the summit of the ridge alongside the road to Cefn Cribwr village was common land. It is unlikely that it was much used by the Burgesses to graze their livestock because of its distance from Kenfig, and as the Municipal Corporations report compiled by James Booth indicates, it seems local farmers were allowed to graze their cattle upon it in return for a fee.

As to the houses already existing in this area the only ones I am aware of prior to the 19th century were three farms – Pencastell; Pwllygath; and Llwynhelig – the latter being the large house set at right-angles to the main Cefn Cribwr road near the cenotaph (known as London Road). What industrial activity there was in the area (other than the sporadic coal mining activities on the Rugge) seem to have been confined to the Margam lands on the north side of the Kenfig River. Mention is made of drainage problems in a "coal works" at Bryndu in 1729 (James B, 1987: 40), by which time another mine was in existence at Havod Hallog (now Hafod Heulog). The colliers that worked these levels presumably found what accommodation they could on local farms and were perhaps responsible for establishing the little hamlet at Penybryn near which relics of early workings have been noted in the past (James B, 1987: 38-40). Mr James apparently believed these to be monastic in origin, but the description he gives suggests they belong to a later date.

William Weston Young One of the earliest would-be developers to come knocking on the door of Kenfig Council seeking to exploit the mineral wealth beneath their land at Cefn Cribwr was a charismatic character called William Weston Young (1776-1847)(Wiki). Today he is principally remembered for his connection with the Swansea and Nantgarw china works and the high-class porcelain these produced. Young not only played a major part in setting up the latter but was also responsible for decorating the ware produced from both sources which today is eagerly sought after by collectors and has earned him world-wide renown. At the time, however, both ventures were commercial failures and Young's partnership in the enterprise at Nantgarw resulted only in bankruptcy – one of several which punctuated his life.

He was in fact a man of many parts (Jenkins, 1968: 61-101), a native of Bristol who had arrived in South Wales in 1797 to take up a lease on a corn mill at Aberdulais near Neath. When several unlucky or unwise business speculations brought his operations there to an end in 1803 he moved to Swansea to become a decorator and 'draughtsman' employed by Lewis Weston Dillwyn at the Cambrian Pottery. On his own account he designed salvage equipment for recovering cargo from ships lost off the coast, and successfully employed this to recover copper and other material from the *Anne and Theresa* in 1806. With the proceeds from that operation Young then set himself up as a 'general dealer' in Newton Nottage where he was ideally placed to continue this work on the wrecks that littered the coast between Nash Point and

Worms Head. In fact the success of his salvage operations was such that it was murmured in certain quarters that perhaps many of these maritime disasters were not entirely accidental and that he was a secret 'wrecker' who had lured these vessels to destruction in the first place!

William W Young was also a surveyor whose talents in this field found employment locally following the death of John Williams of Newlands Farm in 1811, but the fortune he amassed during this time was subsequently lost when he invested most of it in his ill-fated attempts to produce high-quality porcelain.

It was during his time at Newton Nottage that Young approached the Kenfig Corporation with a proposal to open a clay pit on the common at Cefn Cribwr. This was nothing to do with his proposed porcelain factory, but yet another scheme aimed at producing a superior type of fire brick of his own invention for use in blast furnaces. The Borough minute books record that the Rev John Morgan and William Loveluck were authorised to negotiate with Young on the Burgesses' behalf, but the proposal apparently came to nothing as there is no further mention of it.

THE ONLY KNOWN IMAGE OF
WILLIAM WESTON YOUNG
IN THE QUAKER SILHOUETTE
STYLE (WIKI)

An improved brick to line furnaces was desperately needed by the industry at this time because advances in technology enabled such high temperatures to be attained that conventional bricks crumbled and disintegrated in the intense heat. Later in life Young did indeed produce samples of his brick using a silica-rich clay from Dinas Rock near Glynneath to which he added one percent of lime. This produced a brick of sufficient durability that it is (so I understand) still used in furnaces world-wide, and in Russia is known to this day as a 'Dinas'. Sadly William Weston Young never fully benefited from his invention for when it went into production he was still an un-discharged bankrupt.

Of more significance in the industrial development of the area was John Bedford's iron works at Cefn Cribwr which he began building in 1782. Whilst it seems that this was still not in production by the time he died nine years later, the enterprise nevertheless promoted renewed interest in the availability of iron, coal, and lime in the immediate vicinity, and this was further intensified by the subsequent arrival of the Dyffryn Llynvi & Porthcawl Railroad (DLPR) in the 1820s.

On 10th June 1825 a Bill (James B, 1987: 45-6) was placed before Parliament "for making and maintaining a railway or tramroad from ... certain place called Duffryn Llynvi in the Parish of Llangonoyd ... to or near a certain bay called Pwll Cawl, otherwise Porth Cawl, in the Parish of Newton Nottage". Permission was also sought to build a pier, jetty or other harbour installations at the latter place, the supporters and sponsors of the Bill expressing the belief that the construction of the railroad would lead to the opening up of the mineral resources "under or near to the said line of railway or tramroad".

Once the Bill became law its backers lost no time in acquiring the land needed. On 14th September a memo in the Borough Minutes indicates that an agreement in principle had been reached between the Borough Recorder, Joseph Rees and Mr Morgan Price Smith on behalf of the DLPR allowing the company to buy as much of the Burgesses' land on Cefn Cribwr as it needed for the railway at £9 per acre (B/K ALE). A month later, on 14th October, the same source notes the receipt of the sum of £32 from the DLPR as a down payment for the land required.

As indicated on the tithe map of 1846 the railway track ran through the Waun Cimla enclosure, and some Burgesses obviously lost land from their parcels of hay. The council took its time mulling over this until finally declaring in January 1831 that "each and every Burgess and Burgesses' widow enjoying a piece of hay ground on Gwain y Cimla" would be paid ten shillings out of the purchase money received from the DLPR to compensate for "the loss they sustained by carrying and running the Dyffryn Lunfi and Porthcawl Tramroad through and across the said several pieces of hay ground". That decision having been taken the big pay-out duly followed on 25th February (B/K ALE).

By this time the new railway was already in being, having probably started operating sometime in 1829. The trains were hauled by horses, and the track therefore followed a rather winding route so as to reduce the gradient as much as possible – the terminus at Dyffryn Llynfi being some 490 feet above sea level at Porthcawl. In fact the

overall gradient along the railway's 16¾ miles is just 1/180, a tribute to
the skill of the engineer John Hodgkinson (James B, 1987: 56).

Once the railway was operational it wasn't long before potential
developers began looking at the mineral resources beneath the Rugge.
There is a brief reference to a mason named Morgan Thomas quarrying
stone at a previously abandoned quarry there in 1825, but this seems to
have been an illegal and unauthorised operation as the Burgesses
ordered him to cease work immediately, demanding twenty shillings
for the damage he had caused else they would sue him at court
"without any further notice".

The first Company to approach the Burgesses for permission to
exploit the minerals under the Rugge was the Maesteg Iron Company
who sought and received permission "to quarry stones to the use of the
said iron works on Cefan Cribor". The memorandum concerning this
agreement in the Borough Minute Books is dated 7th January, 1831, and
the company agreed to pay a royalty of 2d per ton on the stone it
quarried. Others were to follow, but it is likely that mining operations
were already underway elsewhere in the vicinity as by this time the first
houses of the village that was to become Kenfig Hill were already in
being.

Permission to build the very first cottage was granted to a
labourer named Thomas Hopkin on 30th November, 1827 (B/K ALE). Its
location is described as "on the left Hand in going into the said
Common" which evidently meant something at the time but is now
quite meaningless. The Corporation specified that the walls of the
building were to be 12 feet high and that it was to be roofed and
beamed with Memel deal. Hopkin agreed to pay an annual rent of
sixpence for each perch of land he enclosed for the cottage, and was
promised a lease for three lives which thereby secured his subsequent
tenancy. It was, we may note, a continuation of the practice employed
by the Margam estate whereby the tenant bore the expense of building
the cottage but ownership subsequently reverted to the landlord.

Half a dozen permits were then issued on 10th July, 1829 (B/K ALE),
five of which were to men who were apparently building new homes to
let or sell to others. A sixth permit relates to the house already being
built by Thomas Hopkin, allowing him to enclose a further 20 perches
of land as a garden. His name is a common one in the area at this time,
but he may be a Thomas Hopkin mentioned as a resiant of Pyle in 1821

and 1823 (PM9219,9229), who signed his name to the first of these documents as the Petty Constable.

The five new builders were Morgan Rees; Thomas Thomas; Charles Porter; John Evan and William Esaias. A list of resiants at Pyle in the Margam MSS (PM9229) lists no less than three persons named Morgan Rees, one being a cordwainer who, between 1824 and 1835, had at least six children by his wife Ann, and at the time of his death in 1861 was an elder of Capel y Pil (PPR, GFS, 1984). He may, or may not be the same person.

Entries in the Parish Registers indicate that William Esaias buried a son named William in 1809, and his wife Ann the following year. He then married a Margaret Richard in 1819 at which time he was apparently living in Cornelly. A man of this name also sat on an inquest jury at Kenfig in 1841 and is listed as a cordwainer and a resiant of the Borough two years later. At the time of his death in 1849 at the age of 80, he is described as living at Pyle.

Of John Evan I know nothing, but Thomas Thomas and Charles Porter were both Burgesses of Kenfig. Thomas was by trade a mason and at this time the licensee of The Corporation House. Charles was the eldest son of Thomas Porter of Caeau y Gollen (Glasfryn), and so far as I have been able to ascertain never married. He was admitted as a Burgess in 1823, but only played an active role in the Borough from 1830 onwards.

Of these five therefore at least three certainly never lived in the cottages they built at what we now call 'Kenfig Hill'. The use of the name Kenfig Hill or Mynydd Kenfig only developed gradually during the next few decades, and on the tithe map for the parish of Pyle and Kenfig (1846) it is called 'Cribbwr Village'– apparently being considered an extension of the one at Cefn Cribwr. These cottages were being built or financed as houses to let or sell to others. This in turn implies a pressing need for housing in the area and also that some industrial development was already taking place in the vicinity. The location of the plots of land upon which the cottages were to be built is not given, and it may be that in some instances each plot contained more than a single dwelling. In Thomas Thomas's case, for example, the amount of land involved was 78 perches (about half an acre) – nearly twice that required by Thomas Hopkin for his house and garden.

The income from these various developments could not have come at a better time for the Burgesses who were apparently still struggling with debts accumulated through the refurbishment of *The Corporation House*. As late as November 1827 in fact they had been forced to borrow the sum of £20 in order to complete repairs required to the roof of their hall, but the developments on the Rugge over the next decade ensured a steadily increasing flow of cash into the Borough Treasury.

Kenfig's Own Coal Mine   It was against this background of increasing interest in the mineral resources beneath Cefn Cribwr common that one of the most bizarre episodes in the history of the Borough was played out when, at a Hall Day held on 10th December 1832, the Portreeve and Council decided "to employ workmen to try and dig for coal on Cefan Cribor at the expence of the Corporation". This, no doubt owed something to the fact that the current Portreeve was Jehosaphat Powell of Llanmihangel Mill, the son-in-law of Griffith Thomas who had achieved some success exploiting the coal measures beneath his plot of hay at Waun Cimla. Certainly the Council made him responsible for superintending the operation and placed a limit of £10 on the sum he was allowed to spend.

The entire concept is totally unbelievable! Jehosaphat was a mill operator with, so far as is known, no experience of mining other than what he may have picked up from his father-in-law. For their part the Corporation apparently seriously believed that £10 would be a sufficient sum to prospect for and locate a viable coal seam, then sink a pit to exploit it! Needless to say the entire thing turned into an absolute shambles.

Surprisingly perhaps some coal was located and worked, for in September the following year it was agreed to "pay the Cefan Cribor colliers two pence per bag for working the said coal", and it was also decided that "a man be fixed to measure and sell the same". This suggests that, rather like Jehosaphat Powell's 'superintendence' they anticipated that this role would be carried out by one of their number on a part-time basis and, hopefully, free of charge!

By March 1834 the entire ramshackle enterprise had collapsed, and the Burgesses let the mineral rights on their Cefn Cribwr land to James Hodgkins Allen for 50 years at an annual rent of £100 with an additional rent of ten shillings an acre for any land on the surface he might require. They also set royalty rates on any minerals such as coal, iron ore, and clay that he subsequently raised.

In December the Burgesses sold off the equipment (such as it was) that had been used in their mine – an old saw; two wheelbarrows; and some wrought iron. The task of supervising the abortive colliery had, as we have noted, fallen upon Jehosaphat Powell who was evidently not happy that they apparently had no intention of recompensing him for the hours of work he had put in. The row between them rumbled on until April 1838 when the Corporation finally agreed "to pay Mr Jehosaphat Powell the sum of Ten Pounds for his trouble in superintending the Coal Works on Cefan Cribor in the year 1833 which turned out fruitless". Ten Pounds, we may note, had been all the money they had been willing to invest in the entire operation in the first place!

There is, indeed, a distinct impression from the entries in the minutes relating to the developments on the Cefn Cribwr Common at this time that, faced with the pace of developments there, the Burgesses were now floundering and totally out of their depth! One cannot help but recall the words of James Booth in 1833 that these were indeed men who were "little conversant with business".

Housing Developers In March 1834 William Henry Buckerfield was granted two or three acres of land for no specified purpose, on the common "on the right [side?]in entering the said common from Pyle long side the highway so far as the land is level" for 21 years at a rent of 15s an acre per annum. [This perhaps relates to Prince Road.]

A few days later the Corporation realised they had not required him to fence this land or nominated a date at which payments of rent was due to due to start, so the original was amended accordingly. Two years later and, apparently at Buckerfield's request, the term of the agreement was extended to thirty years, and the Burgesses took the opportunity to add certain additional requirements not in the original, which apparently prevented him actually building upon it. The purpose for which he required this property is therefore something of a mystery.

Collecting the rents from those who had now built cottages on the common was also proving to be a problem, and by January 1838 several tenants were already two and three years in arrears, forcing the

Council to threaten them with legal action. The probable underlying reason for the reluctance displayed by these tenants only becomes apparent in 1839 when it seems to have dawned upon the Burgesses that other people had for "some years since built cottages on Cefan Cribowr without applying to the Court for licences to do so"! In all nine new cottages had been built and the occupants had been living there quite happily rent-free. No wonder those that had gone through 'proper channels' had been so reluctant to pay up!

Alongside the nine illegal dwellings (for which formal permission was given in July 1839), eight new licenses for cottages were granted in the period 1836-39, and this added impetus to the expansion of the village was undoubtedly due to the construction of Bryndu Iron Works which commenced production in 1839.

The housing development on the common was completely haphazard. Applicants simply chose a particular plot that took their fancy and built their homes there. There were no streets beyond the pre-existing roads and tracks, and no 'overall plan' to indicate how subsequent development was to proceed. Neither, presumably, was there any piped water, drainage, or sewerage facilities. This layout is evident from the tithe maps from Pyle & Kenfig and Tythegston Parishes drawn in 1846-7, their common boundary bisecting the area where the new community was developing. They show a random sprinkling of houses principally adjoining existing roads, but some are situated well into the common land itself.

In 1839 too, the Burgesses stumbled upon another unforeseen result of these developments and rushed through a new Ordinance setting out a scale of charges for villagers pasturing livestock on the common land that adjoined their homes. Two shillings and sixpence a year was set as the fee for an ass whilst a shilling each was charged in respect geese and pigs.

Caught up in all this was a dispute involving the Burgess Howell Evan who (apparently at the Corporation's request) had cleared the timber from the 'underwood' at Tir Garw and sold it for the handsome sum of £40. He was not, however, very happy with the fee being offered him by his fellow Burgesses for this work, and held onto the money whilst negotiating better terms. Their wrangling continued until June 1839 when the Borough angrily ordered him to accept their final offer of £5 and pay the £40 to the Treasurer within 24 hours .. or else! As we hear no more of this presumably it brought the matter to a close.

The clearance of the commercial timber on Tir Garw was presumably bound up with an agreement the Borough had concluded with William Mallins to whom in 1839 they let three acres of land on "the lower part of Gwain y Cimla below the Tram Road, to the eastern part thereon" to build either a furnace or cottages. Mallins also took over the mineral rights previously held by James Allen and the general tone of the agreement suggests that he had great plans to develop an industrial complex on this site.

This agreement was concluded in the February, but the following November a new agreement was signed allowing Mallins to have three acres 'above' the tram road rather than below it, and also extending his agreement on mineral rights to include Tir Garw. In the event it seems no furnaces were ever built, nor did Mallins apparently make any serious attempt to exploit the minerals lying under the common.

Permits to build another 17 houses were granted in 1840 but by now the Burgesses had had enough! They were total amateurs in this brave new world of the Industrial Revolution, and were by now realising their own inadequacy. What was needed was somebody to supervise and oversee all these developments; collect the rents; ensure that building regulations were adhered to; check the live stock on the common, etc., etc. This was a full time job, but it never seems to have occurred to them to hire an agent or steward to carry out these duties on their behalf. Then again perhaps it did, but the thought of a non-Burgess handling so much of their business may simply have been too much for them to stomach! Whatever the reason the Burgesses now considered their property at Cefn Cribwr more trouble than it was worth, and in May 1841 determined to sell it off to Christopher Rice Mansel Talbot of Margam.

No price is mentioned in the letter to Talbot's solicitors from the Recorder Joseph Rees dated 22nd May(B/K ALE), but he did include the interesting suggestion that if an agreement were to be reached between them no money need actually change hands. Instead the Burgesses would invest the entire sum with Talbot and accept an annual payment in the form of the accrued interest due upon it.

Their proposal having met with a favourable response, the Burgesses, on 2nd April, set the asking price on the property of £2,000, and suggested that the interest subsequently paid by Talbot should be at the rate of 5% per annum. Whilst the solicitors acting for Talbot were quite agreeable to the proposed rate of interest, to the disappointment of the Burgesses they completely rejected the asking price for the property as too high.

Accordingly the Burgesses met again at a Hall Day held on 23rd April to consider their options. Talbot, they thought, had undervalued the property "and yet they would rather Mr Talbot to have it provided he would make good sixteen hundred pounds". The pace at which these negotiations were proceeding suggests that no attempt was made to find an alternative buyer, and one wonders in fact if Margam was using the influence it wielded over so many of the Burgesses to ensure that such a course was never even considered.

The amended offer was certainly more to Talbot's liking, and at a Hall Day on 27th May 1842 a conveyance for the property was placed before the assembled Burgesses who unanimously authorised their Portreeve to accept the same and "affix the common seal [of the Borough] thereto". The great irony of this of course is that, although neither they nor Talbot were aware of the fact, we now know that they were actually selling him property that was rightfully his anyway!

This signing and sealing of the conveyance formally concluded the transfer was made effective from the 25th of March the previous year. The first payment of £80 annual interest on the capital had therefore already been received by the Burgesses on 19th April. It was a sum that was considerably less than the £100 per annum they had been receiving for the mineral rights alone even without the additional income from cottage rents: building land; letting of pasture rights; and the royalties due on any coal, iron, stone or clay being mined. They were nevertheless no doubt greatly relieved to be rid of the administrative problems these involved, and there remained only the question of what now to do with this new source of annual income.

Sharing the Spoils Sad to say the Burgesses of Kenfig had now degenerated to the point where each individual considered himself entitled to a share of any new income received by the Borough. We have seen how a large proportion of the money received from the sale of land at Waun Cimla for building the DLPR was shared out amongst them with those individuals who held plots of hay there (being the most affected) receiving enhanced payments. These plots having now been sold off, they were now no doubt quick to argue that they should be properly compensated. Their case was valid enough, but the 'compensation' the Burgesses awarded themselves was not just more than generous – it was even extended to those who were not plot-holders as well!

The decision taken was that out of the £80 received, each Burgess that had held a parcel of hay should be paid fifteen shillings "and that the remainder be divided, share and share alike, amongst the whole number of Burgesses within the Corporation". This was not, however, a simple one-off payment. The following year every Burgess was given a pound and the remainder distributed evenly amongst the 29 former plot-holders as a kind of bonus. In 1844 the division was £1. 16s. 0d. to the plot holders and £1 5s. 0d. to the others with the "six shillings balance left on the hands of the Portreeve to be reserved towards paying incidental expences". This thereafter became the norm – every year each and every Burgess received a sum of money with enhanced payments for the holders of the (now non-existent) plots, and the residue paid into the Borough Treasury.

It was an arrangement that blatantly pandered to the Burgesses' self-interest, especially when one considers that previously all income from the properties on the Rugge had been paid directly into the Borough Treasury! Not surprisingly therefore the Burgesses were always a little coy about this source of income. When The Swansea Scientific Society visited here in 1892 (six years after the Borough had been abolished) they were told that the annual income of the Trustees who now administered its former assets amounted to about £120 per annum (Griffiths, 1997:22). The report continues "We could not learn the exact manner in which this income is disposed of, but gathered that a certain number of the oldest and poorest Burgesses get so much a year". Earlier, in 1848, James Motley (also of the Swansea Scientific Society, Wiki) had got rather closer to the truth when, during the course of a visit to Kenfig, he dismissed the duties and responsibilities of the Burgesses as "confined to dividing among themselves the rents of some lands which they still hold".

These payments continued to be made to Burgesses long after the Borough itself ceased to exist, and the late Ted Davies CBE recalled how as a Trustee he delivered such payments annually to John Thomas, the very last of their number. Because of this, the minute book (which ends in 1852) solemnly records the subsequent transfers of parcels of hay at Waun Cimla even after the sale of 1842 exactly as though they were still in existence for the theoretical 'possession' of such a plot continued to attract an enhanced payment.

Towards the end even the 'residential' qualification of Burgesses entitling them to these payments became somewhat stretched. Chris Ensor of Cheltenham, himself a descendant of a Burgess family, told me that his aunt - the widow of a former Burgess and therefore entitled to his former share - lived fifty weeks of every year outside the Borough, but spent a fortnight 'on holiday' with her brother who still lived at Kenfig. This, it seems, was accepted as a suitable period of 'residence' so that she could be paid the money. It was all a far cry from the previous and jealously guarded 'in-dweller' status of the original Burgesses.

PART OF KENFIG HILL (HERE REFERRED TO AS CEFN CRIBWR) ON THE TITHE MAP FOR THE PARISH OF PYLE & KENFIG, 1846. THE EASTERN PART (OFF THE TOP OF THE MAP) WAS IN THE PARISH OF TYTHEGSTON.

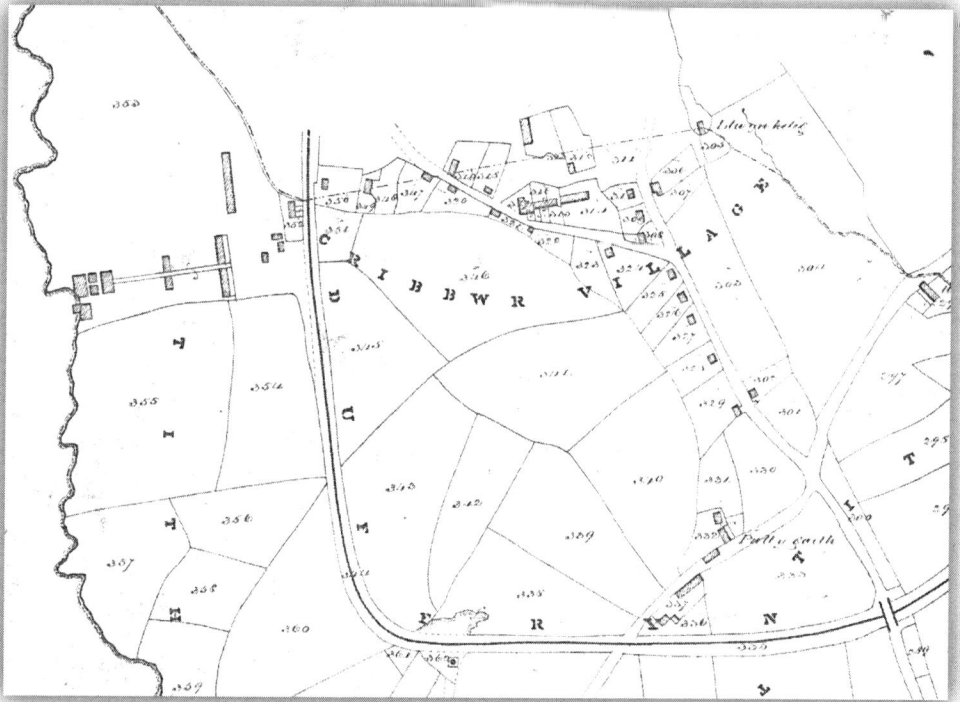

Chapter 18

Rabbits & Railways:
The 1820s, 30s & 40s

The long war with France which lasted until Wellington's victory at Waterloo in 1815 created an artificial boom in agriculture which benefited both the local farmers and their landlords. In order to ensure that they received their share of the benefits the Talbots reverted to the practice of limiting the number of leases issued to their tenants and let their properties 'at will' instead. In 1789 the total receipts from the manors of Higher Kenfig and Kenfig Borough (rounded up to the nearest £) were £160 and £265 respectively (D/D Ma 39). In 1816 the equivalent figures were £323 and £488 (D/D Ma 58,59), rises of 101.8% and 84.1% in just 26 years.

Whilst these figures may be dramatic they only reflect the increasing prosperity within the farming community that enabled such increased payments to be met. There is nothing in contemporary documents to indicate any wide scale collapse such as had occurred during the first half of the 18th century when the ailing Margam estate had previously attempted rent rises on such a scale. Indeed, as Thomas (1968) illustrates under the artificial stimulus created by the conflict for home grown produce, the pace of improvement in farming practices speeded up and the programme of enclosing waste and common land within the Principality reached its zenith. At the end of the war the bubble burst and the value of agricultural land slumped dramatically. With an eye to the future the Talbots of Margam were nevertheless quick to plough back some of the profits made during the boom years into properties which now came onto the market at knock-down prices. Three of these lay within the Borough of Kenfig.

Despite the struggles of the preceding century and a half, there still remained within Kenfig Lower a considerable body of freehold land. It was divided into three sections, one known as Paschal Hill Hold, another simply as 'Free Rents', and a third for which only a nominal rent such as a peppercorn or a red rose was paid annually if and when specifically required by the Lord of the manor. In practice the nominal rents for the latter group had never been requested, and well before the end of the 17th century all reference to them in the Margam rentals had ceased.

The Free Rents were fixed sums payable annually – generally 2d per acre or less – and included payments from the Lords of North and South Cornelly in respect of their manors, and also from the owner of Sker and the Burgesses in respect of their respective portions of Kenfig Down. The Paschal Hill rents, however, related entirely to the fixed payments due upon landholdings within the Lower Borough, and were less than the two (old) pence per acre rate due for those listed under the Free Rents. Although only included in the Margam rentals as a lump sum after 1692, the fluctuation of the annual payment of the Paschal Hill rent does therefore provide a useful indicator of the fortunes of the free-holding community as set out in the table below.

Increases in the total amount paid under this heading occurred when the Lord of the manor allowed tenants to take in fresh land from the waste, whilst reductions occurred when the estate bought up individual freeholds that became available, and re-let them at more realistic rates.

The reduction of the amount of Paschal Hill freehold land apparent in the third quarter of the 17th century may perhaps in part have been tied up with the Restoration of the Monarchy in 1660 and the problems it caused for the local Nonconformist community. Half a century later the massive economic and social

Paschal Hill Rents 1650-1850			
Year	£	s	d
1650	1	7	0½
1661	1	7	2¾
1675	1	3	9
1692	1	2	4½
1707	1	2	5¼
1724	1	2	7½
1739		14	11
1750		10	8½
1764		10	8½
1781		10	4
1799		10	4
1816		10	4
1830		9	8½

problems at Kenfig during the first half of the 18th century are graphically illustrated by the huge drop in the totals between 1724 and 1750 when many local freeholders sold up and left the area for good. Nevertheless, in the early part of the 19th century more than a third of the original freehold land still remained, though much of it now belonged to other landowners such as the Knights of Tythegston or the

Bennets of Laleston rather than local 'owner-occupiers' as had originally been the case.

Presumably what was true of Paschal Hill also applied to the properties in the other two freehold categories, though in the case of these I can offer no comparable statistics. Amongst them was the former farm at Ty'n Towyn and The Angel Inn. The site of the former farmhouse was occupied by a fine new dwelling house built by Matthew Forster, but the land and the inn remained in the ownership of Rees Daniel until his death in 1820. So far as I can discover he never married, and upon his death his executors put the property up for sale by public auction.

The sale took place at Pyle Inn on 28th October 1820, the property having been widely advertised including the *Cambrian* Newspaper (21st Oct), as 34 acres of enclosed land; "about 5 acres of unenclosed sand land"; and "a public house and croft adjoining in the possession of David Yorath". The agents for Margam secured the properties for the estate, and the following year they appear on the annual rentals for the first time. During the same period, however, two other local properties far closer to the Talbots' hearts also came onto the market.

As we are aware Llanmihangel and Marlas farms had passed to the Briton Ferry Estate under very dubious circumstances in 1741, and whilst a copy of the document covering the transaction apparently existed within the Margam archives (PM 1532) nobody there seems to have been aware of its existence. The Talbots knew nevertheless that these two valuable properties had once been part of the estate of their Mansel ancestors and were evidently keen to secure their return.

Following the death of Lord Vernon of Briton Ferry, his successors indicated a willingness to sell, and accordingly negotiations were begun and a valuation of the two properties despatched to Griffith Llewellyn the Talbot's agent. This document (PM 6662), and Llewellyn's rough (and partly illegible) notes which accompany them, are undated, but from other information we can deduce that they belong to the years 1819-20.

Of Rabbits, Children, and the Iron Horse As the year 1820 dawned the agreements made by the Burgesses with the Loveluck family and Jenkin John which allocated them the right to cull rabbits on certain areas of the common had been in force for nearly 30 years. By any standards it had been a huge success. The Leaseholders patrolled the common land adjoining their warrens and culled any rabbits straying beyond their borders. The threat to the villagers' crops, fields and gardens had been removed; and the annual rent provided the Borough Treasury with a steady source of income. Not a single complaint concerning rabbits appears in the minute books during this thirty year period. In December 1816 when the licences came up for renewal the Corporation was perfectly happy to do so. Yet less than four years later, everything suddenly changed.

In February 1820 the Portreeve ordered a special Hall Day to be held on 3rd March and, when it met, William Loveluck and Jenkin John faced the full fury of some very enraged fellow Burgesses! The pair were accused of deliberately stocking the common land they were leasing from the Borough with rabbits and effectively turning them into extensions of their commercial warrens. The cordon that had hitherto checked the spread of the rabbits was thereby removed, and the pair had proved as incapable of restricting the pests to these enlarged warrens as they had been in the case of the originals. The rabbits therefore quickly spread in numbers across the dunes so that now "the pasture of the Burgesses's lands commonly called Kenfigg Down, and also the North Common which commonly is called Windmill Hill, is wrested from the Burgesses".

Already farmers and tenants whose land bordered the common were starting to experience a return to the bad old days when rabbits broke into their fields and gardens and consumed their produce with impunity. William Loveluck for his part had further exacerbated the situation by "hunting rabbits on the Burgesses' lands with dogs & nets by day and night, by which unjust acts he disturbs the Burgesses' sheep on the common and drives them into the roads"

In a lather of righteous indignation the furious Burgesses warned the men that they would have no hesitation in disenfranchising them if they continued to employ such disruptive hunting tactics and then delivered the final blow by revoking their leases upon the common land bordering their warrens, "for they shall remain tenants thereof no longer"!

With that the angry Burgesses probably felt that they had dealt the pair a punishment they richly deserved, and only gradually did it dawn upon them that they had in fact simply cut off the communal nose to spite its face. Loveluck and John's commercial warrens still remained and there was little or nothing that the Corporation could do to prevent these being over-stocked! Effectively they had sanctioned a return to the bad old days prior to the granting of the licences. Nor, or so it seems, were they willing to put in place an alternative means of preventing the spread of the rabbits from the warrens into the common. If any of their more ancient members tentatively suggested a return to the practice of stopping up rabbit-holes, then it was evidently met by a stony silence!

Following the angry scenes in the Town Hall that day there was no question of the Burgesses going back on the decisions they had taken despite the fact that up to this point the arrangement with the warreners had worked effectively over a long period. Against the best efforts of the men of Kenfig, the conies had scored an unlikely and improbable victory! One final question arising from these events nevertheless still begs an answer. Why, after operating their side of the agreement effectively and without the least hint of offence for nearly thirty years, had William Loveluck and Jenkin John suddenly introduced practices guaranteed to upset their fellow Burgesses?

The Final Act of the 'Rabbit War': Here, or so it would seem, the answer lies in the activities of the enterprising William Weston Young of Newton Nottage who came to our notice in the previous chapter which dealt with business matters at Kenfig Hill. Amongst Young's many business activities his biographer Elis Jenkins (1968) tells us that he established himself as a 'general dealer' at Newton Nottage, and from the details he includes about it, this was no mere village store! Young, it seems, traded in a variety of goods which he often bought and sold in very large quantities (Jenkins, 1968: 78) and included oysters, slates, timber, linen as well as "rabbit skins by the thousand at ten shillings a dozen". These he was able to ship to Bristol from Newton via the twice-weekly packet-boat service that now connected the two ports, and there dispose of them via his family business contacts within the city. Suddenly there was an increased demand locally for rabbit pelts, and William Loveluck and John Jenkin had therefore increased production in order to take full advantage of this upturn in demand.

The final act in the 'Rabbit War' followed shortly afterwards in 1826. On 3rd November the Portreeve Rees Rees and his Eight Elected

Burgesses met in solemn council where they agreed to eradicate the rabbit problem on their common once and for all "by digging the same out and destroy[ing] their burrows or nests"*(BK/ALE)*. Brave words maybe, but so far as I can discover they were never followed up with any practical action. Indeed this motion was followed by another which reveals their awareness of the true hopelessness of the situation in view of the continued existence of the commercial warrens.

Having resolved to totally eradicate the rabbit population on their land they also determined to send a delegation to meet with Thomas John Llewelyn, current Constable of the Castle, to inform him of the proposed action "and also the great loss the Burgesses suffer by the said rabbits as well on the common as on the inclosed lands, which is as unjust as [it is] unsufferable".

The delegation consisted of five of the leading farmers and Burgesses from Kenfig – Owen Howell (Penymynydd); Thomas Thomas (Llanmihangel); John Rees (Kenfig Farm); Thomas Thomas (The Prince of Wales) and Joseph Rees (Kenfig House Farm), but it is difficult to understand what they hoped it would achieve. Did they honestly expect Llewelyn in his capacity as Agent for the Margam estate to intercede with his master to have the warren completely shut down? If so, they were doomed to disappointment, and the warren continued in the hands of the Loveluck family up to, and well beyond, the end of the period covered by my studies in 1850.

The rabbits in fact continued to flourish right across Kenfig Burrows until almost exterminated by myxomatosis a century or so later. Ted Davies* CBE and others who lived at Kenfig prior to World War II have invariably described them to me (with perhaps a pardonable touch of

---

* Edwin ('Ted') Davies CBE, JP, 1915-2008, had been President of the Kenfig Society for many years, as well as significant involvement in local government and as Chairman of the Trustees of Kenfig Corporation. Although a native of the Swansea valley, he lived most of his life in Kenfig and his love for the area, its people, its history and its future was evident in all he said or did. [ed.]

hyperbole!) as numbering 'millions', recalling how they carpeted the golf course fairways in the first light of dawn showing little fear of any human approach - "The damned things just sat there and stared at you!" It is almost as though they had their own memory of past attempts to eradicate them, and were expressing their contempt of the humans they had so comprehensively defeated!

A Tragedy in the Dunes: In 1832 the Kenfig conies claimed their first and (so far as I am aware) only human casualty, a fourteen year old boy named David Powell. Born on 7th June 1818 he was the illegitimate son of a spinster named Mary Powell by a labourer named David William. At this time Mary was said to have been living at Waun y Mer, but three years earlier, whilst living on Heol Las she had also given birth to another illegitimate son by a labourer named Edward Griffith. Finally, in 1823 she bore an illegitimate daughter named Sarah to Robert Rees the middle-aged bachelor farmer at Kenfig Farm before marrying a labourer named Evan Evan in 1826.

Whilst Mary's morals may have been somewhat questionable, it has to be noted that at a time when there was a suspiciously high mortality rate amongst illegitimate children, her other two offspring survived into adulthood, and neither she nor her husband Evan can be blamed in any way for the untimely death of young David.

On 13th December 1832 Thomas Thomas of Pool Farm spotted the lad's feet protruding out of the side of a sand dune just north of Mawdlam church. With the aid of Thomas John, a local carpenter he dug young David out of the dune but found that the boy was already dead, the discolouration of his face indicating that he had died of suffocation. At the inquest the jury concluded that he had been digging "for rabbits" into the side of the dune when the tunnel he had made collapsed upon him.

Some thoughts on Mortality in that time: I had originally intended to use this sad little tale merely as a postscript to the story of the Burgesses' long struggle to eradicate the rabbits on their common, but (as is so often the case) one thing led to another and I got to thinking about the dangers of childhood two centuries ago compared with today. My immediate thought was that despite the unfortunate accident to young David Powell, the times in which he lived was a far safer one in which to raise a family compared to the modern era with its ever present potentially lethal dangers such as road traffic, drugs and child molestation to name but a few.

Then I recalled the horrific infant mortality rate of the early 19th century that I had calculated from the parish registers, which claimed the lives of almost one in three infants under the age of three due to the lack of proper health care and medical facilities. Taking that thought a stage further I also realised that one occupation I had never ever found mention of amongst the Kenfig folk was that of a doctor. The nearest such would have been at Bridgend or later Porthcawl, but would the average local family have ever been able to pay the sort of fees he would have demanded for his services? Perhaps the lack of a physician within the community is in itself an eloquent enough answer to that question.

Midwives are occasionally mentioned in contemporary records, but these were local women without any formal training who did what they could based upon experience and lore handed down from others who had practiced the art before them. They undoubtedly did their level best for the mothers in their care, but I suspect that many of them would have been the first to admit that given their lack of knowledge and facilities, the mortality rate amongst the babies they delivered was distressingly high.

Against this, they seem to have succeeded in achieving a surprising level of success in ensuring the survival of the mother, for the numbers that died in childbirth apparent from the parish registers are not as high as I would have believed. Nevertheless there are many instances where the baptism of a child is followed shortly afterwards by the burial of the mother, and in some instances these ceremonies were conducted on the same day. It was, in fact, a rather touching ceremony known to have been practiced elsewhere in South Wales where the baby was christened over the mother's coffin prior to internment. In this way she was still included at the baptism of the child for whom she had died to give birth.

Even once those crucial early years of infancy had been negotiated however, the world was still a dangerous place for the young. Young children, boys in particular, are notoriously inquisitive and adventurous, and like young David Powell have little or no concept of the potential hazards of the environment in which they live, either then or now. During the quarter of a century between 1825 and 1850 the Borough Minute books record details of 17 inquests conducted by the Kenfig Portreeves into sudden, violent, or unexplained deaths in their area. Four of them relate to bodies washed ashore on the beach of which only one was ever identified. The remaining 13 enquiries all relate to local inhabitants of who six – nearly half – were children, all of whom died 'by misadventure'. Interestingly too, most have a story to tell over and above the one related in the bare details of the inquest record. Fourteen year old David was the first of these, and the following year his inquest was followed by that of a young girl.

The inquest on Ann Thomas – and her father: one of the two girls amongst these unfortunates. She was Ann Thomas aged 11, and the daughter of Thomas Thomas [1795-1841] a carpenter from Pyle (an out-dwelling Burgess of Kenfig, admitted in 1824). The horrific accident that ended her life took place at Llanmihangel Mill on April 31st, 1833. What business she had in the mill we will never know, but it is worth recalling that this was probably the only piece of machinery that local youngsters had ever seen prior to the arrival of the main railway line in 1850. Like the steam trains of the latter, the powered machinery within the mill undoubtedly fascinated local children and maybe Ann had merely sneaked her way in undetected to watch it working.

The interior of the mill was the stuff of which a modern Health and Safety Officer's nightmares are made, there being little or no protection provided from accidental contact with the moving parts and no safety devices to shut these down if and when this occurred. Ann's clothing became entangled in the mill machinery and, in the brief and pithy words of the inquest record, "whirled her about with such violence as to mangle her whole frame in such a shocking manner as caused her instantaneous death".

A verdict of 'accidental death' was brought in by the jury, and in the context of the time and the brief details provided by the inquest record it is one that it is difficult to quarrel with. What I found surprising, however, is that the Portreeve who presided at the hearing in his capacity as the Borough's Coroner, was none other than Jehosaphat Powell – the mill proprietor! Perhaps this accounts for the fact that whereas normally local inquests were held within a day or two of the discovery of the body, this one was not held until the 17th May, allowing time for this possible conflict of interests to be sorted out.

Only two deaths are known to have occurred at Llanmihangel Mill, and by a strange coincidence the second death was that of Ann's father, Thomas Thomas which happened on 29th September 1841. He had been called in to make a repair to the water wheel, and apparently chose not to have this stopped whilst carrying out the work. Whether his foot slipped or became entangled in the wheel nobody could be certain, but he evidently lost his balance and the wheel crushed his head against the wall. It is almost as though the place had a personal grudge against this unfortunate family!

The noted death of young Evan Lewis The death of 13 year-old Evan Lewis on 2nd September 1837 is remarkable because it subsequently became a minor local legend. Born in 1823 he was the son of Thomas and Margaret Lewis of North Cornelly, but at the time of his death was living with his employer Charles Amici who resided at Duck Cottage in Kenfig.

Until recently (2008) Amici had been something of a mystery to me. He had arrived in Kenfig earlier in 1837 and was evidently a person of some substance being styled "gent" in local records. When I connected to the internet, his was one of the first names I fed into the search engine facility on the basis that it was rather an unusual one, and this put me in touch with a descendant, Mrs Roz Cawley. Her own research into the family history is still ongoing, but she told me that Charles' father was a London merchant of Swiss and possibly Huguenot origin.

Born in 1792 Charles was a businessman, and it may be that his initial visit here in 1837 and another in 1840 (when he sat on the jury at the Court Leet) were made in this connection. On his next visit in 1842 he stayed at Pen Plas cottage (now Cae Rhyd near the former Windrush restaurant) and this time brought with him his new bride Frances Sarah Williams, the granddaughter of a former Rector of Coity. He was 50 and she was just 27, and the reason behind their visit becomes apparent in the parish registers which record the baptism of their first born child Ann Sarah on 28th February – only a few months after the wedding. Francis, as Roz puts it, was "a bit of a girl!

The following year (1843) they were back here again staying at Albert Cottage (now divided into four dwellings) on Heol Las for the birth of their daughter Mary. He is mentioned as living at Albert Cottage in 1845, though whether this represents a continuous period of residence or just another visit to the area it is impossible to say. The last mention of him comes in 1847 when he and Frances baptised a daughter named Emma Mariah and were living at Hall in North Cornelly. He died at Bristol in 1849, and within about six months his widow had remarried a local innkeeper. She did not long survive for her death is mentioned near Lewes, Sussex in March of the following year when she can only have been in her mid thirties.

MARY AMICI WHO WAS BORN AT ALBERT COTTAGE IN 1843 (PHOTO ROZ CAWLEY)

It is a further indication of Charles' status that he owned a coach, and on his first visit in 1837 employed young Evan Lewis as a live-in servant. On 2nd September he instructed Evan to wash down the coach and so, harnessing up the horse to the vehicle the lad took it down to nearby Kenfig Pool. The inquest record merely states that whilst there "the said Evan Lewis, was in the water of the said Pool then and there suffocated and drowned", and the Parish Register notes his burial two days after the inquest.

All straightforward and very simple, but perhaps something of the true circumstances surrounding this incident survive in a story told to Thomas Morgan ("Llyfnwy") on a visit he made to Kenfig some twenty years later. He was gathering material for a history of Kenfig which he entered for a local Eisteddfod and which was subsequently serialised in 1857 by *The Bridgend Chronicle* (Lyons&Griffiths, 1996: 4). Llyfnwy is the same person who inadvertently created the current version of the legend of the Maid of Sker, but sadly the history of Kenfig he wrote, whilst sufficient to win first prize at the Eisteddfod, contains little information of any merit today.

During his visit the locals regaled him with the story of the "City beneath the Pool", and when he expressed doubts that this was anything more than a story, hastened to assure him that their fathers and grandfathers before them had seen walls beneath its waters.   They also told him the tale of how "one Evan Lewis drove a carriage through a portion of the water to cross it [Kenfig Pool], and, unfortunately, the wheels were caught by the old masonry [of the sunken town], so that his watery career was stopped; man, horse, and carriage disappeared and were never more seen"!

Maybe therefore young Evan, carried away by his promotion to driver of a horse and carriage, had been showing off a little and, drove the vehicle faster and further into the lake than was prudent, causing it to overturn and bring about his premature demise. As for the horse and carriage I cannot vouch, but the record of the inquest and the parish registers confirm that the sad remains of Evan Lewis were recovered and properly interred!

The New School at Kenfig. The school that William Lloyd attended at Kenfig was a recent arrival and was situated (as had been the previous ones) in the Town Hall. In this instance, however, it does not seem to have been initiated by the Burgesses but was a private venture by a school teacher named Thomas Kneath who appears to have hailed from the Swansea area. On 24th March 1844 he reached an agreement with the Corporation to rent the hall for £2 a year with the Burgesses reserving priority use as and when required. As the agreement was back-dated to the April of the previous year it would seem that the school had already been in existence for anything up to twelvemonths.

Kneath presumably charged parents a fee to educate their children and thereby earned himself a living, but although the school he founded was destined to survive for many years, he himself departed at the end of 1845 in rather acrimonious circumstances. When they re-let the premises to a new schoolmaster – a Mr Taylor – in December that year the Corporation specifically warned him that if "Mr Kneath should have any concern in this undertaking, a notice to quit will be given immediately"!

Despite this Thomas Kneath does seem to have had his loyal supporters in the area. The 1851 Census shows him living at 3 Nelson Terrace, Swansea which he had apparently turned into a school with three of the boarding pupils being members of the Powell family of Llanmihangel Mill, though here described as being from Pyle.

A Commissioner for the Inquiry into the State of Education in Wales visited Kenfig on 5th March, 1847 and mentions the existence of this school without however making any report upon it. He also says that there was a Sunday School being held at Kenfig – a branch of the Calvinistic Methodists at Cornelly – and one presumes that this too was held in the Town Hall as the only suitable location. This mention came as something of a surprise since although a Sunday School was held in the Town Hall until terminated due to lack of support in the year 2000, its banner proudly proclaimed that it had been established in 1861. What its relationship was to the earlier one is therefore unclear.

SUNDAY SCHOOL AT KENFIG.

THE PICTURE ABOVE SHOWS A CLASS IN PROGRESS AT THIS LATER SCHOOL.(ITS POOR QUALITY IS DUE TO THE FACT THAT IT IS A BLACK AND WHITE PHOTOCOPY OF A WATER-COLOUR PAINTING PUBLISHED IN THE SOUTH WALES EVENING POST 22ND JAN 1944). THE ARTIST WAS W GRANT MURRAY (1877-1950), HEAD OF SWANSEA ART SCHOOL AND IT "WAS HUNG IN HIS RECENT EXHIBITION AT THE NATIONAL MUSEUM OF WALES IN CARDIFF UNDER THE TITLE 'SUNDAY SCHOOL AT KENFIG'". THE ARTICLE ALSO ADDS THAT "IN THE PAINTING THE WALLS ARE A VIVID 'RECKITT'S' BLUE AND PINK"!

The day-school did not survive for anything as long as the one held on Sundays. It was still in existence when *Llyfnwy* (1857) visited here in 1857 though he claims that it was originally founded in 1838 "and with slight intervals had drawn on a lingering existence until the present time". He clearly implies that the school was struggling to survive, but the following brief notice in the *Glamorgan Gazette* (15th May, 1868) seems to indicate that it was still in being in 1868 (unless it is the Sunday School that is the one in question).

> **Mawdlam.** We have received intelligence of some persons visiting the Guildhall, Mawdlam, last Saturday, and carrying away a quantity of the school books, and damaging others so as to render them useless. Such conduct is very reprehensible and as the manipulators have been pretty well traced, they would act wisely by returning the books. We cannot expect such persons to show their contrition by making reparation for the injury done but it should be made compulsory that they do so

If the 'manipulators' were indeed discovered, then there is no report of the fact in subsequent issues, and allowing for the fact that I have not particularly searched for material relating to the school after 1850, this is the latest mention of it that I have so far discovered.

The Arrival of the Age of Steam The 1840s was a time of mounting excitement in Kenfig and the surrounding area as news filtered through of plans to build a railway through the district that would connect Swansea to Cardiff and London. Although the old DLPR was still in existence this was still only a tram road on which the wagons and trains were hauled by horses and mules. The locomotive power on the new line would be steam engines capable of hauling long rakes of carriages and wagons to destinations across the entire country far more rapidly, and at a fraction of the cost of the stagecoaches that travelled the main highway through Pyle.

Travel beyond the confines of the world they knew would now become a possibility for the people of Kenfig. The market towns of Swansea, Neath, Bridgend and Cardiff were suddenly within easy reach – catch a train at the station in Pyle, and be back the same day! Local farmers would be able to ship their produce to booming markets in London and the Midlands where the mineral produce of the district was also in demand by the new factories and industries of the age. Some, however, were less enthusiastic. On discovering that these noisy rushing engines would be thundering by just beyond the back door of their home the Jones family at Stormy Isha Farm near Kenfig Hill promptly abandoned the house and moved to a new one built high above on Cefn Cribwr ridge at Pencastell!

The Borough Minute Books note on 17th September 1847 that William Loveluck the Recorder was served with a notice from The South Wales Railway Company that they required part of the Burgesses' common land for the new railway, and engaged Adam Murray of Briton Ferry to value the land and negotiate on their behalf. Permission was given for the work to start immediately.

It was also agreed that the purchasers would pay 5% interest on the eventually agreed purchase price from this date until such time the money was actually paid. By the time payment was made in 1852 therefore the sum totalled £30 which, needless to say, was distributed amongst the Burgesses as a bonus on top of their normal share in the annual interest payment from the Margam estate.

If only for this reason therefore one assumes that they welcomed the arrival of the railway, but then most of them were living well away from the new line. One Burgess who lived considerably closer to the proposed route was certainly not so happy, especially when work actually began at the railhead near his home.

At Kenfig in 1848 old Thomas Porter of Caeau y Gollen (Glasfryn), now well into his 70s, viewed the approach of the new railway with considerable trepidation, and his misgivings increased as construction work proceeded on the new bridge across the Kenfig River and the approaches to it. By 25th August he had worked himself up into a state bordering upon hysteria as is apparent in two letters written by him that day to William Llewelyn of Baglan, the Agent for the Margam estate[*].

To appreciate the alarm and dismay the construction work was causing him, it has to be appreciated that hitherto, as was mentioned earlier in this chapter, the only piece of working powered machinery in the area was the local corn mill. The loudest noise one heard was a clap of thunder, the ringing blows of the blacksmith working at his anvil, or the rumble of a wagon along the highway. Suddenly this peaceful

---

[*] These are in the possession of Mr Neil Prior of North Cornelly, and I am greatly obliged to him for his permission to make copies of them and utilise the information they contain.

world was shattered by steam engines; steam shovels, pile-drivers, and hundreds of navvies swarming everywhere, all working flat out dawn to dusk within a hundred yards or so of his front door! Caeau Gollen was owned by Margam, and William Llewelyn or one of his minions had evidently visited Thomas and told him about the arrival of the new railway, but nothing they said could have prepared him for this milling cacophony of men and machines!

Woken from his slumbers at the crack of dawn Thomas rushed out of his house to discover work already in progress with the railway line apparently heading "along the inside of the field leading from the flood gate towards my garden"! Furthermore the area where work was taking place extended well beyond what he understood to be the line of the actual railway. Angry at having his rest disturbed at such an ungodly hour; furious at the damage being caused to his land by what he deemed 'unlawful trespass', and no doubt not a little unnerved by all the bustle and commotion, Thomas charged from his home and sought out a Mr Matthews who was responsible for supervising the work.

Clearly something of a heated exchange took place between the two with Porter taking Matthews to task for extending the construction work outside the line of the actual railway and the early hour at which his men had started work – did he not realise what time it was?

Doubtless many similar encounters took place as Brunel and his engineers drove their railroad through the quiet rural countryside with all the speed and efficiency that the technology of the age could muster. "Yes", responded Matthews in a tone which indicated that it was a matter of complete indifference, he knew exactly what the time was! Porter's accusations of trespass he dismissed out of hand. "He said they had a right to take what they pleased for their convenience within a 100 yards off the line", the old man wrote incredulously. Adding for good measure that Porter's power to do anything about it was virtually 'nil', Matthews then turned his horse and rode off leaving the old fellow seething with rage.

Matthews had nevertheless agreed (or rather Thomas Porter believed that he had agreed) to suspend laying track across the field and to contact Llewelyn to clarify the position. Scuttling back to his home the old man immediately penned his own letter to the Margam Agent, urging him to come in person and view the "great trespass" the railway builders were committing on his fields, for "if they are allowed to go on, I presume the land ought to be measured and valued immediately and paid for or enter into an agreement for that purpose."

For a time it seems that the construction work on Porter's fields was indeed suspended, but later that day work recommenced and with no sign of Llewelyn, Thomas Porter despatched another short, desperate appeal to him later the same evening. "Since I wrote to you this morning to say that Mr Mathews w[oul]d stop railing across the fields He has given orders again to his men to proceed with the Railing. They will not stop or take notice of anything I say to them, therefore I hope you will take means to prevent them immediately, and make them pay Trespass".

Against the might of the railway company, and the indifference of the landowner with whom, as Matthews indicates, issues of rights of access to land for temporary spoil heaps had already been settled, Thomas Porter had little chance of securing any redress for the disruption to his farm and lifestyle. It was a rude introduction to the age of industry and one which he did not survive. It seems that he went to live with one of his family at Pyle, and there he died less than twelve months later in September 1849 at the age of 74.

Unlike his fellow Burgesses therefore he was not amongst the crowds lining the trackside across the common on 18th June 1850 when, as the Recorder noted proudly in his minute book, "the South Wales Railway was first opened". The inaugural train steamed proudly past en-route to Swansea station; the Kenfig folk waved and cheered; the gentlemen in the coaches raised their hats in polite acknowledgement.

Chapter 19
The Final Chapter 1850-1886

[This is the last chapter which Barrie wrote, and as you can see, he takes the story up to 1850. Actually the Ancient Borough of Kenfig lingered on until 1886, but perhaps nothing much happened in the last 38 years that was worth a mention! Ed.]

To wind up my 700 year story of the Kenfig folk I could think of no better way than to take an imaginary perambulation through the lower Borough [south of the Kenfig river] about the year 1850 when the main railway line opened. This portrayal of Kenfig is possible thanks largely to three documents created in the decade 1841-1851. The first two are the Census returns for 1841 and 1851, whilst the third is the tithe map for Pyle & Kenfig parish dating from 1846. By using these in combination it is normally possible to work out where the farms and dwelling houses of the day were situated, and some (though not always all) of the people who inhabited them.

One thing I've discovered in compiling this chapter is that there are more 'heads of households' listed in the Census returns than there are houses on the map! The reason, or so I suppose, is that often a single room or rooms within a house were sub-let to a family, thereby creating a separate household in the same building. Unfortunately it is normally impossible to identify the houses where such arrangements were in place. Sadly too it is impossible to reconstruct a similar tour of Higher Kenfig [along Water Street] as no tithe map was ever made of Margam parish since all land there was 'tithe-free' – a relic of the days of the medieval monastery. Without the map the scant information contained in the Census returns regarding location is normally insufficient by itself to indicate the site of a particular dwelling.

Caeau y Gollen (now Glasfryn Kennels) Our tour starts in the extreme north of Kenfig Lower at the former home of Thomas Porter whose brush with the railway contractors was noted in the previous chapter.

By 1850 old Thomas was dead, and the house and farm were in the hands of his son Charles (1798-1870). The curiosity about Cae y Gollen was that whilst the house and some of the fields belonging to it stood on the south side of the River Kenfig (in the parish of Pyle & Kenfig), the bulk of its land stood on the opposite bank in the parish of Margam. The Margam estate regarded it all as being part and parcel of the Manor of Higher Kenfig, but for taxation and other purposes the house and its occupants were assessed under Pyle & Kenfig.

In the 1851 Census Charles Porter is described as farming 23 acres of land (which must include the fields on the north side of the Kenfig) and the only other occupant of the house was his 50 year old live-in servant, Sarah Lewis. There is no mention of any wife or family, and so far as I can discover Charles never married. The Census tells us that he employed one man and a boy to work the farm, and they evidently lived locally – probably in the group of nearby cottages adjoining New Mill Bridge (Pont Felin Newydd) on Water Street, of which little trace now remains.

Although admitted as a Burgess in 1823 Charles seems to have taken no part in Borough affairs until 1831, which probably indicates that he was living away from home during this period. Leslie Evans states that he held the office of Portreeve in 1859, and his burial is recorded in the registers on 31st March, 1870.

Twyn Cottage & The Plwryn Caeau y Gollen stood on the northern edge of land once known as 'Tir Ffin' nestling in the wide bend of the Kenfig River between Pont Felin Newydd and its confluence with the Afan Fach (Goylake) stream. This name, which means 'Land's End', takes us right back to the days of the medieval town with which we began Kenfig's story when this was the land of the Borough furthest away from its town and castle.

The southernmost part of Tir Ffin ended in a ridge known as The Twyn ('Dune') which overlooks the lane from Mawdlam to Pyle. On it in 1850 stood two cottages, one (now called *The Plwryn*) is still there; the other stood a little distance further west and has long since decayed into a ruin that is totally buried beneath the undergrowth of its former garden. By 1850 the latter had acquired the name *Twyn Cottage*.

Both cottages have a long history, though ones that are rather tricky to follow. A commercial corn drier was being operated somewhere in this vicinity as early as 1633, and I get the impression that it was in some way connected with the origins of *Twyn Cottage*, though the details are unclear. Two centuries later it was the home of Jenkin John - the warrener of that name who got himself into hot water with his fellow Burgesses for misuse of the common land adjoining his warrens. He died here in 1832 at the ripe old age of 79, and was succeeded as the tenant by his son, also named Jenkin.

It was Jenkin junior (1797-1874) and his wife Martha who were living at *Twyn Cottage* in 1850, and during this period the place seems to have been quite a hive of industry! Jenkin himself was a shoemaker, as were two of his sons, whilst two of his daughters are listed as dressmakers. Also packed into the tiny cottage were three younger teenage children; Jenkin's 34 year old nephew from Neath and his second cousin Elizabeth Forster, 'of independent means', (also from Neath) who had been living with him for over ten years. They were a staunchly Nonconformist family, and were members of the congregation at Capel y Pîl in North Cornelly where Jenkin and Martha lie buried in the tiny graveyard.

With regard to the nearby cottage *The Plwryn*, I can trace the history of the fields adjoining the house right back to 1632 when they were a freehold property owned by an Eleanor Gronow. The cottage however seems to have been built somewhat later, probably between 1667 and 1682 when the property belonged to a Howell George who rented it out to other tenants. Acquired by the apothecary John Thomas of Marlas it passed from him to the Bennet family of Laleston with whom it still remained in 1850. In the early part of the 18th century the house itself fell into ruin but was apparently restored by William Leyson who took up residence there following his eviction from *The Prince of Wales* in 1806. He subsequently moved on to create a small farm based upon a house on Heol Las, and the occupant in 1850 was a Richard Yorwerth.

Marlas Farm. Although lying outside *Tir Ffin*, this seems an opportune place to make some brief mention of Marlas Farm as, like the previous holdings, it lay some distance from the main settlement area. The farm and its inhabitants have played a major role in my history of Kenfig amply covered in earlier volumes, so what follows is merely a brief synopsis of that story.

Marlas is, without doubt, the oldest continuously inhabited site within Kenfig Lower, though it was never (as has sometimes been claimed) a grange of Margam Abbey. Arguably its origins lie in the second half of the 12th century, and it is virtually certain that by 1199 it was the home of the Grammus family who gave their name to Grammes Hill – the ridge upon which it stands. The house there today was most likely built by Thomas Richard (fl 1593-1646) during the closing years of the reign of Queen Elizabeth I, and it was his increasing financial problems that led to him disposing of the property piece-meal to the Mansels of Margam during the first half of the 17th century.

Over the years the quality of the house attracted tenants who were of good social standing – notably the 'retired' London apothecary John Thomas (1659-1723) and Richard Jenkins (1721-1783). Acquired for the Briton Ferry estate by Bussy Mansel under rather dubious circumstances in 1741 together with neighbouring Llanmihangel, the two properties were bought back by the Talbots eighty years later. At this time Marlas was in the hands of Richard Jenkins' daughter Mary, an elderly spinster.

By this time too, part of the house had been turned into a brewery, and the premises were becoming rather run down, so having persuaded Mary to surrender her lease in return for an annuity, the Margam estate installed a new tenant named Thomas Joseph in 1826, and he and his family were still living there in 1850.

The tenant that succeeded Thomas Joseph at Marlas was Robert Morgan (1810-1881) who had probably taken over the farm by 1859. I have found references to him in the Parish Registers as a farmer in 'Pyle Village' as early as 1837 when his daughter Elizabeth Lougher Morgan was baptised, and he is the ancestor of the two Morgan families that still inhabit the house today.

Llanmihangel Mill lay just across the Kenfig River from Marlas in Higher Kenfig and was in the parish of Margam. It is nevertheless, worthy of mention at this point if only because of the active role played in Kenfig's story by its tenant, Jehosaphat Powell. It also enables me to include a mention of his involvement in local agitation against the Bridgend Turnpike Trust and his subsequent death.

Agitation against the manner in which the various Turnpike Trusts were operating their toll gates had become widespread across the country during the early years of the century, and nowhere more so than here in South Wales where it boiled over into the Rebecca Riots of the 1830s and 40s. These involved attacks upon the property and employees of the Turnpike Trusts by men dressed in women's clothing who smashed the gates and burnt toll-keepers' houses. Whilst equally furious at the manner in which the Bridgend Trust was operating the local people chose to express their outrage in a rather more dignified and civilized manner.

    This story properly belongs to the history of Pyle through which the turnpike road ran, but on 24th October 1843 a mass protest meeting was held at *Croes y Ddadl*, the site of the ancient 'Taddlecross' near Mawdlam. It drew protesters not only from the local community, but also from as far away as Margam, Newton Nottage and Tythegston. It is a measure of the respect in which old Jehosaphat Powell was held that those attending, who numbered several hundred, chose him as their chairman and spokesman. Accordingly, he drew up a document outlining their grievances which was signed by 229 of those present and forwarded to the Trust (no ref). It was also perhaps Jehosaphat that enlisted the support of CRM Talbot of Margam who, in a separate letter to the Trust not only gave his backing to the protest but added one or two pithy observations of his own for good measure.

    In the short term it did little good as, although the Trustees admitted the justification of many of the allegations, they were unable to take any action. They had contracted the collection of the tolls to a man named Mr Bullen, but whilst they agreed that he had exceeded his mandate in this respect, the time limit for any legal action to be taken against him had expired. Nevertheless the days of the turnpike system were numbered, and Thomas Joseph of Marlas ('Thomas Marlas') was one of a delegation of local people who made representation to members of a Parliamentary Commission subsequently appointed to look at the operation of the turnpike system. The result of this nationwide survey was that the system of maintaining the major highways of Britain by virtue of the turnpike trusts came to an end. Jehosaphat, however, did not live to see this, nor was he a member of the delegation that gave evidence to the Commissioners, for on 3rd December 1843 he had suddenly and unexpectedly passed away peacefully in his sleep "by visitation of God".

Heol Fach After crossing New Mill Bridge (Pont Felin Newydd) Water Street continued as 'The Cartway'. This is now called 'Heol Fach'/B4283, (which is as it is shown on A-Z maps but not Google Earth). It eventually joined up with Heol Las (which is now divided by the M4) at Cornelly Cross in North Cornelly. At the time of the Tithe Map there were no local houses on this road, so our perambulation of the Borough goes directly (via the Porthcawl road, which Barrie identifies as 'Heol Kenfig') up to Mawdlam village.

Heol Las now starts by Mawdlam Church, as a turn-off from the road to Porthcawl. In the early part of the 17th century it had been known as 'Green Street' or 'The Greenway'*, but by 1850 the name long in use was Heol Las. This is now Mawdlam village, and along Heol Las several cottages were scattered on both sides of the road, and interestingly it seems that many of them were occupied by craftsmen rather than agricultural labourers who tended to congregate in the houses towards the southern end of Heol Kenfig (past *The Prince of Wales*).

A little further along Heol Las from the cross (where the smithy built by Richard Yorwerth a century earlier still continued in operation) was the ancient tithe barn – Scibor Degwm which stood on the north side of the highway - roughly where the old wooden welfare hall stands today. Even by 1850 it was probably already falling into decay, and just beyond it the tithe map shows a group of 7 houses, 4 on the north side of Heol Las and three on the south.

The house shown as occupied by Jenkin Evan, with a garden opposite was known as *Albert Cottage*, and was rented by Charles Amici on one of his visits to Kenfig during the period 1843 to 1845. It was actually owned by a William Powell who was almost certainly the man of that name who was the tenant of Eglwys Nunnydd Farm, Margam. It must have been a dwelling of some size, for it is still there today though now divided up into four separate cottages. Mrs Megan Berry of Heol Las, who has lived all her life in the area, tells me that she was told that the one nearest the camera in the photograph was originally a dairy,

---

* Although Barrie took 'glas' in its usual translation 'blue', in this case it should be 'green'. According to my Oxford *Pocket Modern Welsh Dictionary* (2000) "*Glas* is also used to refer to the green of vegetation; in this use it is ...of common occurrence in place names". Thanks to Margaret Bird of Cardiff for help in this matter. [ed]

and if this was so, then at some time in its history it was evidently the centre of a small farmstead.

The house that occupies the site today is known as Elmsfield and at the rear is the barn (indicated on the tithe map) depicted in the photograph above. It incorporates several elements of an ecclesiastical nature which led Thomas Gray to believe that it was the medieval chapel dedicated to St Wenduin that served the village of North Cornelly. My own research indicates however that this probably lay on the opposite side of the village on the former road that connected it to Pyle, so it would seem that when this barn was built the old chapel was in ruin and some of the masonry was re-used here in its construction.

[You can find out more about the inhabitants of these cottages in Volume 4 of this series, which gives details of all the people and their houses which Barrie discovered by his ceaseless labours in the field.]

Heol y Lane: is the minor road which today runs past the front of *The Prince of Wales* and then continues around the back of Ton Kenfig. Some clues might be expected from the records of baptisms and burials in the Parish Registers, but it seems that the name 'Heol y Lane' was falling into disuse at this time and there are few mentions of it in these documents after 1840.

One resident deserves a note here: William and Lena Rees were classed as paupers and lived in the second cottage on Heol y Lane, having married in 1799. Lena had her moment of destiny when, in her 90s and living with William and Mary Hopkin, she met Thomas Morgan ('Llyfnwy') and supplied him with details of the woman she knew as 'The Maid of Sker', and so she inadvertently created the legend with which we are so familiar today.

Kenfig Down: where the family farm at *Penymynydd* stands, is part of Ton Kenfig. Further south along the eastern boundary of the common from Penymynydd Farm the tithe map shows a building standing in one of the fields named *Tair Erw Bakehouse*. This undoubtedly indicates that the building was, or had been a bakehouse constructed at a time when such buildings were set away from the main house to reduce the fire risk.

This perambulation through the Lower Borough as it was in 1850 brings my History of Kenfig to a close. During its course we have followed the story of its people from their modest burgages in the medieval town, frequently destroyed both by Welsh attacks and the forces of nature, through to the 'straggling village' of the 18th and 19th centuries. How the eyes of these people would have popped to see the sumptuous and luxurious homes that are the village of Kenfig today! The story of that transition would indeed be a fascinating tale to research, but is a task that I must nevertheless leave to some future local historian.

As you will have gathered if you have indeed had the stamina to read this history from start to finish, my work is far from over! There are still ample documents to research and many new facets of the Kenfig folk yet to be uncovered during my chosen period (1145-1850. This promises to keep me fully occupied for many years to come then, who knows, if I still possess the ability and the enthusiasm, I may just re-write the entire story all over again!

POST-SCRIPT
[This section has been added by the Editor]

In a poignant entry towards the end of *The Buried City of Kenfig*, by Thomas Gray (1909: 324) it is reported that: —

> On the 9th of September, 1886, a notice headed 'Kenfig' — a dry, unsympathetic notice—was sent to the Constable of the Castle, Portreeve, and Burgesses of Kenfig in the County of Glamorgan, dissolving the ancient Corporation. Trustees are to be appointed to manage the property of the Burgesses. They are twelve in number, and 'shall be called the Trustees of the Kenfig Corporation Property'. Four to be appointed by the persons whose names shall be on the Burgesses' Roll ; four by the Rural Sanitary Authority Bridgend and Cowbridge Union ; four by the Margam Local Board.
>
> The Trustees shall stand possessed of the interest of the Corporation in Kenfig Common, referred to in the Schedule to the scheme. Upon trust as follows ; that is to say : —

1. To permit the persons whose names shall be on the Burgesses' Roll as Burgesses or Burgesses' Widows, who now have, or as Burgesses' Sons or Widows who hereafter acquire, right of pasture and of cutting fern on the said Common, to exercise and enjoy the rights aforesaid as fully and effectually, and for such time, and in such manner as he or she, by any Statute, charter, byelaw, or custom of the Corporation in force at the time of passing the Municipal Corporation Act, 1883, might or could have had, acquired, or enjoyed, in case that Act had not been passed

2. Upon the extinction of the aforesaid rights of all of the said Burgesses and Burgesses' Sons and Widows to allow all the inhabitant householders of the said place of Kenfig to exercise such rights.

3. Provides that if previous to the extinction of the said rights the number entitled to enjoy the said rights shall fall below the number of persons so entitled on the formation of the Burgesses' Roll, then the rights of pasture and cutting fern may be let at the best rent they can obtain, etc. The Trustees shall stand possessed of the income derived from the property, including rents received by the letting of rights on Kenfig Common, also any fines, fees, or sums of money paid to them subject to Manorial rents.

Upon trust to pay, etc.

1. In payment of interest, salaries, and other lawful expense and cost of administration of the scheme.

2. In recompensing existing Officers of the Corporation who, by reason of the dissolution of the Corporation, have been deprived of any emolument of pecuniary profit, etc.

3. In payment annually of 11 s. to each of the Burgesses or Burgesses' Sons or Widows who represent the Burgesses who were the original holders of parcels of the Common called Gwaunycimla or Le R u g g e.

4. The residue to be equally divided between the aforesaid persons.

5. Provides, for the division of the said residue in case the number of persons falls short of the number on the Roll, and a " Surplus Fund Account " to be formed.

Six articles follow, providing for the management of the scheme and the sending in of claims of persons entitled to be Burgesses Widows, or Burgesses' Sons or Widows etc., etc.

SCHEDULE.

The Public House called the Prince of Wales Inn, now let with the plots of land next mentioned to Mrs. Wrath at a rent of £10 per annum.

A garden, a pond, and a field containing 1a. 2c. or thereabouts, known as the " Croft," and let with the said Prince of Wales Inn as aforesaid.

The interest of the Corporation in Kenfig Common or Down, containing 1,200 acres or thereabouts.

The franchise of free warren on a certain portion of the said Kenfig Common, now let at a rent of £35.10s. per annum.

Sums of £1,600 and £100 now in the custody of Christopher R. M. Talbot, Esquire, M.P., on which interest is paid to the Corporation at the rate of £5 per centum per annum.

Chattel property, including silver mace, cup, sets of weights, scale furniture, and documents. (These are of late date—George II., I believe.)

And with that, over seven centuries of the Borough of Kenfig came to an end.

APPENDIX

The Kenfig Courts

In Parts 1 & 2 of my history readers will come across frequent references to various courts held at Kenfig, usually in the Town Hall. This part of the Appendix therefore looks at what these Courts were and how, so far as I can discover, they operated within the Borough.

The courts in question were only of local importance. Prior to the Act of Union in the time of King Henry VIII the Borough, as the centre of the Hundred of Kenfig, was the seat of criminal trials for the area and, as mentioned in Part II, could even impose the death penalty. With the introduction of the Act this function passed to Newcastle and the local courts dealt mainly with purely manorial matters. Since there were two manors within the Borough, there were therefore two separate sets of manorial courts.

Those for Higher Kenfig were held at Pyle alongside those for that manor as explained in Part II. The only surviving record of its proceedings prior to the mid 19th century are in the Margam collection of MSS at Aberystwyth, and cover the years between 1666 and 1703. Only fragments of the records for the sittings for the courts of the Manor of Kenfig Borough during the same period have survived. This seems to be because prior to 1692 the Portreeve of Kenfig acted as the steward of the manor and kept these records himself.

The surviving Minute Books for the Borough of Kenfig commence in 1729, and contain a record of sittings of the courts of the Manor of Kenfig Borough from that date, but only in a very limited form. This was because responsibility for all property held directly to the Lord of the Manor was now in the hands of the Margam steward whose records have not survived. The Portreeves, being still responsible for the freeholders, kept only records of those transactions relating to them. Unfortunately these entries are usually very brief and rather patchy.

There were three types of manorial court – Courts Leet; Courts Baron; and The Court of Pleas. Since the records for those in Higher Kenfig have not survived, these notes relate solely to those for the Manor of Kenfig Borough.

Courts Leet

This was a manorial court that was held twice a year in Spring and Autumn, and were presided over by the Constable of the Castle (in his capacity as the Margam Steward) sitting with the Kenfig Portreeve. These courts are sometimes described as petty criminal courts, though in a modern context the term can be misleading. The most serious (and most frequent!) offence dealt with by the Kenfig court was the failure of tenants to properly trim their hedges alongside highways! As a matter of convenience the Leet Court was held alongside the monthly Court Baron, so effectively it dealt with purely manorial matters at the same time.

Every tenant, landholder, and resiant was required to attend these courts, and were fined if they failed to appear to answer their name when the Suit Roll was called at the start of the proceedings. From those assembled a 'Jury of Presentment' was then selected which usually numbered anything between twelve and sixteen members. They then 'presented' or reported to the Constable all matters that fell within the court's field of responsibility that had occurred since the last sitting for his consideration and judgement.

To assist him in making his decisions the Constable had two Assessors appointed at the commencement of proceedings. Their role was to advise him on the custom and practice within the manor when it came to imposing any fines and penalties, and they were therefore usually (in the quaint words of a manorial survey) 'two of the annciet burgesses' of the Borough (PM 9620). Occasionally, however, a younger burgess of high social standing was chosen, the guiding principal apparently being that they were persons whose word would be accepted without question by tenants.

At Kenfig the Autumn Leet was also the venue for the selection of the officers of the Borough for the coming year. Three names were put forward to the constable for all posts except that of the two Aletasters where four were nominated. He then selected the most suitable candidates. Since this aspect of the proceedings affected the entire Borough burgesses from Higher Kenfig also attended these sittings.

Courts Baron

These were almost identical in form to the Courts Leet, but were presided over by the Portreeve who sat without Assessors. They dealt with purely manorial matters and sat every month but, as already mentioned, the Kenfig Minute Books record only those jury presentments relating to freeholders. Nevertheless an entry was made every month in the minutes noting such sittings on a given date though usually no business is recorded. From this I would assume (for there is no specific statement to that effect) that two courts were held on the same day. At the first (which finds no mention in the books) the Margam steward presided and dealt with matters involving Margam tenants, and then the Portreeve took over for those involving freeholders. At the same time it is worth remembering that according to the manorial survey of 1633 (PM 1280) Courts Baron at Higher Kenfig were only held when specifically requested by the tenants.

In the main these courts dealt with changes in the tenancies or ownership of property within the manor, noting any heriots due to the lord on the death of the occupant and formally admitting his successor. It settled boundary disputes between neighbours, and locally during the 17th century was particularly involved in ensuring that the tenants of the Lord maintained his property to an acceptable standard as we have seen at Higher Kenfig in Part II of this history.

The entries in the minute books also seem to indicate that the Court Baron was frequently used as a convenient forum for routine matters that were properly the responsibility of the Hall Day Courts (see below).

The Court of Pleas

This was a civil court which was held, in the words of the 1660 Manorial survey (Gray, 1909: 246) to 'hear and determine all manner of suits, actions and plaints between party and party'. In theory they were held every month alongside the Courts Baron, and were presided over by the Portreeve. In practice they only are occasionally mentioned and unfortunately little or no details are given beyond the names of the parties involved. According to the survey these courts were then empowered to deal with actions *'to any value whatsoever'* but by 1729 this had been limited to cases involving sums under £2 which seems to have also been the limit imposed on the earlier courts in respect of Higher Kenfig.

As a general rule such courts were only held very infrequently, and had virtually died out at Kenfig by the start of the 19th century.

Other Courts

In addition to the above two other types of court were held at Kenfig, the first of which was the **Hall Day** which was called by the Portreeve as and when required to consider matters relating purely to the administration of the Borough itself. Although all burgesses were apparently expected to attend the business was conducted by the Portreeve with the advice of the Eight Elected Burgesses who formed his council. The manner in which these were selected, and their function, has already be given in Part 2 (page 126).

The most frequent business dealt with at such sittings relate to the parcels of hay at Waun Cimla and those of fern on Kenfig Down. The Council supervised the various changes of ownership and the maintenance of the fences and boundaries at Waun Cimla rather in the manner of the manorial courts, and often such routine matters seem to have been dealt with at the end of a sitting of a Court Baron. A Hall Day was therefore only normally called to discuss other matters. They are rarely, if ever mentioned in the earliest minute book prior to the middle of the 18th century, though there seems no reason to doubt that they were being held at that time. Although mention of Hall Days occur from the 1750s onwards, but initially little or nothing is said about the business transacted. Alterations in the way the Borough was administered are certainly apparent in the minutes, but there is no record of the Hall Day at which such changes were adopted.

This may well be because of the secretive nature of the burgesses themselves. As the books recorded the proceedings of Courts Baron and Courts Leet they would presumably have been open to inspection by the Margam steward, and the burgesses had no wish to have him prying into affairs that were properly not his concern. Perhaps the Recorder kept a separate record of such transactions, but if so, then that record has been lost. Only towards the end of the 18th century did Recorders begin making entries in the minutes regarding these courts that give us a better insight into the workings of the Borough.

From the end of the century too the books contain a record of **Coroner's Courts** for the Borough. This office was held by the Portreeve, though how long this had been the case I cannot say. Inquests were held in the case of any sudden or unexplained death and were required to determine the identity of the deceased; how and when he or she died; and to identity any person or persons considered responsible for that death. Normally held at the Town Hall (though some of the earliest ones took place at the location where the death had occurred) the Portreeve sat with a jury, normally about eight in number. Having heard all the evidence it was the responsibility of the latter to deliver the verdict.

PRINCIPAL SOURCES

Documentary Sources

B/K	Borough of Kenfig MSS (Cardiff Record Office)
BTT	Bishop's Trancripts for Tythegston Parish (National Library)
D/D Ma	Margam MSS (Swansea Record Office)
D/DP	Penrice MSS (Swansea Record Office)
D/D Ty	Tythegston Estate MSS (Cardiff Record Office)
DJ	David Jones of Wallington, Notebooks (Cardiff Central Library)
LL	Llandaff Diocese MSS (National Library, Aberystwyth)
Llandaff Wills	Llandaff Diocese MSS (National Library, Aberystwyth)
MPR	Margam Parish Registers (Photocopies- Swansea Record Office.
PM	Penrice & Margam MSS (National Library, Aberystwyth)
PPR	Pyle & Kenfig Parish Registers (Photocopies – Swansea Record Office)
PRO	Public Records Office, Kew.

Published Sources

Andrews, C Bruyn (1934) *The Torrington Diaries of Hon John Byng*

Appleby, A B (1978) *Famine in Tudor & Stuart England,* Liverpool University Press.

Cambridge (1985)*The Cambridge Agrarian History of England & Wales, Volume V, Part II,* Cambridge University Press

Carlisle, Nicholas (1811)*Topographical Directory of the Dominion of Wales"* which was published in 1811.

Carr, Yvonne (1995) *Wrecks Around & About Kenfig*

Commissioners on Proposed Division of Counties And Boundaries of Boroughs, (1832) *Swansea District, Report on Kenfig*

Commissioners on Municipal Corporations in England and Wales (1834) *Report*

Denning, RTW (ed), (1995) *The Diary of William Thomas* Glamorgan Historian

David, John (2004) *Porthcawl and its coastline* The Author

Davies, J *(1962)The Parish of Penlline,* 'Saints & Sailing Ships' (Stewart Williams ed)

Dillwyn, L W, Extracts from the Diary of, South Wales & Monmouth Record Society, Publication No 5 (1963)

Mr Dillwyn's Diaries (1998), Dillwyn Lewis Weston, p 24 Swansea Museums Services (10 Oct 1998)

Donovan (1805) *Descriptive Excursions through South Wales and Monmouthshire in the Year 1804* London: The Author

Evans, A L (1960) *The Story of Kenfig* Port Talbot; Author pub.

Evans, A L (1964) *Sker House* Port Talbot; Author pub

Evans, E D (1993) *A History of Wales, 1660-1815* Cardiff; University of Wales Press

Evans, Frederic (1912) *Tir Iarll (The Earl's Land) : comprising the ancient parishes of Llangynwyd, Bettws, Margam, and Kenfig* Cardiff : The Educational Publishing Co. Ltd. Mid Glamorgan Libraries (reprinted 1993)

Evans, T C (1887)*History of Llangynwyd Parish*, Mid Glamorgan Libraries (reprinted 1992 from 1887 original

Gilpin, William,(1783) *Observations on the River Wye"* (1783) pp 76-9

Glamorgan (1974) *County History Vol IV. Early Modern Glamorgan from the Act of Union to the Industrial Revolution.* Glamorgan County History Society.

Monumental Inscriptions at Capel y Pil transcribed by the Bridgend Branch of the **Glamorgan Family History Society**, 1984. GFS (1984)

Grant, Raymond (1988) *On the Parish . An Illustrated Source Book on the Care of the Poor Under the Old Poor Law* Glamorgan Archive Publications (1988)

Grant, Raymond (1978)*The Parliamentary History of Glamorgan 1542-1976*, Swansea; Christopher Davies

Granville, N.(1980) *Cefn Cribwr - Chronicle of a Village*, Stuart Williams Publishers, 1980

Gray, Thomas (1909) *The Buried City of Kenfig*, T Fisher Unwin

Griffiths, Barrie (1990) *Sturmi's Land* unpub. but copies have been deposited with the Glamorgan Record Office and the Bridgend Library Service

Griffiths, B, *Kenfig as Others Saw it"* (1997)

Guy, John ed (1991) *The Diocese of Llandaff in 1763 - the clergy's answers to Bishop Ewer's visitation queries of 1763*, South Wales Record Society

Hibbert, Christopher (1987) *The English, A Social History,* Guild Publishing

Higgins, L (1968) *Newton, Nottage and Porthcawl*, Gomarian Press

Hopkins , T J ed. (1965) *C.C.'s Tour in Glamorgan, 1789* Glamorgan Historian Vol II, 1965

James, Brynmor (1987) *DLPR The story of a railway and its background* Kenfig Hill, The Author (pub.).

Jenkins, Elis, (1968), *William Weston Young Glamorgan Historian V*, Cowbridge, Stewart Williams

James, B.L.I. ed., (1983) *Morganiae archaiographia: a book of the antiquities of Glamorganshire, by*Rice Merrick, South Wales Record Society

Jones, B (1981) The Population of 18th century West Glamorgan *Glamorgan Historian XII*, Cowbridge, Stewart Williams

Jones, D R L (1994) *"Vicars of Llangynwyd"* (1994)

Jones, Dennis (1997) *"What the Paper Said v1"*, a series of booklets published by The Kenfig Society

Langdon (c.2000) *Aspects of Kenfig* pub. by Society of the Ancient Borough of Kenfig

Leland, John *The Itinerary in Wales of John Leland in or about the years 1536-1539 see* Smith (1906)

"Llyfnwy" **Thomas Morgan** (1876) *Cupid*, 3e, Maesteg; John Jones

Lyons, John & Griffiths, Barrie (1996) *Llyfnwy's History of Kenfig,* Kenfig Society

Martin, Joanna (1981) Landed Estates in Glamorgan c 1660-1760; *Glamorgan Historian Vol XII*, Cowbridge; Stewart Williams

Martin, Joanna, (1995)"Shook to Death. The Travels of the Talbots of Penrice and Margam in the Georgian Period", *Morgannwg* Vol XXXIX

Martin, Joanna,(1993) *The Penrice Letters 1768-1795,* South Wales Record Society

Motely, James (1848) *Tales of the Cymry: with notes illustrative and explanatory* Llanelly, Thomas

Reed, Michael (1983) *The Georgian Triumph 1700-1830*, Routledge & Kegan Paul

Rees, T (1861) *History of Protestant Nonconformity in Wales*, John Snow

RCAHM(W) (1988) The Royal Commission on Ancient & Historical Monuments in Wales, *Inventory of Ancient Monuments in Glamorgan, Vol IV, Part 2, Farmhouses & Cottages*, HMSO

Smith, Lucy (1906) *The Itinerary in Wales of John Leland in or about the years 1536-1539* London; George Bell and Sons

Spencer, Mrs Marianne Robertson (1913) *Annals of South Glamorgan* (1913; reprinted 1970),

Stratton, J M (1969) *Agricultural Records AD 220-1968* New York; Augustus M Kelley

Thomas, David (1963), *Agriculture in Wales during the Napoleonic Wars*, University of Wales Press, 1963

Thompson, MV(ed) (1983)*The Journeys of Sir Richard Colt Hoare Through Wales and England 1793- 1810,* Alan Sutton Publishing

Thorpe, Lewis (trans (1990) *Gerald of Wales*, Penguin Classics

Warner, Revd. Richard (1798) *A Walk Through Wales, in August 1797* R. Crutwell London

Wyndham, Henry Penruddocke (1775) *A gentleman's tour through Monmouthshire and Wales: in the months of June ...*

Family Historians

John Lyons, formerly of Maesteg and now living at Narberth in Pembrokeshire to whom I am extremely grateful for this and many other items of his own research that he has made available to me over the years.

My sincere thanks are due to the following family historians who have kindly shared the results of their own research.

Allan Bleddyn, Aberavon

Chris Ensor, Cheltenham

Jean Evans, Cowbridge

Anne James, Cardiff

Brian Ll James, Cardiff

Sharon Janousek, Vancouver, Canada

Chris Jenkins, Maesteg

Averil Jones, Bridgend

Caryl Jones, Brynamman

Howard & Sonia Lewis, Pontardawe

John Lyons, Narberth

Lynne Miller, USA

Mrs Terry Robbins, Porthcawl

Phillip Thomas, Cardiff

Margaret Williams, Neath

David Yorath, Laugharne

Mark Yorwerth-Middleton

INDEX

Wyndhams 50

Over the years the Kenfig Society has published many booklets on the History and People of Kenfig including:

1994	Yvonne Carr	Shipwrecks around and about Kenfig (available as a re-print)
1999	Barrie Griffiths	A Spy for Wellington Sir John William Waters 1774 - 1842. (available as a re-print)
2000	Barrie Griffiths	The House at Sker Point (1e) 2002 (2e)
2001	Barrie Griffiths	The Inn at Pyle (available as a re-print)
2002	Terry Robbins	Digging Up Kenfig (in print)
2004	Dennis Jones	What the papers said Vol 7 Jan-Dec 1881 (in print)
2005	Barrie Griffiths	Once Upon a Time in Kenfig (in print)
2005	Dennis Jones	What the paper's said Vol 8 Jan-Dec 1882 (in print)
2007	Barrie Griffiths	Time Trekker (in print)
2008	John Blundell	From Kenfig to Ogmore: A personal history of the coast (available as a re-print)
2012	Barrie Griffiths	Welcome to Kenfig (revvised and updated in print)

For more details log on to our website:

www.kenfigsociety.org

KENFIG FOLK PART I:
The FIRST BOROUGH of KENFIG: 1147-1439
"The abiding value of this book is in its account of the abandonment of the 'old' town. This, the final chapter, shows the author at his best, telling with dramatic detail how the advancing sands constantly troubled the town's inhabitants and how they were unable to bring themselves to take the counteractive measures that would put an end to their livestock grazing.

"This attractive book is rounded off with a bibliography and a very useful index. It will be of value to anyone interested in the towns of Glamorgan, and as a topographical study is exemplary. The Kenfig Society has done Barrie Griffiths proud." (from the review by Tony Hopkins in *Morgannwg LV*, 2011) Published May 2011.

KENFIG FOLK PART II:
KENFIG IN TUDOR AND STUART TIMES: 1485-1699
How could the town of Kenfig survive when its people were driven out by the on-rush of sea and sands? But Kenfig lived on! It still had its Charter and its Council led by the Portreeve. We can follow their battle to keep the Borough organisation in being, by adapting its institutions to meet their altered circumstances. But the battle against the sand that had claimed their medieval town and castle was far from over. More fields, buildings, and even a small hamlet were lost during these years. Then there were the religious changes spawned by Henry VIII's break with Rome which split our tiny community to its core with rival groups of Catholics, Nonconformists and Anglicans. Published June 2012

STILL TO COME (as an e-book)
KENFIG FOLK PART IV:
THE PEOPLE AND PLACES AROUND KENFIG
Barrie Griffiths unearthed a wealth of detailed information about families such as the Lovelucks, Yorwerths and Loughers and the houses and farms they lived in. This will be of great interest to family historians, and includes many family trees. It is hoped to make this available in early 2014.